# Intermediate Riding Skills

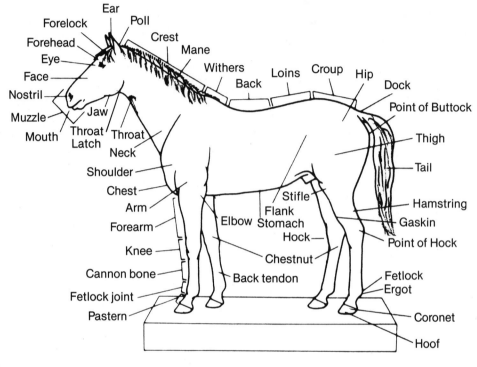

Points of the Horse

# Intermediate Riding Skills

*by*
Robin Hirst-Fisher

*Photographs by*
Margaret Thomas

*Illustrations by*
Heather St. Clair Davis

*For Judy*                    *June 1990*

*Best Wishes for you and
your daughter*

*Robin Hirst-Fisher*

**HOWELL**
BOOK HOUSE
New York

Howell Book House
Macmillan Publishing Company
866 Third Avenue, New York, NY 10022
Collier Macmillan Canada, Inc.

Library of Congress Cataloging-in-Publication Data
Hirst-Fisher, Robin.
  Intermediate riding skills / by Robin Hirst-Fisher.
    p.  cm.
  Includes bibliographical references.
  ISBN 0-87605-882-9
  1. Horsemanship.  I. Title
SF309.H638 1989
798.2'3--dc20        89-24545        CIP

Macmillan books are available at special discounts for bulk purchases for sales promotions, premiums, fund-raising, or educational use. For details contact:

Special Sales Director
Macmillan Publishing Company
866 Third Avenue
New York, NY 10022


10 9 8 7 6 5 4 3 2 1

Printed in the United States of America

# Contents

# Prologue

THERE ONCE WAS a "Captain of Industry" who was smitten by a lady at a small, elegant dinner party. Wanting to impress her, he mentioned that he was an advanced skier and had ocean-raced sailboats in his spare time, between making international deals. "How interesting!" she replied, "But do you ride?"

Remembering that in his youth he had gone on chaperoned trail rides along the beach, he felt safe. "Sure," he replied.

"Would you like to join me on a fox hunt in Virginia?" she invited.

Not wanting to miss on opportunity to be with the lady, he quickly agreed.

When he arrived at the fox hunt meet, he discovered that no one else was dressed in khaki slacks and army boots. No one was even wearing a sweater. And they all had funny hats.

Then he went to the barn to meet the lady and the horses. Noticing his attire, she quickly understood that he hadn't a clue what a fox hunt was. "Well," she suggested, "why don't we just hilltop and mosey along at a slower pace?"

Meanwhile, the groom had appeared with a bridled and saddled Thoroughbred. As the Captain of Industry noticed that the horse was over six feet tall at the shoulder, the beast snorted and danced a little, anxious to go.

"That's your mount," the lady cheerfully told him. "He's my best horse. He's a top-level three-day eventer. His name is Orion because he's such a fast, wonderful hunter, too."

The Captain of Industry realized that the horse was larger than a two-story house and as enthusiastic as Man O'War. The horse bore no resemblance at all to the little fat riding stable horses of his youth. His eyes glazed over, and he nervously approached Orion.

Trying to mount, he discovered that he had to get his foot above his ear to reach the stirrup. Meanwhile, Orion was wiggling, making the stirrup play peek-a-boo. The lady suggested waiting until the hunt left and then mounting when the horse was quieter.

During the momentary reprieve, they went outside to watch the hunt move off. As the Captain of Industry watched, the whole group, including the swarm of hunting dogs, jumped an enormous boundary fence. Even the little children on little ponies got over. The Captain of Industry blanched. The lady observed him and gently asked, "Never jumped before, have you?"

Manfully, he admitted that it was all a bit different from what he had in mind.

So, instead of hunting, they rode the horses in an indoor arena until he learned where Orion's gears were. She mentioned to him that Orion was trained to change pace and direction with the rider's shift in balance.

Feeling more confident, the Captain of Industry suggested going outside for a trail ride. He liked Orion a lot. He was mentally comparing him to a Ferrari he had once had, when he tensed up a little and shifted weight. Orion left like a shot, at a full racing run. The tighter the Captain of Industry clung, the faster the hunter went.

"Circle him!" the lady called from behind him, as they flew by.

Finally, he became exhausted and loosened his death grip on Orion's neck. The big horse gently came to a stop, waiting for the next command.

The Captain of Industry had two thoughts. One was that horses and what he thought of as "riding" were not anything like what he had just experienced. This was a whole new sport. The other thought was that it was the most exhilarating thing he'd ever tried. He also concluded that he had better learn how to stay on and steer if he was to survive at all.

When the lady joined him, full of concern, he asked her if she would show him how to ride.

They then spent many hours together riding over great billowing meadows. The Captain of Industry developed his riding to the point of acquiring his own hunter. Finally, one day he was able to go to the fox hunt and jump all the fences. Greatly admired by all for his perseverance and obvious enjoyment of riding, he was most admired by the lady he desired.

This is a true story. This book is the result of the many questions asked by the Captain of Industry, James B. Fisher.

And, by the way, he got the girl, in the end.

# Introduction

THERE ARE few exact definitions for the various levels of riding skills.

A beginner is someone without significant previous riding experience—equivalent to the person applying for a learner's driving permit. He or she may have had a few brief lessons as a youngster in summer camp, but the likelihood of these being of any use in a more advanced environment is remote.

However, as a beginner becomes more comfortable mounting and dismounting, or just sitting, a horse, and is able to do slow trail riding without serious anxiety, the novice level is approached. Roughly, it is a psychological transition. The novice starts to like riding and feels able to *affect* the horse—that is, to steer reasonably well, stop and start when desired, and generally act rather than react to the mount. He learns to walk, trot, and canter and can develop some control of his horse in a group.

When the rider wants to develop further in affecting the horse, he becomes an intermediate. At this level, the skills of a horseman are nurtured. The rider learns that the outcome of the ride depends on a complete understanding of the needs and relationship of horse and rider. In addition, it makes good financial sense, with an investment as large as a horse, to understand how the needs of the horse are met. A horse is very fragile. Well cared for, he can prosper for years, increase in value, and become a close friend. If he is not well cared for, he can quickly deteriorate and die.

*Intermediate Riding Skills* is designed to aid the rider's transition from novice to horseman. Hence, not all riding skills are mounted. The first concerns are learning to care for the horse and rider—comfort, appearance, proper care, selection, and adjustment of saddlery, health, and, most important, safety. Along with this goes the ability to handle with greater control gaits on the flat. This includes walk, trot, canter, and gallop.

The next big step is learning to jump, and what a thrill that is. Little hops over low-cross-rails come first. As confidence and balance grow, rail fences, coops, and other obstacles offer exhilaration as in no other sport.

As the novice masters control of all gaits, some basic dressage (or at least good steering and control), and, finally, jumping up to one meter (3 feet, 3 inches), the rider has been graduated to intermediate level.

At this point, our new intermediate can handle all kinds of trail riding, cross country, fox hunting in most territories, horse showing, and even competitive three-day eventing at the training level. It's a wonderful feeling, and that's what is called *Intermediate Riding Skills.*

# 1

# Selecting a Horse

---

WHEN ONE FIRST LEARNS TO RIDE, the kind of horse needed changes with one's abilities and skill level. Like skiing, one starts with very short skis and then works up to competition length.

## BEGINNER HORSE

For the basic beginner horse, what you really want and need is a horse that doesn't scare you to death. This paragon should be extremely quiet, with its first thought to stand still rather than run away. A beginner horse will put up with a great deal of misinformation and be kindly about it, forgiving the rider for his many mistakes. The beginner horse is frequently an older mount—at least ten or twelve years old or even older—who has had a lot of experience with teaching new riders. The horse's mental attitude needs to be unflappable. He's willing to do what you want him to do but only with a great deal of persuasion. If one wants to walk or trot, it takes a nudge or perhaps several nudges to get him to move. When the rider stops impelling the horse forward, the horse stops. That way the horse always feels controllable to a new rider.

The horse needs to be somewhat sound but not incredibly so. In other words, if he can walk, trot, canter a little, and take light exercise, you've really gotten your money's worth out of a beginner horse. A beginner horse frequently is a quarter horse or a quarter horse cross, an Appaloosa, or a miscellaneous-grade horse of no particular breeding but very calm disposition. Frequently, a draft horse or a partial draft horse works very well for this purpose.

Arabian: refined, short-backed, straight croup, high head and tail carriage, head is very small with dished face, large eye and tiny muzzle. Temperament is hot, very intelligent, tremendous stamina and heart. This breed is used to upgrade others.

# INTERMEDIATE HORSE

The next step is a horse that is a little bit more willing to go forward. The second horse in the learning hierarchy comes as the rider is learning how to jump. He is now comfortable with basic steering, and basic brakes. At this point, the rider is trying to go exactly where he intended to go. In order to be able to make the dressage figures, he will want to make precise turns, and develop straightness on his straight lines. He has to have that degree of skill level and compatibility with the horse in order to jump, since 90 percent of successful jumping is how you get to the jump.

The intermediate horse is also an older horse who has had a great deal of experience in the field of endeavor you want to pursue. As an intermediate or beginning rider, *never* buy a young horse or a green horse who has not had his training. It is not safe, because the horse makes many mistakes. He's learning, and a beginning–low-intermediate rider cannot compensate for these as easily and is more likely to have falls. In addition, it's a lot less fun. The made horse makes everything you do seem easy, comfortable, and a joy to do. A young horse has so many questions that he's worried about, and he relies so heavily on your having the right information at the right time, that he can be a very difficult ride. It would be the same as starting skiing as a novice and going to the top of an expert slope. Your chances of having a fall are excellent.

# CONFORMATION

For virtually all of the purposes we discuss in this book, the horse that the intermediate rider needs for dressage, eventing, or jumping would be one whose withers are level with the top of the croup or higher than the top of the croup. That is to say, when you look at his top line, it appears to be built either level or uphill. If his withers are higher than his croup, or level, it is easier for him to shift his weight to his hindquarters and lift his forehand. This makes it possible for the mount to be a more comfortable ride as well as enabling you to jump more safely. For dressage, it means you can rebalance the horse to his hindquarters, making it easier for him to do the dressage movements. A dressage horse may have a fairly flat croup on its top line and be able to have a great deal of power for the movements on the flat. Frequently, German warm bloods, especially Hanoverians, Trakehners, and Austrian Lippizaners, will have that kind of hindquarter. It works quite well for dressage, but it is a more difficult jumping configuration. The hindquarters on a jumping horse tend to drop from the point of hip, creating more angulation through the hindquarters. It is easier for the horse to compact and spring in through the vertical motions of the jump.

Short-backed horses tend to be quite agile and very easy to turn. In addition, they tend to have fewer back problems. On the negative side, they

Thoroughbred: athletic, medium- to long-backed, sloping powerful croup, 45-degree angle in shoulder and pastern, long slender neck, head is straight, refined with a good-sized eye. Temperament is hot, can be intelligent, with stamina and heart, incredibly athletic, bred for racing but superb in jumping and other high-intensity sports.

frequently interfere with their own feet. A horse that's properly in proportion is almost visually in thirds as you look at his top line—he gives the feeling of being square overall.

A horse that is long-backed can be weak through the back and haunches and is more difficult to gather together for dressage or for jumping. On the other hand, they are frequently favored as open jumpers—if the rest of the configuration or conformation works together, the horse can use the long back as a spring to throw himself over the larger fences. The Selle Français horses are particularly noted for their long backs and narrowness in the shape of their necks. It's a long, slender package that looks almost like a greyhound. They've been quite successful on the open jumping circuit. They have not been as successful in eventing, and they are rarely seen in the foxhunting field. Sometimes, a very short-backed horse, such as the Arabian, has difficulty jumping because of a lack of suppleness occasioned by the presence of too few vertebrae. As a result, the horse will jump with his head high in the air, hollowing his back. The result looks like an upside-down rainbow.

If you plan to jump a horse, you should watch him over fences before purchasing him. You do not want a horse who hangs his knees, because he can hook a knee on a fence and flip with you. Ideally, you want a horse that has his upper, front legs level on the horizontal or tucked up toward his chin. The horse may not show this kind of form on a little fence. But at around three feet or so you'll start to see the form improve and he'll begin to put it together.

Horses can get in deep—that is, too close to the fence—and be able to climb their way up and over the fence, but their form tends to be very irregular; it's not balanced or pleasing to the eye, and their knees don't come up evenly. If the knees come up unevenly, there is a possibility of a knee being left behind and getting caught in the fence, which will mean a fall for you.

A horse that leaves too early or leaves out a stride before a fence is also a very difficult prospect. He can misjudge his fence and fall into the fence on his descent to the ground because the bascule of his jump is too far forward and not centered over the fence. Both jumping too deep and jumping too early can be rider faults instead of horse faults if the rider cues the horse improperly. A made horse will compensate for the rider's error and get himself out of trouble. He may even make it look good while he does it.

Some of the things that you're looking for in the mental celerity of the horse is his attitude toward new and different experiences, how quickly he assimilates new information, and whether he loses his composure. Frequently, you can find out a little about his reactions by placing him in a slightly new and surprising situation to see what he does. Often, a made horse will perk up his ears, maybe snuffle a little bit, and might possibly put in a bit of shy. Then he will figure out what the problem is and get on with the subject at hand. A young horse or a green horse who has not had much training will make a much bigger fuss over the new surprise. This element is terribly important when you're riding the horse because in fox hunting you don't know what you are going to be doing next. He has to judge from the reactions of the other horses

Quarter horse: heavily muscled, short-backed, straight shoulder and pastern, exaggerated sloping croup with low tail set. Very round withers and thick short neck; head short, thick and wide with large eye. Temperament mild, kindly and gentle, intelligent and forgiving. Bred for short-distance racing, cutting cattle, and can jump small fences.

what to expect ahead. In eventing, he doesn't even have the movements of the other horses to help him. He must analyze each of the fence combinations as he comes to them. At the higher levels of preliminary and above, he has to make multiple decisions quickly as to how to handle the changes and terrain. The horse decides whether a fence is a bounce or whether it's too narrow to do a bounce and has to be flown as an oxer.

## TRYING A PROSPECT

You want the horse to be enthusiastic about going forward, but not too enthusiastic. He needs to respect you, want to please you, and care about your input. It's important when you're riding the horse to feel that he is paying attention to your aids. A horse that is totally ignoring you will not be satisfactory in the long run. A horse that does not understand any of your cues just may be confused and, therefore, is dropping out most of the information that you're giving because it's contradictory. A sensitive horse just may get agitated until you calm down all your cues and try to give him one or two very clean ones without the contradictions. Bear in mind another factor when trying horses. Frequently, you the rider, in going to a new barn and a new situation, will be more tense than you normally are if you were on your regular horse. After all, it is a new experience for you, and most people, when they are faced with a new situation, have their adrenaline go up a bit. The adrenaline also makes them stronger, so their legs suddenly become more viselike and the horses tend to go forward more. It helps to take several deep breaths after one has mounted and try to relax before asking the horse to do too much.

You can tell immediately upon mounting a horse whether he's a forward-moving horse or whether he's going to be quiet and want to be pushed. He'll react to the way you have mounted and the feel of your weight in the saddle. Assuming that you have mounted without kicking him in the ribs, or thumping him on the back, and have landed beautifully, gracefully, and lightly, he will either move forward into your hand ready to tackle what new challenges are out there or he'll stand very quietly and wait for your signal. If he requires only a tiny nudge to get him to go, then you know that he's going to be pretty forward. If he requires a lot of effort, he's also going to require more pushes later on.

When a horse walks, you want to watch his movement from the ground. If the hoofprint of his front foot is covered by the hoofprint of his hind foot, he's "tracking up." If he's built well, he will overtrack by twelve inches—that is, the hoofprint of the hind foot will be twelve inches or so ahead of the hoofprint left by the front foot. This overreach is what makes the horse feel smooth when you ride him, and is an important attribute to look for. In dressage, the walk is counted double of the other movements because it is considered to be of such importance to the whole springiness of the horse and his comfort level.

Ideally, the horse that you pick would have a 45-degree angle with his shoulder and a matching 45-degree angle in his pastern for shock absorption. Warm bloods, draft, and quarter horse types will be a little bit more upright and will have a more fleshy wither, which is known in the vernacular as "mutton-withered." The more upright the shoulder, the greater the concussion to the rider. If the hindquarters are straight, then the horse can't push off properly and will leave his hind feet out behind him rather than having them underneath him. The camping out from behind makes the horse very weak and consequently of less use to you.

Ideally, when a horse trots straight toward you all of his feet move in a straight line toward you without side motion. The more sideways movement, the more likely he is to knock into his opposite foot in the process of motion. In addition to wasted energy, it seriously cuts down on his ability to cover ground comfortably. It can also lead to long-range problems with joints if you use high speed. At high speed, the oscillations of the hooves become greater and torque more severe so the joints are more severely stressed.

## THE COMPETITIVE TRAIL HORSE

The conformation of a competitive trail horse should allow for smooth ground-covering movement. Arabians are particularly well known for their incredible endurance and ability to cover ground without tiring. As a result, they tend to be the favorite breed for competitive trail riding. Some people are too big to ride a pure Arabian so they cross the Arabian with other breeds to produce a larger-bodied horse to compensate for their height. It is important for a competitive trail horse to have a cheerful, willing attitude, happy to cover mile after mile. The shortest of the competitive trail rides is usually twenty-five miles, and they go up from there to one hundred miles. For a horse to do that comfortably, he has to have the correct attitude: he doesn't like to quit. A field hunter needs to have a fairly decent conformation for his jumping capabilities, but he does not have to be a great beauty. This is also true of competition trail horses. For both of these, form follows the function—if they can get around capably, that's just fine.

## FIELD HUNTER

Frequently, some of the slower fox hunts or first-season fox hunters use Appaloosa or quarter horse crosses because they're easy to control and are willing to go on. But at the same time, they're not going to run off with you and try to pass the fox. They have a phlegmatic, follow-the-leader attitude that makes it much easier for their rider to maintain his place in line and not overtake the horse in front of him. Half-bred horses are also quite nice because of their mellow attitude. Because of their heavier build and thicker-through-the-neck-and-throat latch, they are a little harder to stop because they don't flex their necks easily and shift their weight to their hindquarters. They're not quite as agile, but they're terribly comfortable and a very easy ride. They also have an excellent sense of self-preservation.

When one is out for four and a half or five hours on a regular basis, the horse soon learns not to waste any extra energy fussing because he's going to need it a little later on. They are especially careful conserving their energy going up and down hills. The seasoned hunter will measure his jumps, and jump only as much as necessary to get the job done, if he's economical in his style.

If you want to fox hunt, you would buy a field hunter that has hunted for at least three seasons and is very quiet. You check his references in the hunt to find out how quiet he really is. If at all possible and you are already jumping at the skill level to do it, you hunt the horse. If not, you find an expert rider you trust to fox hunt the horse for you to find out what he's really like.

## EVENT HORSE

If you're looking for an event horse, you want the horse to have the bulk of his experience already in competition. The United States Combined Training Association keeps records from the preliminary level of every competition that the horse enters, and a breakdown of how he did in each section of that event. An intermediate rider who wants to go on the eventing circuit needs a preliminary horse that has had several years of safe jumping experience. It is critical that he be able to get around a cross-country course without falling and with few refusals. The event horse has had dressage training so he already knows the cues to teach his new rider how to do the maneuvers. Frequently, the horse is so experienced he can almost do the test by himself.

Similar to the fox hunter, the event horse is more a type rather than a particular breed. He is often half Thoroughbred crossed with something else or half draft, half Thoroughbred. Occasionally, you'll find Appaloosa or Standardbred.

The horse that has the ability for jumping will have more angulation to his hindquarters, so he can compress and push off when he's jumping. A field hunter will frequently be very quiet and is not interested in being the first horse out in front. An event horse, on the other hand, wants to be first. He can be quite enthusiastic about hunting and be a harder ride in the hunt field because of his desire to go forward, a desire that is critical to your success in cross-country when he is the first horse in line. Event horses can be any size but usually are around sixteen hands. He can be smaller than that successfully at the lower levels through preliminary. Usually, you don't find a small horse above that level.

Show hunters are entirely different—they're usually finer, almost always a Thoroughbred, with a generally hotter temperament and very attractive to the eye. They may not have any brains. It is sometimes difficult to find reputable professionals who will tell you straight facts about a horse, so one needs to be even more careful with one's vetting program to make the sure the horse is sound and sane. Again, with a show hunter as with any other competition horse, such as an event horse or a dressage horse, the American Horse Show Association keeps records of the horses' wins and places in the various rated shows. You can communicate with the agent in the New York office for a copy of the transcript to find out if the owner is being straightforward about what the horse has done. With dressage horses, the Dressage Federation keeps that material as well as the AHSA.

## SOUNDNESS

A field hunter needs to be very sound but not quite as sound as an event horse. Frequently, ex-event horses become field hunters in their old age and do an excellent job of it. A field hunter will only be going out once or twice a week and he has rest days in between. He also usually has the summer off or has light hacking during that period. An event horse is in a much more strenuously athletic program, with a lot of trotting and a certain amount of canter work on a prolonged basis. As a result, an event horse is more likely to develop problems.

When you pick out a horse to buy, it is of great importance to have the horse vetted by a reputable vet who has no connections whatsoever to the family, trainers, etc., of the horse. The veterinarian will attempt to evaluate the horse's soundness for your intended use. Since there are different levels of soundness, it's important to tell the veterinarian exactly what you plan on doing with the horse.

Frequently, for an event horse or a dressage-oriented horse, X rays are made of both the front ankles and feet and also the hocks behind. At the higher levels, there is much stress on the joints from the concussion of the jumping and from the changing weight distribution of the dressage. Unfortunately, in these times, drug abuse for horses is something to be considered. If you are not absolutely, completely positive that you know everything about the person you are buying the horse from, you should spend the money to have drug tests done to make sure he is not on tranquilizers or on a pain-masking substance that would cover up lameness.

Some tranquilizers are effective for as long as two weeks. So, even if you took the horse home on approval, at the end of two weeks you may have an entirely different beast from the one you had at the beginning. While many drugs do have tests, there are a few that tests have not been devised for. You must hope that you are not buying from an unscrupulous dealer.

If you look at a horse that seems unusually quiet and there is blood on his neck at any point, be highly suspicious, because a badly done injection will leave a lump on the neck and will occasionally bleed. It's a tip that something is wrong with that horse. Be sure and mention it to your veterinarian as well.

Occasionally, with young horses, if the horse is not fit and has been ridden hard the day before, he will be very quiet and saggy. A gelding will even drop his penis and let it swing as if he were tranquilized. A veterinarian ought to pick up on that clue and look for a tranquilizing problem. However, a horse who is just tired can pull himself back up, whereas a horse that's tranquilized cannot.

## THE QUESTION OF PRICE

What you can expect to pay for the right horse, once you find him, will depend on numerous factors. The condition of the economy in general is one: a pleasure horse is a luxury item and the demand is often dependent on the amount of disposable income available at the given time.

The kind of horse you are looking for is, of course, another factor. Some breeds customarily fetch a higher price than others. The kind of competition the buyer wants a horse for will surely come into play as well as the horse's age, condition and training. Also, prices may vary according to the area the seller is living in.

The prospective buyer would be wise to ask professional riding instructors and experienced equestrians for some ideas on what to pay for the kind of horse he or she wants and where such horses may be available.

Be wary of very low asking prices. There may be some serious problem attached to the bargain horse that might not be obvious until you get your purchase home. Auction horses should be considered carefully and no purchase should ever be made without carefully observing the horses you are considering and getting the opinion of a competent veterinarian before committing yourself to a purchase. Another way of discovering "ball park figures" for different kinds of horses is to consult the various periodicals serving the equestrian world.

## INTELLIGENCE AND HUMOR

An event horse is frequently very intelligent. Horses are similar to people—some are smart and some are not. If you can spend time with a horse and observe how he reacts to you and to new situations, you'll learn a lot about how he thinks. Ideally, you'll find a horse who quickly figures out a complex puzzle, which might show up as an ability to undo all the locks in the barn or take the phone off the hook and make long-distance phone calls by wiggling his nose around the dial. He might enjoy turning himself around in the trailer or playing tricks on other horses or trying to dominate them. While occasionally one will find a lovely event horse who is very proper and wouldn't dream of doing anything wrong, usually there is a sense of humor hidden deep within the equine brain.

When gold medalist Might Tango was on vacation after the world championships, he was very frustrated from being out of work. To ease the angst, he had been allowed to wander loose in the stable area as if he were an oversized dog.

One day, perturbed at his slightly smaller than usual share of adoration and jealous of the attention the other horses were receiving, he uprooted one of the nearby rosebushes. Delicately holding it between his teeth, he waltzed into the barn. There, finding a crosstied equine in whirlpool boots, he dropped the bush on his victim's rump. Gleefully, Tango trotted out of the barn to a sweet cacophony as the startled horse bounced about.

Frequently, horses that have a ponylike sense of humor, intelligence, and a lot of time to be bored will come up with many ways to get into trouble. They develop almost prehensile dexterity with their lips to get themselves out of their stalls, to turn on and off light switches, and to have great fun with turning on and off hoses and faucets. Anything that can be twisted or pushed is fair game. It makes the game a lot more fun if something dramatic happens thereafter, such as the water overflowing.

One event horse, in particular, has made a small career out of his spare time when he was resting between competitions. He opened his stall door, freeing himself of the ennui of confinement. Desiring company, he would then free another horse and the two would then antagonize the rest of the horses in the barn. The dynamic duo acted the classic line of the three-year-old child "Na na na na na. I've got something you don't have. Gee, the grass is greener over here. Do you want to take a good look at it? You can't have it!"

Then, having exhausted that particular game, they meandered over to the automatic waterer and started playing with the bubble that holds the water mechanism in place. They very quickly figured out that if they pressed it a certain way the water turned on, and if they let it go, the water would turn off. So one horse backed up and basically sat on it until he was surrounded by a major pool. In the process, he bent the spigot so when he left the water kept flowing.

Another time, the same horse discovered that the emergency telephone in the grooming area was very easy for him to reach with those big lips of his. He took the phone off the hook and spun the head set about by its cord in large circles. Dropping the head set, he turned his attention to the rotary dial, using his lips to move it. When he got a squawk at the other end, he put his head down to listen to it, pleased with himself. As the squawking got worse, he picked it up and started spinning the dial again. He wasn't caught at this until the first phone bill came in.

To go further, he was bored in the pasture and decided his owners had been playing too much tennis on an adjacent court. Therefore, he let all the horses in the pasture out and herded them over to the tennis court and made them stand on the court until the master showed up. Now, there's nothing to eat on a tennis court. There's nothing to do except stomp around with studded shoes and leave little holes. He did have a wicked gleam in his eyes when he was found by his owner.

12

This particular horse was at his worst when he would be sidelined with an injury that he considered to be minor and his owner considered sufficiently major to keep him out of work. The horse would watch the replacement horse start to get exercise and he would become jealous. Several weeks later, he would then single out the poor replacement horse for a bit of bullying. The rookie would be pushed about the pasture or kicked or generally terrorized. If worse came to worst, the old wounded warrior would let himself into his horse trailer. Once the ramp was down, he would climb into the trailer and wait for somebody to take him somewhere. Becoming annoyed when no one showed up, he'd turn himself around in the horse trailer to complain about the lack of service.

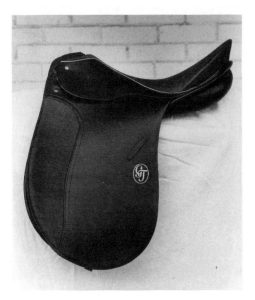

Dressage saddle: very deep through the seat with a long straight skirt, it places the rider in the center of the horse in a long vertical frame.

All-purpose saddle: a jack-of-all-trades, the all-purpose has a deep seat and high pommel with a wide, fairly long skirt. Ideally, with the stirrup leathers let out, one can do dressage. With the leathers shortened, the rider's knee will snug into the jumping support built into the skirt.

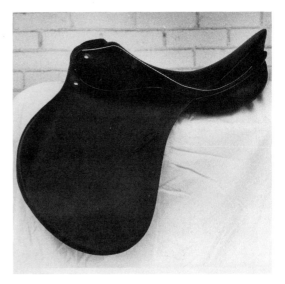

14

# 2

# Saddlery

SELECTION and proper care of correct riding equipment is basic to good equestrianship and the enjoyment of all riding. There is a tremendous variety within all the various components of saddles, bridles, bits, and all the other articles needed for a harmonious partnership between horse and rider.

What constitutes the right equipment will depend on the horse, the rider, and the kind of riding and conditions with which you are dealing. Situations can vary and the rider should be familiar with the tack available to suit a given set of circumstances. This chapter provides sound guidance in selecting tack and equipment and the Bibliography at the back of the book will direct readers to other sources of valuable advice.

## SADDLES

Saddles come in four basic models for English riding. They are the dressage saddle, the cross-country or all purpose, the endurance, and the jumping saddle.

### Dressage Saddles

The dressage saddle has straight skirts to it because when riding dressage, you use a longer stirrup leather to wrap your legs further around the horse and to sit deeper into the saddle. The balance of the dressage saddle puts

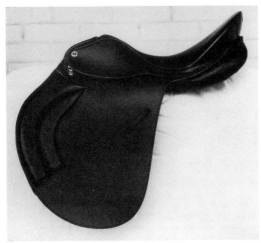

Cross-country jumping saddle: designed to support the rider on drops and banks, the saddle has a low pommel, a deep seat, but not as deep as dressage, and a high cantle. The skirt is molded and padded to create a supporting cup for the knee. A terrific choice for fox hunting and eventing, comfortable for hours.

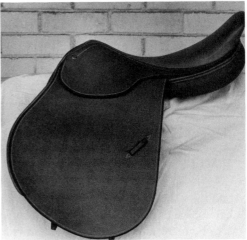

Flat or close-contact jumping saddle: used primarily for horse show and stadium jumping, it allows the rider to move quickly into any position, allowing subtlety of movement. It gives no support to the rider, so it is only appropriate for jumping on flat ground. The seat is very flat with a low pommel and cantle. The skirt has no padding or molding to support the leg.

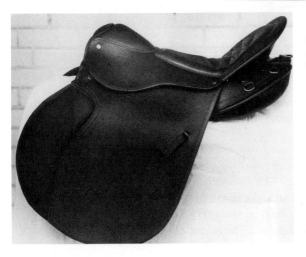

Endurance saddle: designed for competitive trail riding, it has extended panels to spread the rider's weight on the broadest possible surface. It is a hybrid, with an English pommel to allow gallop position and jumping, a deep western seat for long-distance comfort at slow speeds, and dees for attaching equipment across the back, cavalry style. An English skirt supports the leg for jumping, galloping, and steep terrain yet allows the stirrup leather to be dropped to dressage length for slow work.

you into the middle so that your feet are directly under your hips. It's almost as if you are standing up in the saddle.

## All-Purpose Saddles

The all-purpose is a cross between a jumping and dressage saddle. The seat is fairly deep, but less so than a full dressage saddle. The skirts are wide and fairly long, being a compromise between the forward flap on the skirt for the jumping saddle and the longer and straighter for the dressage. If you are going to get just one saddle, the all-purpose is a good choice. As you become more proficient, you'll probably want to sell it and get the saddles that are specifically designed for dressage and jumping.

## Jumping Saddles

The jumping saddle is flatter and the pommel is usually lower than the cantle. It comes in two models. A flat saddle, which has no padding on it, is used for stadium jumping, for show ring riding, and for show hunters. It gives a very pretty picture but no support at all to the rider. The other type, the cross-country jumping saddle, has molding in the knees and usually a suede padded skirt under the knee that helps to support the rider's leg for drop fences or the concussion from a very high jump. It occasionally will also have a small roll behind the leg to hold your thigh in place. This is an unnecessary feature if you have developed your leg muscles. The cross-country jumping saddle has a deeper seat and is very comfortable for four or five continuous hours of riding. The flat saddle tends to be comfortable only for about twenty or thirty minutes.

## Endurance Saddles

The endurance saddle has extended weight-bearing surfaces. If you turn the saddle upside down, the tree has more padding on it than conventional saddles and the tree is extended close to four inches behind the seat and cantle. The padding also extends farther down the side of the horse so that the pressure is distributed much farther than in a conventional saddle. It is a lot more comfortable for the horse. Endurance saddles frequently have extra grommets on the back to tie on the various provisions that the rider will need in an competitive ride, such as sponges, cups, and other paraphernalia. The saddle also generally has a split tree similar to the old U.S. Cavalry saddles and feels a little strange to the rider, but eventually it becomes fairly comfortable. The balance is a bit different, too. Endurance riders often will run alongside the horse and stand in their stirrups going up and down mountains. They may also stand in their stirrups when their horse is galloping. The balance is a bit like the warrior's saddle designed for charging with his lance.

## Fitting the Saddle

In all saddles, when you are buying, you should turn it over and check the padding of the tree. You want as wide a weight-bearing surface as you can manage. You would like the saddle, when placed on the horse, to have even weight-bearing surfaces. If there is a knot in the padding of the saddle, it will apply pressure to that spot and can cause the horse to develop a pressure sore. One way of checking for a possible pressure point is when you take the saddle off, there will be a dry spot where the pressure point is because the sweat glands have been compressed. If a pressure point is allowed to continue to develop, an ulcerated area will result, which might take several months to heal. The horse usually loses skin and hair in that particular area until the healing is complete. There can be muscular damage as well. A saddle poorly fitted can cause lameness. Frequently the lameness will show up as a hindquarters problem in that the horse is not completing the stride with his haunches. If, when grooming your horse, you find he drops away from the brush and the curry on his back, you may have a saddle problem.

As far as the rider is concerned, you want the balance of the saddle to place your hip directly over your heel. The saddle should be totally level. It should be very comfortable to get up easily into a posting trot. You should not feel that you are behind the motion or that you have been thrown on the pommel. In the fitting of the saddle to the rider, you need enough space so that you're not actually pressured in any way but not so much space that you slide around. Trying a saddle on the rack is a whole different ball game from trying it on the horse. It's very important that saddle and horse are comfortable with each other.

## Saddle Pads

Saddle pads come in many different sizes and shapes. The two basic forms are square and contoured. The square, which is seen frequently for dressage and competition use, usually is just a flat pad. It has no particular padding to it. The contoured pads occasionally will be a little bit thicker and have a bit more padding to them. These can be used to adjust the fit of the saddle.

There are also specialty pads, such as the high-density foam pads. Some are designed to have a wedge-shaped thickness to them. These can raise the front or back of the saddle. Another one for the back of the saddle is called a "lollipop," from its shape. You can also have one that goes under the entire weight-bearing area of the saddle, which relieves the pressure points of the tree. The pad will make the saddle a little smaller through the fork of the tree.

The high-density foam pad should be considered a necessity of life if you are spending time on top of your horse. It will alleviate much of the back soreness of the horse. A sore-backed animal will soon develop other ailments in his attempts to protect his injured area.

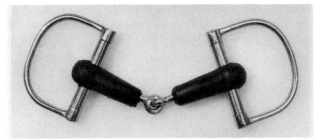

Rubber snaffle: the mildest bit, very thick and chewable, it has "D" cheek pieces to assist in turning the horse without pinching the lip.

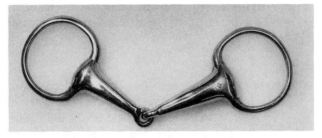

German thick hollow-mouth snaffle: an extremely mild bit, it does not have turning support in the cheek pieces.

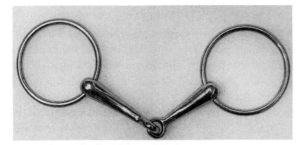

Free ring snaffle: a medium thick bit; the cheek pieces can pinch or slide through the mouth. Frequently, rubber discs are put on the bit at the joint of the mouth and cheek to prevent this.

The pad is especially helpful when you are learning and using the sitting trot. It absorbs much of the concussion of the shock of your body weight against the horse's back. It takes a long time to become synchronized with the horse's movement, so the pad softens your errors for both you and your horse. To make it less noticeable for competition, you can slip it into a matching cover or an envelope section of a regular saddle pad.

### Purchasing a Saddle

When buying a saddle, you should consider getting a used one, one that is already depreciated. You can get a used saddle that is already broken in and is comfortable for both you and the horse. When you get ready to sell it, you will actually end up making money because over the years the saddle will appreciate, as the cost of hand-made leather goods goes up. The point of having it already broken in is important because a new saddle will require about six months' worth of settling.

However, if it does not suit you after just a few months, then you have to sell it as a used saddle, usually for at least a third off. The more expensive saddles hold their value better for the long term than an inexpensive saddle.

### Care of Saddle

A used saddle or saddle purchased new, which you have had for a couple of years, will have its stuffing shift, creating pressure spots and also areas where it is lower, throwing you off balance. Your saddler can raise your saddle by restuffing and adjusting the knots and pressure points, thereby extending its life.

If you have a fall or the horse rolls on the saddle, be sure to take it to a saddler and have the tree checked to make sure it is not broken. A broken tree will damage both horse and rider. You also need to check for broken trees in saddles when you buy them.

## BITS AND BRIDLES

Bits are designed to give control of the horse. This can be done by exerting pressure on the poll, nose, jaw, and mouth. An expert rider can ride a difficult horse in the softest of bits. By excellent timing, he can adjust the horse to his needs. The lower-level rider needs more mechanical help until his timing and coordination improve.

Dressage work will improve the horse's balance and allow the rider to gain more control with less bit. The more severe bits should only be resorted to under expert supervision. The bit action can be so harsh that the horse will refuse to function and may go crazy from pain.

Generally speaking, the snaffle is the mildest bit, then the Pelham, Kim-

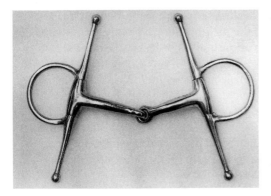

Full cheek snaffle: medium thin mouthpiece, plus extend cheeks, gives more turning and stopping control while encouraging the horse to accept the bit.

Dr. Bristol snaffle: the double-jointed mouth and the plate set on an angle break up the horse's jaw action so he cannot lean on the bit or lock his jaw. With the right side up, the angle of the plate follows the angle of the tongue.

Roller snaffle: a thin mouth with free moving rollers to encourage mouthing the bit, coupled with "D" cheeks to aid turning.

Bar and roller snaffle: this is a more severe snaffle. The bars have a more rectangular shape while the rollers keep the horse mouthing the bit. The oversized egg-butt cheeks help with turning.

berwick, full bridle, and gag bridle. Hackamores are quite difficult to use because horses react inconsistently to the nose pressure. The other variations to bits are: the thinner the mouthpiece or the longer the shank, the more severe the bit.

Many bits have pieces in them to encourage mouthing and chewing of the bit. A wet-mouthed horse will be more comfortable with having a bit in his mouth. Some of the wetness comes from the horse bending his neck at the poll. This releases the production of saliva, further helping movement of the bit. An excellent, specific book on the subject, *The Horse and the Bit,* by Susan McBane (Howell Book House), gives an in-depth look at the entire subject.

### Snaffle

The "D" and the full cheek snaffle are designed with extended pieces on the side to help the rider turn the horse. The extensions put pressure on the side of the mouth and keep the bit from pulling through. The Dr. Bristol snaffle has a plate in the center that is offset so that it moves at a different angle and reminds the horse to pay attention at the bit. More severe than the Dr. Bristol is the twisted wire snaffle, which can cut a horse's mouth if it is not used discreetly. Roller snaffles have bars on the sides and rollers in the middle. Again, each of these gives the horse something to mouth and the nut cracker action breaks up his resistance in his jaw to the bit.

### Gag Bridle

Another kind of snaffle is a gag bridle, which is different in that the bit is not fixed in one place, but slides on a track up and down the cheeks of the bridle. This teaches the horse to bring his head up and helps the rider break resistance on a severely pulling horse. Usually, this kind of horse pulls at a gallop and tends to get on his forehand, refusing to shift his weight to his hindquarters. It's frequently seen on steeplechase horses, high-level event horses, or open jumpers. Most of the time, riders go with two reins, one that goes to the gag action of the bit and the other that goes to the regular section of the bit and creates a regular snaffle effect when the horse cooperates.

### Pelham Bridle

The Pelham bridle is designed to have a longer lower shank plus a curb chain. This creates a pressure behind the horse's jaw line in addition to putting pressure over the tops of his ears by pulling the bridle down behind his ears. The Pelham has two rings, one for the snaffle, which is a straight bar, and then a lower rein to control the curb. The Pelham is most frequently seen in the fox hunting field. Horses who normally would go on a snaffle are so enthusiastic that they need more brakes, and the Pelham does a nice job of giving the rider brakes but not pushing the horse too hard.

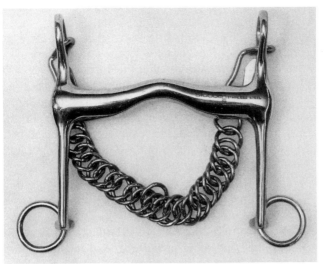

Curb: the curb used alone, is used to flex the horse's head and neck and help with collection. It stops forward movement as well. Curbs come in a variety of thicknesses. This one is a very thick German hollow-mounthed curb with a medium length shank. It would be used for a high-level dressage horse.

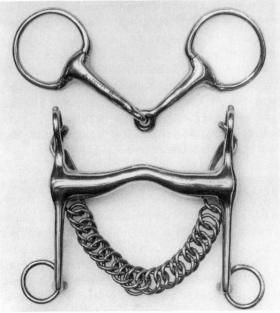

Full bridle: the bradoon is a small-cheeked snaffle that is designed to be worn at the same time as the curb. The snaffle is placed higher in the mouth to allow space for the curb. The thickness of the mouth of this bradoon is appropriate for the thick curb.

23

## Full Bridle

A full bridle or double bridle has two bits to it: a snaffle bit, which is fairly small, and a curb bit. Since the bits act independently, each one has stronger action than that of a Pelham. Occasionally, one will find old school fox hunters using a full bridle for a young horse to help him flex and keep his head up. Usually, it's found on a more advanced horse, who has either been given a lot of dressage training and the curb is used for correction, or for an advanced event horse who needs the extra collection over fences in the stadium area. You rarely will find a full bridle being used in the cross-country phase of eventing because of the difficulty of sliding the reins for drop fences.

## Hackamore Bridle

There is also an entirely different type of bridle called a hackamore. This uses no bit whatsoever, but rather pressure around the horse's nose. This is illegal for dressage and for many of the competitive sports. So, if you are going to use this option, read your rule book very carefully.

## Kimberwick Bridle

The Kimberwick is a curb bit effect bridle. Like the Pelham and full bridle, the curb chain behind the horse's jaw pinches when the rein is pulled. The Kimberwick, however, has only one rein. If the curb chain is not smooth against the jaw, it will become too severe for the horse. You can damage a horse severely with a curb chain that is too tight or twisted. The decision of which bridle to use and which bit to use depends on not only the horse's temperament but what one is trying to do with the horse. For example, a horse who is a quiet ride by himself will go in a snaffle, probably just a normal jointed one. If you ride in company and you decide he's a little enthusiastic, you might go to a narrower snaffle or a Dr. Bristol.

## Controlling Nosebands

If you wanted still more control such as riding a dressage test or a cross-country course where you wanted to keep riding with a snaffle rather than going to two reins, you could add a drop or a figure-eight noseband for cross-country. The figure eight is not used as often for the dressage work, although it is perfectly acceptable. The drop noseband is used in preference for dressage because aesthetically there's less on the horse's face, presenting a prettier picture.

However, for galloping and cross-country work, the drop noseband is unsuitable because it cuts off a certain amount of the horse's capacity for oxygen. He can't open his nostrils as far. The figure-eight noseband has many different points of pressure, so it's a very influencing thing, creating a strong

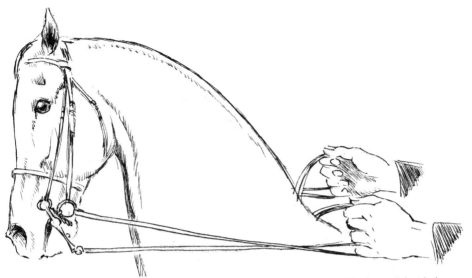

Full bridle: the snaffle bit is adjusted to be higher in the horses mouth with the curb just below it. The flat curb chain is attached to hooks on the curb bit. The illustration also shows the correct way to hold the reins both for the full bridle and the pelham.

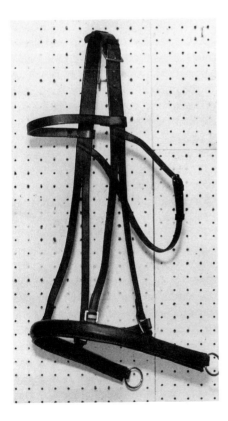

Hackamore bridle: A bitless bridle, its controlling action comes from the nose and pressure on the poll similar to a lunging cavesson. It is very difficult to use because the horse reacts inconsistently.

effect on the horse's carriage. It requires being properly adjusted. You need to adjust and mark all of the pieces and take it in to the saddler. Have him stitch each of the points in place. As a result, the figure-eight is usually for one horse or a horse that's very, very close in the same head shape. Figure-eight nosebands that come straight from the tack shop rarely will work properly.

Tack shops sell a figure-eight noseband that is all sliding pieces. You can buy this particular type of noseband as long as you plan on taking it to the saddler and having it tacked at the proper pressure point. Otherwise, the noseband shifts around about three minutes into the ride. The bottom part that goes around the horse's muzzle falls off. This can be very disconcerting when you're coming up to a large ditch and bank combination.

An alternative to cut the cost of buying equipment is something called a flash noseband attachment. This goes on your regular noseband and attaches on the front of the nose, turning the regular item into a dropped noseband. This works only if you can adjust the regular noseband up enough to compensate for the space that the buckle takes on the flash noseband. It's a handy little device to carry with you in your sandwich case if you're fox hunting. If your horse starts getting too cantankerous with you, it gives a quick fix in the middle of nowhere.

### Breastplates

To hold the saddle forward and in position are two kinds of breastplates. One is called the hunting breastplate, which forms a yoke around the horse's neck and attaches to the saddle at three points. The second kind is known as the polo breastplate. It has a holder over the horse's neck and is attached to the saddle only in two points. The polo breastplate works better for greater rider weight or high-stress situations. The hunting breastplate is nice for less rider weight, dressage, and general appearances.

The rider can hook a thumb or a finger under a hunting breastplate if the horse should start to buck to help the rider keep his balance. It's an alternative to holding on to the mane, which tips you forward and is not good. Putting a thumb under the breastplate for a buck allows you to keep your shoulders behind your hips and ride the buck out more easily.

### Martingales

Frequently, from the breastplates there are attachments for martingales. The martingale is a piece that runs from the noseband of the horse down through the breastplate and attaches to the girth between the horse's legs. Its purpose is to keep the horse from putting his head up in the air in resistance to the rider. If a horse is particularly difficult, a standing martingale is often used as it does not require pressure from the rider's hands.

A running martingale is used for event work because if a rider releases the rein, it releases the effect of the martingale and allows the horse in trouble

Gag bridle: an alternative snaffle for severely pulling horses. The leather cheek pieces go through the metal cheeks of the bit. When the rein attached to the bottom of the leather cheek piece is pulled, the snaffle slides up the bridle, putting pressure over the poll as well as in the mouth. Another rein is attached to the metal cheek and activates the snaffle. One must be a good rider before using this bridle. The hands must be very quiet or the horse will overreact.

Kimberwick: more severe than a snaffle, it acts more as a short-shanked curb. If the rein is attached to the large ring, it acts like a very short-shanked curb. If two reins are used, the upper acts as a snaffle and the bottom as a curb. Horses frequently react inconsistently to this bit. It is mostly used by lower-level riders in the hunt field when they want to use only one rein.

Pelham: most frequently seen in the hunt field. The upper ring takes the snaffle rein while the lowest takes the curb. The little ring in the middle is for a lip strap to hold the curb chain in place.

to correct itself. A standing martingale will not release until it breaks. There are also a variety of running martingales that are either in a bib shape or two rings independent of the strap to the breastplate between the legs.

The German martingale runs up from between the legs up through the breastplate through the rings of the bit and attaches to rings sewn on the reins. This is an automatic version. It's a cross between the standing martingale and the running martingale. It is not legal for three-day event riding.

Occasionally on ponies one will see a crupper strap, which is a strap that goes from the back of the saddle around the pony's tail. These are seen mostly on ponies, because they have very little in the way of withers. If one puts his head down, the saddle pops forward and out over his neck. Occasionally, in high-level dressage exhibitions, one will see a crupper strap for horses such as Lippizaners, who do the airs above ground. The movements create sufficient torque that the saddle is likely to slip.

## Fitting Equipment

Ideally, when you're fitting a bridle to the horse's head, you want to be able to slip your hand under the throat latch when it's done up. Or you can tuck the horse's head into the vertical position to make sure he has enough looseness in the throat latch, that he can still breathe with his head tucked to the vertical. You don't want the throat latch any looser than a hand's worth because the bridle will slide off the horse's head. In adjusting the nosebands around the nose, you want one finger width so the horse can move his jaw slightly but not a lot. The breastplate adjustments are so that the breastplate is snug against the horse's chest where the chest and the base of the neck meet. The strap that runs from the girth up to the ring of the hunting breastplate usually needs to have an extra hole punched to make that strap sufficiently short. If you can find a hunting breastplate with adjustable sidepieces so that the yoke can be adjusted to the neck of the horse, it will make it fit a great deal better. With the polo breastplate, if you slide one of the loops through the girth where the girth attaches onto the billet straps, it will keep it from shifting from side to side or twisting. Alternatively, if you sew loops into the bottom of your saddle pad, you can use the loops to help hold the positioning of the breastplate by putting the breastplate between the loops and the billet straps.

## Care of Tack and Equipment

Saddles need frequent oiling to keep them safe and supple. If your saddle feels hard and stiff, it is in need of oil. The leather should feel pliable and resilient in order to take the amount of torque and pressure that riding creates. The saddle oils are not all created equal and it takes some time to figure out what works best for you.

Two products are particularly good. One is Hydrophane, which comes from England. Hydrophane's point of interest is that it does not stain white breeches. So if you are competing, you want to pay particular attention to that product for areas where your breeches touch the saddle. Anytime you oil a saddle with any other product, you should expect to have stains on your breeches for at least a week and a half afterward. The other product is Tanner's Conditioning Oil, which penetrates very quickly and helps to waterproof and adds sweat resistance to the leather. If you warm the oils before you apply them to the leather, and you have warmed the leather as well, they will penetrate much faster. You don't need to boil the oil; it just needs to be lukewarm to be able to make a difference.

Saddle soaps will clean the leather but do not put the oils and conditioning back. Therefore, you have a two-part series of care on horse leather goods: saddle soaping daily whenever the tack is used to keep it clean, and regular oiling to keep it soft and pliable. Saddle soaps, if applied too profusely, will rot the stitches, but used in moderation they do a nice job. In many cases, a little water goes a long way in solving the problem and you do not need to use the soap at all.

There are several products out for cleaning the silver and brass. Duraglit from England is one that works quite well and is not terribly messy, so can be used for competitions.

If they are not too dirty, the wool horse blankets can usually be washed in a washing machine on the delicate cycle. Hang to dry, or run through the no-heat cycle of the dryer to remove most of the dampness, and then hang to dry. Do not try washing your big heavy blankets at home. They will totally destroy your washing machine, unless you have an extremely heavy-duty one.

# 3

# Feeding and Care of Your Horse

How your horse performs is directly related to what you're feeding him, so the rider needs to take an interest in what his horse is getting for breakfast, lunch, and dinner. The horse that is turned out twenty-four hours a day or twelve hours a day on good pasture does not need a heavy grain supply unless he is in hard use. The grass is usually quite rich except in the winter. It fluctuates, having much higher protein content in the spring and fall. At these high-protein times, one must especially guard against founder in a horse at pasture.

## DIET COMPONENTS

### Hay

Horses need a lot of hay if they are off pasture to keep their intestines working properly. Horses are grazing animals and are used to having a lot of roughage, which the hay takes the place of. Any good grass hay will do the job nicely. Some types of hay that are particularly used for horses are alfalfa and alfalfa-clover mix.

### Alfalfa Hay

Alfalfa is a legume. It is very, very potent, with a large amount of protein in it. You feed less of it than you would, say, a timothy-clover mix because

Your horse looks forward to his grooming.

of its richness. Many horses consider alfalfa to be candy. You don't need to go to alfalfa hay unless you have a horse who is not eating his hay and is losing weight as a result. Alfalfa is a better choice than increasing his grain content and having him becoming hotter-tempered as a result.

### Grass Hay

A timothy-clover mix or an orchard grass/timothy/clover mix are good solid hays for general maintenance of most horses and ponies. They will give a horse hours of pleasure and keep his body regulated. You can expect a horse in moderate work to eat four flakes of hay in the morning and four in the evening. That comes out to about a half bale a day to keep him happy. If you're putting the horse out on pasture in the winter, you might put the hay out with him and give him an opportunity to nibble and graze at picking up his requirements during his outside time. If a horse has something to eat, he's less likely to gnaw on your fences and develop other vices such as cribbing, weaving, or dismantling your stable and pasture. It makes for a happy horse.

When a horse goes into work and is starting to lose weight, you then, in addition to his hay, start giving him some grain. Sometimes, horses react to grain by showing temperament changes.

### Grains

Oats can make a horse very hot and bouncing off the wall. It's especially true for Thoroughbreds. The expression "feeling their oats" is a very real one. Oats can make the horse seem out of control to you and the horse was just fine before. If you have a horse that is very quiet and you want to increase his energy level, oats is a way of doing it. The steamed and cracked or crimped racehorse oats will give you the best value for your money. Most people mix their oats with sweet feed, which is another type of feed that looks like granola. It has molasses, corn, and various other grains mixed into it. While oats have the highest protein level (being about 14%), sweet feed can come in any protein level that you want. Usually if you're mixing it, you want something that is 10 percent or 12 percent to cut the effect of the oats.

Also, the molasses coats the oats and makes it easier for the horse to swallow small quantities of the oats without inhaling too many at one time. Oats all by themselves are a little difficult for a horse to eat because they are dry and may get stuck in his throat. If you have a horse that tends to eat too fast, you can put his salt block (one of the small ones) in his feed tub. Alternatively, you can put rocks in his feed tub to make him work a little harder to get to the grain. This will slow him down a bit so he doesn't choke on his food.

### Bran

Bran is given as a choice to rest the horse's digestive tract. It can be given damp to relieve irregularity. It is used before and after a stressful situation, such as shipping, cross-country competition, or illness. It is high in selenium, which helps prevent tying-up syndrome. It is frequently used on an everyday basis for horses in work.

### Special Supplements

There is a smorgasbord of mineral and vitamin supplements on the market, each of which has varying degrees of success for developing a harder hoof and more gloss in the coat. Your veterinarian will be able to help you sort through the different products and make a suggestion as to what kind to try for your particular horse's needs.

### Hay Pellets

If you have a horse who still seems hot-tempered on straight sweet feed at 10 percent, you can then switch to a hay pellet combination. These also come in different protein levels. You want a low one, probably about 10 percent. These will calm a horse down even further.

If your horse is in work and you've tried the oats and he still seems to be lethargic, you may ask your veterinarian to do a blood scan on him to see whether or not he is anemic. This may be corrected by an iron plus vitamin supplement that can be put in his feed. Frequently, this gets a very strong response. The horse becomes very energetic. He starts acting enthusiastic, spooks and shys, and generally has more energy than he knows what to do with.

## SOME HINTS ON FOODS AND FEEDING

### Buying Hay

When buying hay, you need to check it for quality. Stick your hand into the center of the bale as far as you can and pull out a handful. The hay should have the leaves and the seed heads still intact. The color should be green. The oxidation should just be on the outside. It should not be musty or dusty-smelling. Frequently, hay that has been baled too green and not allowed to cure properly will become moldy and you need to look for that carefully. If you feed moldy hay to your horse, he will develop respiratory problems.

The hay should not be stemmy or have lots of weeds in it. After you've hefted a few bales, you'll be able to discern whether the hay is of good quality or not, in part from the weight. If it's terribly heavy, something is wrong. If it's terribly light, something is wrong.

### Baling Twine

Most hay in the East is put up with baling twine, which, once removed from the bale, has a life of its own. It multiplies in the dark so that every

Fat horse: the fat horse is fat all over his body but not his legs or head. His neck thickens and may appear shorter as a result. The fat is found on the top line and the ribs do not show. There is little indentation along the sides showing bone structure. The horse may have a hay belly as well. Occasionally, a fat horse looks like a marshmallow with four toothpicks for legs.

A

Thin horse: the thin horse shows every bone in his body. He loses his muscling as well, so he has little mass even in his upper legs. He may have a distended belly from hunger or parasites. He is very weak and susceptible to illness and injury. He has trouble maintaining his body temperature and is unwilling to move around. A veterinarian's advice should be used to devise treatment and feeding schedules.

B

Fit horse: the fit horse carries muscle with a thin layer of fat over it. While the topline is rounded, the musculature shows through. The bones do not stick out, but their presence is hinted. The belly is tucked up, going up from the rib cage to the hind quarters. The ribs may show as a shadow. When you pat the horse, his body feels smooth and hard instead of spongy or bony. There is resilience to the muscles. The coat and the eyes of the horse glow.

C

morning when you come down to the barn, there's even more of it. As a horseman, you'll discover that baling twine is one of the most useful pieces of equipment you'll ever have. You can fix a multitude of things. It's quite strong, yet will break if tremendous force is put on it, and the best part is—it's free. As you go around to visit your friends' barns, you'll discover that baling twine has been plaited and is used as extra handles, or for putting together the surcingles on horses' blankets as an emergency measure, for holding water buckets up when a clip is broken, or holding fences shut. It is a remarkable piece of equipment.

### Price of Hay

The price of hay goes up dramatically from the time it is harvested to the dead of winter when you're most likely to run out. Try to organize your stable to be able to put up your entire winter's worth of hay in the summer, when it comes in from the fields. Frequently, arrangements with your supplier can be worked on a year-to-year basis, so that once you've found the best source of hay in your area, you can have a perennial business relationship with your hay supplier.

Most people do not feed horses the large round bales that you sometimes see out in cattle country because it is so difficult to feed in a stall situation. Also, when horses are turned out together, they tend to fight over their hay. It needs to be placed in several clumps so the horses wander back and forth instead of one horse standing guard, hogging it, and not allowing the other horses to eat.

When properly fed, a horse's frame should be rounded out, but not fat, and his coat will look shiny and will dapple. Dapples are the changes in color from dark to light in an all-over pattern over a horse's body. Any horse of any color can dapple. It's a sign of good health when you see it. Dapples will disappear briefly after a horse is clipped, but with some rubbing and brushing, they will come back up again. The horse's eyes will look bright, clear, and he'll just look like a happy horse. The dapples are less likely to show if the horse is dirty, with a long coat, but once he's been rubbed down, they should start showing up. Some people will feed a coat supplement with corn oil to enrich the horse's diet to add more gloss to the coat. You can experiment with this on your own or you could ask your veterinarian for suggestions. Usually, you won't need to use it if you're using good-quality hay and grain, your horse has enough turnout, and is healthy.

## SHOEING

There are several ways to shoe or not to shoe your horse for the specific activities you plan on doing with him. A horse who is on grass, will not be on gravel or crossing hard, paved roads, and is usually on soft footing, doesn't particularly need shoes. Horses maintained on sandy soil can also go without. If the horse isn't being ridden terribly hard, you can have his hooves trimmed every four to six weeks. Whenever the horse is left out for a rest, he can be without shoes for the most part. In the summer, in August, when the ground is rock hard, you will probably need to leave the shoes on on the front feet. The horse will break his feet down stamping on the hard ground.

## Your Farrier

Farriers are among the most difficult artisans to deal with. They're independent, they have no sense of time whatsoever, and they are difficult to get. As a result, one does everything one can to hold on to a good farrier.

If at all possible, you should be there when the farrier comes to work on your horse. If you can't, you need to arrange for someone to hold your horse while he is being shod, so that he doesn't wiggle around and upset the farrier. If you have a horse that doesn't like to stand, you need to spend extra time teaching him to stand quietly while the farrier is working on his feet. You might try feeding him little bits of hay or carrots, or if worse comes to worst, hay pellets to keep him occupied while the farrier is nailing the shoes. This way he doesn't injure the horse, and the farrier doesn't become injured by the horse jumping around. Some horses take a fiendish delight in sitting on the farrier. This does not endear them at all to the farrier's heart. There is no need for a farrier to be rough with your horse. If he hits your horse with a file or seems to be unnecessarily rough, you need to find another farrier.

Thereafter, your horse will require more training time to get him to stand quietly, since he has now had another bad experience. Your horse does not need to stand perfectly still the entire time the farrier is there. It is only when the farrier is actually working on his feet that he needs to be still and quiet. All of your lunging work teaching him voice commands will help keep him standing still.

Farriers need lots of praise about what they do right. They are artists at heart and it takes a tremendous amount of encouragement to keep them happy and coming back. If you tend to correct your farrier many times, you may need another farrier. Rather than his telling you that he's unhappy being corrected by you so many times, he'll just simply refuse to show up. Most farriers, when they pull this number, don't even let you know that they are dropping you as a client, they just don't appear.

## KINDS OF SHOES

### Lightweight Shoes

Generally speaking, you want to use the lightest shoe you can for the purpose at hand. So a training-weight Saddle-lite shoe will work well for a horse that is in training and won't interfere with his movement as much. The heavier his shoe, the more the horse forces his legs up, giving the appearance of climbing.

For dressage competition, you want the horse to look as airy and floaty as possible. Sometimes people will use an aluminum wide-web shoe, which is wider than a normal shoe. This sometimes works better with a lightweight horse, but a heavier horse may twist the shoe into a pretzel.

## Jumping Shoes

Usually if you're planning on jumping, you need some heel caulks for the hind feet. Occasionally, riders will try a polo plate, which has a curved rim all the way around the groove for jumping. This is an alternative way of shoeing that gives the horse quite a bit of traction without too much concussion. In event training, about training level, you will frequently see horses with special shoeing that has screw-in heel caulks. The screw hole is placed in a wider shoe than normal. There are a variety of different-length caulks that can be screwed in for use on the cross-country course for the different weather conditions. These should not be used by a novice. Even the best riders will check with each other to decide what size caulk to use for the particular condition. When these are not in use, which is most of the time, space is filled by a little thing called a "spacer." Alternatively, the riders oil and stuff cotton in the holes to keep the holes clean.

The screw-in studs that are used for eventing are used because of the superior traction they give. They can be adjusted to exact terrain requirements at the moment of competition. It's very similar to a runner having several pairs of track shoes from which to choose, depending on track conditions.

The problem with the studs is that they put a tremendous amount of angled force on the horse's hoof and leg. They jar him with every step he takes because his foot will no longer slide. For that reason, they are only used for competition. The shoes are also very expensive because of the hand detail involved in making them. Jacking the horse's foot up unnecessarily is like making a lady wear four- or five-inch high heels all the time. Eventually, she starts having back trouble or problems with her joints and tendons.

Frequently, a farrier will suggest corrective shoeing for a horse who toes in or out. There is very little you can do to change a horse's way of going without creating new stresses or strains and leg problems. Never do a corrective change without having first checked in with the most reputable, experienced vet you can find. Most veterinarians will recommend the horse's foot move the way it was born to move. They usually don't want you to correct his movement by changing the angle of the hoof walls.

Farriers will sometimes put on just a touch of a trailer to correct for the horse swinging. You need to watch your horse very carefully after this has been done to make sure you haven't made his problem worse instead of better. If your horse starts coming up with back problems or seems sore in any of his joints after you've done a shoeing change, then you've overstressed him. You have to go back to a more normal way of shoeing.

Generally speaking, the less shoe there is the better the horse is going to go. He'll cover more ground, be more comfortable, and he'll stay sounder. The farrier will suggest various heavier-weight shoes following the theory that the shoe will last through more shoeings or because of the weight of your horse. Part of your job as rider and owner is to see how little shoe it takes to get your job done. The cost of the shoe itself is very little, it's mostly the labor to put the shoe on, which you have to pay for anyway when the farrier comes.

## BEYOND HORSE SHOES

### Fox Hunting and Borium

For fox hunting, one frequently goes to a wider shoe that's fairly heavy and will accommodate having a smear of borium put on it to keep the horse from slipping. Borium is a very hard substance that will scratch concrete, tear up stainless steel, and will actually grab into asphalt. Because of its extreme hardness, it gives a horse the opportunity to grab into the ground when he's hunting, and when one goes up and down the frozen gravel roads. If you are planning to ride throughout the winter, borium should be a necessary part of your preparation. When horses have borium on their hind feet, you have to be very careful with turning them out with other horses because they can do a lot of damage if they start kicking each other.

### Snow Pads versus Regular Pads

In the northeast part of the United States, special pads are used for snow. Called "bevel pads," these are designed to pop the snow out of the shoe. They are more expensive than regular pads but are worth their weight in gold if you decide to ride all winter. The pads frequently can be used for the worst months and then pulled and used a second year. In warmer climates, where you're fox hunting and snow is not an issue, you can use a regular pad, which will protect the horse from rocks and gravel. Riders also will frequently use them if they're planning to go to competition. They don't want to risk the chance of a horse coming up lame before the competition.

### Pad Fillings

There are two choices for the filling between the horse's foot and the pad. The traditional method is to stuff oakum. This is a lanolin-and-pine-tar-soaked fabric that's a little bit like flax or linen that has been shredded. It comes in a rope, and the rope is shredded and then packed into the horses' hoof. Farriers like this because it has very easy accessibility. You can pick up large quantities of it at plumbing-supply stores, since it's used for packing around pipes. For the horseman, you need to have the farrier leave extra oakum with you so that you can keep the pads sufficiently stuffed. The oakum will tend to migrate out of the pad on its own and it is more prone to picking up gravel if you do very many stream crossings.

The other alternative is a high-tech alternative: silicone caulk that stays moist and resilient after it is cured. This you can pick up in any hardware store. Usually, you have to get it because the farrier won't pick it up on his own. It's a little more expensive to use and requires greater care on the part of the farrier. It also takes awhile to cure, so you can't have your horse done and then immediately ride him. It will take a couple of hours for the gel to set sufficiently to be able to handle work. But once it does set, it does the same thing for a horse that a running shoe does for a person. The resiliency helps absorb concussion. Once it's in place, it stays in place and is less likely to pick up rocks, gravel, and debris.

Frequently, farriers complain that it burns the sole of the foot when you put it in. Check carefully each of the different varieties of the caulk that are on the market to find one that seems to have the fewest side effects for your particular horse. Also bear in mind that the horse's hoof does tend to be a lot more resilient than one gives it credit for.

### Hoof Epoxy

For a horse that has shelly, brittle hooves that break off and don't hold nails and shoes well, there is now a high-tech solution—a variety of epoxy similar to the epoxy used by dentists. This you can find in many tack shops. There are several varieties using special lamps to cure it. Others are mixed so that they don't require the special lamps. The epoxy coating seals the outside of the hoof, hardening it with a resilient finish that will act as a protective barrier for the hoof. Since it's only used on the outside hoof wall and leaves the cornet band free, the horse still gets the moisture and nutriments that it needs. The epoxy comes in various colors and clear.

## YOUR VETERINARIAN AND YOUR HORSE

Your veterinarian can also tell if your horse is anemic or starting to get run down. Frequently, a horse that gets put into fairly heavy use, such as fox hunting or preparing for a training level or a competition, will after being in training for a couple of months have a drop in his blood count and require a little extra help from the veterinarian to get his blood work straightened out again. Your veterinarian will be one of your best friends when your horse starts looking a little droopy around the edges, or you run into a problem in your training. Often, your vet can tell you if there's a physical basis for why the horse is doing what he's doing.

For example, if the horse is throwing his head a lot, and refuses to take the bridle, perhaps he is very difficult about his bit, refuses to go on the bit and tries a number of evasive maneuvers, it may be that he has problems with his teeth and needs to have his teeth floated. Your veterinarian can ascertain that if he comes out and checks the horse for you. He can also check to see if there is a problem with his ears or some other physical base for the problem you're having. Frequently, your vet is also a horseman and he may be able to give you some practical suggestions that are easy to follow on changing the horse's behavior.

The money that you spend on your vet is an inexpensive way of picking up your education. Eventually, you'll learn enough about veterinary medicine so that you'll know what is an emergency, what is something that the vet will deal with when he can, and the things that you can do yourself. There are veterinary books on the market that are designed for the lay person that can give you first aid information. An excellent choice is *Horse Owner's Veterinary Handbook* (Howell Book House).

### Worming

Your horse will need to be wormed on a regular basis, which is usually about every two months to break up the parasite cycle. There is no way of permanently getting rid of parasites, so what one tries to do is to keep the cycle broken up enough so that the horse does not carry a large load of parasites at any one time. Horses that have parasite problems are much more prone to have heart attacks, colic, and gastrointestinal problems, which can be fatal. Your veterinarian can go over with you an appropriate worming schedule for your area and number of horses that are grazing the property where you have your horse.

### Immunizations

The vet will also suggest the shots that you need for immunizations in your area. In most parts of the United States, horses require eastern and western sleeping sickness shots, tetanus, flu, and rhinopneumonitis every year. These are usually given in combination so that the horse doesn't get as many needles as there are shots. Your veterinarian can tell you what is important for your area and should also be consulted if you're going to move your horse from one part of the country to another, especially if you're transporting commercially or if you're going to competitions in other parts of the country. If you have decided you're going to take the horse out of the country, you will need a passport for the horse and your veterinarian will help you with the paperwork.

### Colic

Colic is a massive stomachache for a horse. It can be caused by worms, by being overstressed, and by having the electrolyte balance get too far out of normal range, among other things. It is a very serious acute condition that requires immediate veterinary care. If you find that your horse has any of these symptoms, he may have colic.

- Sweating profusely
- Biting at his sides and stomach
- Looking distressed at his sides or stomach
- Kicking at his stomach
- Thrashing at his stomach
- Thrashing around the stall
- Lying down and getting up repeatedly
- Trying to roll
- No interest in food
- Cannot pass manure
- Has trouble urinating
- Looks as if he's bloating
- Generally seems extremely miserable

You need to keep the horse up and walking until the vet can get there. This is one case where if your first vet can't come for a while or doesn't respond to the call, keep calling other veterinarians until you find someone who can come. You don't want to wait until morning if you have a colic case.

A colicky horse frequently can be heard banging in the stable from your house because he will be thrashing against the walls. If a horse rolls with colic, his intestines can twist and create a blockage. The horse will die if he does not receive immediate veterinary intervention. Usually, the horse has to have surgery to straighten his gut out again. This is why it is so important to keep the horse up and walking and not let him roll if he's colicky.

Horses are particularly susceptible to colic after a long shipping. Before the trip, your veterinarian will suggest oiling a horse. This means giving him a lot of mineral oil to keep everything working through his digestive system while he's on the trip. Keeping hay in front of him will also help to keep the digestive tract working. Frequently, the good commercial carriers will stop every couple of hours and offer the horse water to keep his system up and running.

### Founder

Colic and founder are two major acute diseases or attacks that a horse owner is always on guard for. Founder is likely to happen if a horse gets wet and chilled while his protein level is very high. It sometimes happens to mares after they have foaled and their hormonal system is shifting. It can also be brought on by high fever. If your horse does not wish to move and seems rooted to the ground, you need a veterinarian immediately. Do not try to move the horse yourself, as you can injure him and tear muscle. Founder is a disease that changes the shape of the bone structure inside the hoof. This makes the horse go lame. It can be severe enough so that the horse needs to be destroyed.

## Tying Up

If the horse has had a massive charley horse of his body, it is known as "tying up." Usually, it comes from having an electrolyte imbalance and stressing the horse too much. He will be unable to move and you will feel his hind end getting very stiff. You can feel the difficulty in his being able to walk. Don't ask him to move if you can possibly help it. For both founder and tying up, cover the horse and keep him as warm as possible. Get a veterinarian immediately.

## Cuts and Anemia

If your horse has had a cut that is severe or he has been on work and seems lethargic, you can check for anemia by examining his gums to see if they have turned pale. A horse with a serious cut should be brought to a veterinarian as soon as possible. Also any abrasions or saddle sores of a serious nature should be brought to the veterinarian's attention.

## Tendons

Every day before you ride, when you are grooming your horse, you should run your hands over the horse's legs, especially down his tendons. This way, you will learn how they feel when they are normal. You will be able to feel all of the hard structures and the tendons behind the knee that run down to the fetlock. Your vet can help you with identifying each of these tendons. By checking every day, you can tell if your horse has hit himself and picked up a knot on a tendon or if he has injured the bone.

A horse will not necessarily show lameness at the start of tendon injury. If you get the veterinarian in quickly to help you with managing the injury, your horse may be only out for a couple of weeks. If you work a horse with the beginning of a tendon injury, you risk the chance of seriously injuring the tendon and having the horse out for a year. There is the distinct possibility that he may not come back to the same level of flexion to the tendon that he had before. This means that the horse would not be able to do more strenuous work.

Some horses will injure their tendons by hitting them when they're playing, twisting, and bucking. A rider can injure a horse's tendon by galloping him too hard and too long for his level of fitness and can literally break the horse down. You frequently will find bow tendons, which is a tendon that has been overstressed and injured, and has lost its shape as a result. Tendon injuries can be found frequently in horses that have been raced and did not receive sufficient conditioning before they raced. However, this injury can turn up at any time with any breed if the tendon has been stretched sufficiently.

# OTHER CARE COMPONENTS

## Turnout

Ideally, the horse is turned out every day in a large pasture or paddock so he can stretch his legs and exercise himself. The more turnout time a horse has, the happier he is and it keeps his disposition from getting sour.

Horses do not do well in cool, rainy conditions. If they get wet and chilled, they are likely to founder. There are rugs called New Zealand rugs that are waterproof, so you can throw one on a horse and on most days if it's not pouring, you can get the horse out for at least an hour or two to clear the cobwebs. Ideally, he's out as much as possible, at least a couple of hours a day, but twelve hours if at all possible. Occasionally, you'll be very fortunate and run into a situation where the horse can have unlimited access to the outside and have a shelter that he can go to if the weather is really bad.

The turning-out time, in addition to being important to his psyche, also helps to maintain him in good health, because he gets a chance to use all of his muscles. If one can turn one's horse out after fox hunting, he will walk out most of the stiffness and swelling in his legs that would show up if you had him just standing in his stall.

Occasionally, if the weather is very cold and you want to get him out, there's nothing wrong with adding more blankets. In some climates, that can be three or four blankets before he goes toddling on out into the snow or the bitter wind. He'll still be grateful for his time out.

## Long Coats

If the horse is not getting used, his coat will grow long in the winter, and by rolling a great deal, he'll build up a lot of dirt in his coat that acts as an insulating felt to keep him warm. The problem with a long coat is that if you were riding heavily enough for him to sweat a great deal, he will chill off; his skin and body will drop in temperature before his coat dries out. You can thus get the phenomenon of having an athlete sitting around in a wet coat that he can't get out of. This situation is also likely to cause founder. If you choose the coated option in the winter and your horse does get damp, you can use an antisweat sheet, which looks a bit like a hole-ridden undershirt, with a cooler over it. Give him the option to dry out slowly with a little extra warmth and protection.

## Clipped Coat

If one is planning on riding regularly enough to make the horse sweat, then one can consider trace clipping, which is a modified trimming pattern on the horse that helps him stay a little cooler. If he is still getting soggy, you might want to go to a blanket clip, which has a bit more skin showing. If you

Turn-out is important to the horse's physical and psychological well-being.

After riding, many riders like to hose down the horse's legs.

are riding a great deal, you might end up going to a full hunter clip. This leaves a lot of fur on his legs, which protects him from jagged plants and the winter winds, but his body is clipped, as is his neck and head. This particular clip is very useful if a horse is doing a lot of galloping, such as for fox hunting, but it requires an entire wardrobe of different-weight blankets to keep the horse warm and comfortable when you aren't riding him. You've taken away his natural protection.

Blankets can be made of wool or Cordura nylon on the outside and be fleece-lined. Many have surcingles attached, which hold the blanket in place. Clips can be sewn into the liners to fasten them to the outside of the blanket to help prevent shifting.

## Stabling

If the horse is clipped, he'll need to have more protection from the elements and will require stabling at night in the winter to try to keep his temperature a little warmer. On the other hand, horses don't do well with artificial heating or air conditioning. So heating a barn is not a great idea for the horses, as nice as it is for the humans. Horses need quite a bit of air flow in their stabling to keep them from coming down with colds and allergies. Frequently, barns are built with a small opening at the bottom of the stall to the outside that is used for venting the ammonia fumes away from the horse's head when he's lying down. In a well-designed barn, there is a lot of open work at the upper part of the stall so the air circulates freely. Horses are very gregarious and they like to see each other and see what's going on, so, again, the ideal barn would be very airy and bright on the inside with a lot of open space so the horses can see out and feel themselves a part of what's going on.

The more amused a horse is, the less likely he is to develop stable vices out of boredom. Stable vices are something along the lines of cribbing, which is chewing on wood or any other surface a horse can hook his teeth into. He will literally inhale hunks of whatever it is he's latched onto, be it metal, wood, or any other surface. There are cribbing straps that go around his neck, which hopefully will persuade him not to swallow air, but it's a very difficult thing to stop a horse from doing. Another thing a hungry horse will do frequently, even if he's turned out in a paddock that has no grass, is to chew on wood because he has nothing else to do, he's bored and he wants to gnaw. You can prevent a lot of vices by keeping hay in front of horses most of the time. Four flakes in the morning and four in the evening go a long way toward abating a horse's urge to gnaw and roam. Being grazing animals, they are used to taking in a lot of roughage and covering quite a bit of ground while they do it. If a horse is stabled, giving him something to do with his spare time is helpful. Some people put toys in the horse's stall, such as a tether ball that he can bounce with his nose. Children's bathtub toys can be placed on top of a water bucket that he could nudge and play with. Usually, if a horse has enough turnout time, and he can see what everyone else is doing, he'll be happy.

# 4

# Outfitting and Conditioning the Rider

$I$N THE SAME WAY as tack and furnishings are selected for the horse, appropriate dress is necessary for the rider. The rider's attire is dictated in part by tradition, in part by the demands of the activity. However, even the most wonderfully turned-out rider is at a disadvantage if he or she is not physically fit to meet the often stringent demand of trail and arena.

## RIDING CLOTHES

Riding jackets are made of a special wool that has more oil than regular wool and is designed to have a certain small degree of water repellency. To maintain the natural oils in the coat, do not dry-clean unless you have fallen in a swamp and it smells terrible. For the wear and tear of a day's fox hunting, let it dry, then you can brush off most of the mud and use a damp rag to spot-clean it. If it was a dusty day and the whole coat is dusty, you can put it in the dryer on the no-heat cycle with a damp rag for fifteen minutes or so. It will pull all dirt out of the coat without damaging it. Some people like to tape the buttons so they do not clank.

With riding breeches, the art form is keeping the leather from shrinking and getting stiff. Some of the saddlers and tack shops carry a leather-washing solution that can be put in the washing machine with your breeches that will keep the leather soft and prevent shrinking. This product is usually made in West Germany, although the English also have one. Leather is very sensitive to heat, so it is rare that you can put your breeches in the dryer. Usually, you end up having to line-dry them turned inside out in the shower stall or some other spot. If they are still soggy at the moment you need to wear them, pop them in the dryer on delicate for a few minutes. This will get the inside dry enough so that you can bear to put them on your body.

## Hats

There are many different varieties of hats on the market. These vary between bowlers, safety helmets, top hats, and derbies for English riding. Ideally, you need a safety helmet that will have inside it an imprint saying that it has passed the safety test of ASTM and is U.S. Pony Club approved. These helmets come in a variety of styles and they all have safety harnesses.

Some of them are designed to have a variety of cap covers on them such as the jockey helmet. Others are designed in black velvet to have a permanent hunt cap look. Your head is one of the few parts of your body that you really cannot do without. Head injuries can be greatly reduced or eliminated by the use of the helmet. If you have had a fall and your head, and helmet, have hit the ground, or if a horse has stepped on your helmet, you need to buy a new one. Even though the helmet looks fine from the outside, the fracture pattern inside may make it give way the next time you have a fall. It is very foolhardy to ride without a safety helmet.

You will find riders who believe that they are invincible. They will choose the older forms of headgear because they like the look and tradition, and they do not care if they have a head injury. The top hat is very dramatic and looks beautiful but is very unsafe. It is most frequently seen for dressage, where one hopes to have greater control over one's destiny than out fox hunting. However, it is also seen in show ring and fox hunting.

The derby was required for many years by many hunts as the preferred headgear for members of the field, and the diehards will still use that in preference to a safety helmet. Derbies have no safety features to them at all and are almost as dangerous as top hats. Since neither cap has a safety harness, they can flip off as soon as any object starts to strike them.

The traditional hunt cap offers more protection than the derby and top hat, but since it does not usually have a safety harness, it will still flip off when you do. In addition, the front of the cap is likely to break your nose if it tips forward when you hit the ground. The back of the helmet can also slip and hurt your spinal cord.

Riding is an adrenaline sport and can be as dangerous as skiing. Like any other sport, if care is taken, you can greatly reduce the chances of injury, and if you should get injured, the injury will be of less magnitude.

## Boots

A rider's boots are usually his first major investment in horsemanship. While it is possible to ride in old hiking boots, with pinched, rubbed, and blistered legs, it take takes most of the *joie de vivre* out of it.

Very few people can ride comfortably in "stock" boots. As a result, custom models are important to the rider as soon as possible. Several bootmakers produce excellent well-crafted boots that will last for many years with proper care. They are wonderful for hard use, fox hunting, and eventing.

Your first pair of boots should be black dress. These are appropriate for anything. Later on, you might get a pair of field boots for less formal events. Ask for cuff-lined, as the boot will break in faster and be more comfortable. Some people prefer three-quarter-lined, but the boot is much stiffer. The break at the ankle settles differently in larger folds. Therefore, it is more likely to rub the back of your ankle.

Ideally, you are measured for custom boots wearing two pairs of heavy socks and heavy breeches. You'll be grateful for the extra room both in the winter and in the summer, when your feet swell—not to mention when holiday banquets catch up with you. Boots can be stretched somewhat larger if necessary.

Putting on new boots can be very difficult. Try to locate a spray can of silicone like electricians use. This will make the boot inside very slippery. One caution; it makes everything around the boot slippery, too, including the floor. Another method is baby talcum powder.

One of the major problems with riding is preventing the sweat stains. The salt in horse sweat will literally eat through the boot in a twinkling of an eye. If you apply warm mink oil and silicone mix to the leather, it will sweatproof and waterproof it. About once every month or so is plenty. You'll know that you should reapply when the leather starts to feel stiff and becomes discolored. The mink oil softens the leather, making it more supple and resilient.

For polish, Properts dressing conditions as well as buffs to a deep gleam. Many riders don't polish the parts of the boot that rub against the horse, since it immediately comes off on the saddle pad.

### Protective Vests

There are protective vests on the market now. Information on them is available through the AHSA, or the U.S. Combined Training Association. Occasionally, saddleries will carry them, but usually they have to be special-ordered. These protective vests are designed to take the force of the fall. Some of them are made with Kevlar, which is used for bulletproof vests. Others are made with a high-impact resistant gel product. Many of the high-level event riders are now wearing these for competition. They can be designed so they don't show under your hunt coat. There are other models that are worn over your cross-country clothes. The heavy men's fox hunting coats help absorb some of the shock on falling, too, although not as much as a protective vest.

## EXERCISE AND CONDITIONING

Many aspects of horse care are very helpful for burning off excess calories. An example of this would be mucking out stalls and grooming your horse.

If you're into jogging or running, you can try to catch your horse out in a larger pasture, which will give you a fair amount of cross-country running on uneven ground. It's also helpful for your tennis muscles in that you will be making quick starts and stops as the horse changes direction.

For practice away from the stable, you could go to a health club that has Nautilus equipment. Or, if you decide that's too expensive, you could buy a copy of Arnold Schwarzenegger's *Encyclopedia of Modern Bodybuilding* and get a few ankle weights. You would thus be using many of the same muscles that you would by working around your horse. For example, if you curry your horse using big circles and pushing really hard, working until you feel the burn, you will have come up with an exercise for the latissimus dorsi muscles that work your shoulders and upper back. Those are also the ones you'll need for doing the half halts when you're on the horse, so they'll come in handy. Plus, your horse will love you more for making him feel so good.

Another area for exercise centers around your trapezius muscles, which run from your neck to your shoulders. With those, you can either do "dumb-bell shrugs" in "upright rows" or you can carry a full water bucket in each hand, which also gives you a happier horse. It gives you the added benefit of carrying extra weight if the water sloshes out into your shoes.

Another familiar exercise is for the gluteus muscles, which help support your lower back. For these, one does squats and half squats with feet even with the shoulder, and one's toes pointed slightly outward. Those will come into play when you are attempting to pick up your horse's hooves to clean, or brushing off his belly and his legs.

For strengthening your legs while riding, you can post without stirrups or try riding in a half seat (that's up in gallop position, roughly), making a point to stretch your muscles out in your legs and your tendons by dropping your heels. Another handy exercise to be done at home is standing on the edge of stairs on your toes and dropping your heels down below the height of the step that you are standing on. You can raise and lower yourself by standing on the toes and then sinking down until your heels are as far down as they will go. This also helps to stretch out your calf muscles. If you want to add weight to that, you can always carry your hay back and forth from the hayloft or a twenty-five-pound bag of grain.

Your abdominal muscles can be strengthened by doing a sitting trot without stirrups, or by doing a large quantity of conventional sit-ups without the horse. One occasionally tries doing sit-ups on the horse, but usually this is after a branch has brushed one flat back and one attempts to regain the center of balance.

If your horse is quiet, you can sit on top of him and do the old-fashioned stretching exercises for your upper body that you remember from high school. Spin your arms out to the side, making little windmills and twist your upper torso with your arms extended. These will help stretch out your side muscles and the middle of your body.

Another exercise is to stretch your legs and shake them out away from

Mucking stalls keeps you fit while it trims the bills.

51

the saddle so that your leg comes farther down and around the horse. Think of limp, wet rags wrapped around the barrel of your horse and it will help you think your legs lower. Or think of your back as being straight and flexible like pearls on a string.

Riders share one of the same problems that runners have, in that the hamstrings and leg biceps muscles that run the length of the back of your thighs and connect up to your pelvis and down to your heels can get very strong. If they get tight as well, they become so strong that they can pull the pelvis out of position, causing a great deal of lower-back pain. Therefore, to keep that set of muscles stretched out, runners' exercises help a great deal.

One of these is to seat yourself flat on the floor with your knees straight, legs outstretched, and with your toes up. Reach for your toes. Don't bounce and don't tug. You just slowly let the stretch relax the muscles and you feel a small give when you let go.

Another stretch for riders who have very wide horses can be found in most yoga books, and in Jane Fonda's workout. This is a stretch for the inner thigh muscles and groin. For this one, sit on the floor with your knees bent outward and the soles of your feet pressed together. Then with a straight back and lifted chin, lean forward slowly until you can touch your feet and pull yourself into a good stretch. You can also use your elbows to help stretch your knees toward the floor. Yoga is very helpful for learning balance and stretching. The Sally Swift book, *Centered Riding,* gives a lot of yoga exercises and visual images to think of to help you relax and to visualize what you're trying to do with your body.

### Saddle Sores

A frequently heard concern of riders is saddle sores. The image of the cowboy or the novice rider standing up to eat dinner is one of the first thoughts most people have. Saddle sores can be avoided in ways other than by not riding. The chafing on your knees that comes from a lot of galloping can be reduced or eliminated by using a skin barrier product before you ride. These usually have some silicone in them and make the surface of your skin sufficiently slippery so that it doesn't snag and cause chafe. This cream can be liberally applied to any part of your body that needs it. One of the best on the market is sold through professional pharmacies. The product is called *UniDerm* and a little goes a long way. A jar of it will see you through fox hunting, and probably through an entire year of riding.

If you are getting saddle sores on your seat, in addition to using a skin barrier, you should consider taking a serious look at your saddle. If you're slipping enough to have a saddle sore, either your saddle is tipping and the balance is incorrect, forcing you to tuck yourself forward to maintain your balance, or the saddle is built incorrectly for you and is so flat that you can't maintain your position. Unless you can correct the slippage problem, you will continue to have saddle sores every time you ride.

You can stretch your legs out before you ride to help prevent cramps and muscle damage.

Stretching your muscles before you start schooling the horse.

If the saddle is balanced and the slippage is minimal, you might be able to put the sheepskin seat saver on the top of your saddle. This is a piece of sheepskin with a leather back that will tend to hold you in place and will make you a lot more comfortable. Many riders use these for training, especially if they're spending five or six hours a day on a horse. One problem with a seat saver: it is not legal for competition. So you may be comfortable for your training, then, when you actually get to the competition, you'll have a problem. Another consideration—if you have a very hard time of it—is that the saddle does not fit you. You need to get another saddle. You do not have to be miserable. It's the same as buying a hat. If it's too tight and you have headaches, you will associate headaches with riding.

### Protecting Your Skin and Eyes

Riders may take superb care of their horses and equipment but forget about themselves. If you don't want to have your face look like old leather by the time you hit your fortieth birthday, remember the sunblock. Between the elements of wind, sun, and cold, your face doesn't have a chance. Since riding, like skiing, requires a lot of time outside, you are at a greater risk for skin cancer, too. Sunglasses can help with protection in addition to shading your eyes. Worn for cross-country or fox hunting, they help prevent dirt clods, branches, briers, and dust from damaging your sight. At a gallop, they help reduce tearing.

## DRESSING FOR THE WEATHER

### Winter Riding Clothes

Another complaint of riders is being too cold in the winter or too hot in the summer. The too cold is easy to remedy by going to a ski shop and getting some long winter underwear. Silk works very well and it's quite thin so it doesn't show under your riding breeches. It is gossamer enough that you can get your legs into your boots once you put the long johns on. There are also silk and wool combinations that are warm and quite thin. The polypropylene tends not to do as well for this particular sport. It's a little harder to maintain because it melts if you forget and stick it in the dryer. All silk tends to be less warm than the silk-wool combination, but if you have a chafing problem, you'll find it more comfortable. Some riders swear by using pantyhose underneath the breeches with a couple of layers of socks.

One of the topics of fox hunting, once the weather starts to turn cold, is whose long johns work best. Endless speculation and a lot of exchange of information is reviewed around the check while waiting for the fox, who has gone into his nice warm hole and doesn't want to leave.

There is now an alternative to riding breeches on the market. This is a variety of ski pants that have been adapted to riding use with a leather strip down the inside. They are very comfortable in cold weather. For hacking out, their ski pant qualities make them wonderful for riding in the snow, which is a real treat. Also, in the winter, one can find insulated riding boots or go to a snow boot with a heel. There are many of these on the market now that are made with Gortex and are quite flexible.

In gloves, deerskin leather continues to be quite pliable even when wet and frequently comes with a wool liner. You can also purchase a silk liner. Have a variety of weights or an alternate pair to warm your hands if one pair of liners become soggy. Frequently, when you're fox hunting, you'll carry a spare pair of silk liners inside your coat pocket in case the weather turns or if your gloves have gotten too damp to use and your hands are growing numb.

One can use a skimobile outfit if you're really anxious to get out when it's quite cold. You can think in terms of skiing in order to imagine something that keeps you warm. Some riders like putting chaps over their pants and find that works to help keep the warmth in.

## Summer Riding Clothes

In the summer, there is the opposite problem, trying to cool off. You need to remember that your safety helmet is solid and doesn't necessarily have very good air flow through it. Therefore, you need to take breaks, remove your hat, and be in the shade.

There are quite loose camp-type shirts that permit free air flow and allow maximum cooling. Sometimes you can find these in tennis shops or specialty catalogs.

There are also breeches now on the market that are made with much more cotton so they provide better air circulation. Gloves come in a driving style made with openings on the back to let your hands breathe.

When the temperature climbs up to around 100°F, unless you have been working hard for competition and must continue to practice, you'll find that everything goes better for you if you either give the horse the day off or ride very early or very late. The temperature is coolest at dawn. Many riders will get up before dawn and have their horses saddled and ready to go as the light breaks so that they get the maximum use of the time. Other riders are fortunate enough to be able to ride under lights in the evening. When the weather is very hot, you want to avoid stressing the horse too much. Horses are just as prone to heat prostration as people are. Therefore, one wouldn't do gallops and canters if the weather is hot.

In the winter, when it gets very, very cold, the horse will enjoy moving on in a trot. Again if the ground is hard frozen, the concussion is hard on his legs if you go faster. Snow pack gives some resilience but still requires caution.

## Falling Safely

How to fall is an acquired art. When one is leaving the company of one's horse, over his shoulder, either voluntarily or involuntarily, the idea is to tuck and roll in a somersault. When you land, you are in a ball and the force of the fall is dissipated. This also has the advantage in that you can keep on rolling and get out of the way of the horse if he is coming down, too. Most falls have you over his shoulder, forward and off to one side. While there is a small amount of time, try to tuck your head into your chest and start the spin. This way you will be landing on a shoulder and then rolling over on your back in a curled-up fashion similar to a fetal position.

When falling, don't try to take the reins of the horse with you. If your hand gets tangled up in the reins, the horse may end up dragging you, or if he starts rolling as well, the reins will pull you into him. In addition, if he gets up before you do, he can dislocate your shoulder.

You may want to practice falling and the roll at home on the ground or on a gymnastic mattress. Many health clubs will give you a hand in learning how to do the gymnastic somersault. If you explain what it is that you want to learn, they will even help you with doing it from a little height. Ideally, you do not want to fall over backward because it is much harder to curl up and break the force of the fall.

The saddle has a stirrup leather bar that is a safety catch. When it is locked in the upright position, the stirrup leather and stirrup will not fall off. When it is opened to the release position, if you have a backward fall, the stirrup leather will release from the saddle and you will not get dragged by your foot, cowboy style. This looks painful in the movies and can be fatal in reality.

# 5

# Horse Transportation

---

**A**FTER THE RIDER has acquired a steed, he quickly discovers a wealth of new opportunities away from the barn. Friends offer invitations to ride with them, and lessons with different instructors, low-key horse events, and, occasionally, vet and farrier appointments all require leaving home base.

Horse transportation can be solved in a number of ways. If one is fortunate to board with a reliable barn, the manager may be able to ship his horse for him. This is a rare and very expensive service. Commercial vanning, which will be discussed later, is expensive and has its own deadlines and timetables that rarely work for short, spur-of-the-moment local jaunts.

The rider develops a pressing need for horse transportation that he can call his own. Private transportation consists of two major options, trailers and vans.

## THE HORSE TRAILER RIG

The horse trailer rig consists of two vehicles: a pulling vehicle and the trailer. At this time, pulling vehicles include large vans, large pickup trucks, truck-based station wagons, and, rarely, large station wagons. The pulling vehicle needs to have:

| | |
|---|---|
| • Power | A large engine that is at least 125 horsepower, and usually six to eight cylinders. One will appreciate it when one has to go up hills, enter interstates and fast-moving traffic, or pull out of a field. |

- Extra-heavy wiring

  The wiring should be factory installed in a "trailer package." Regular wiring heats up and quickly burns out the fuses, affecting the whole vehicle. The light circuits are the first hit. Use a breaker for brakes instead of in-line fuses.

- Extra-large radiator plus a second radiator for transmission

  These are also usually installed in the factory "trailer package." The second radiator will save the owner many new transmissions since it cools more effectively.

- Long wheelbase

  The long wheelbase helps to even the weight distribution with the trailer. Short-wheelbase vehicles tend to jackknife more easily.

- Easily accessible doors and hatches

  The trailer hitch can make opening rear doors and hatches difficult to impossible.

- Power steering, brakes

  The driver needs all the help he can get, especially on long trips, with tight turns and windy conditions.

- Automatic transmission

  These can give a smoother ride for the horse. Some horses object to the extra lurches that a manual transmission gives. The driver will still need to use lower automatic gears for special situations.

- Extra-large gas tank or extra tank

  The fuel consumption will be incredibly fast when the rig is fully loaded.

- Extra-heavy-duty frame

  The heavy-duty hitch is bolted on to the frame of the vehicle, not just the bumper. The frame is usually included in the factory "trailer package."

- Heavy-duty shock absorbers

  These will help getting around fields and country roads and help compensate for the movement of the trailer.

- Very good tires

  No recapped tires. The tires take double abuse and require more frequent care and replacement.

- Storage space

  The horseman always needs it.

- Vinyl or washable interior

  After the hoof dressing and one's lunch spill at a traffic light, one still can make the interior look normal.

- Automatic or reachable windows

  Inevitably, as one is in the middle lane of the interstate, a thunderstorm comes up and one's stock flies out the window. Try to arrange all control units within reach of the driver.

• Comfortable seats

Driving a rig can be exhausting because a high level of attention is required. A comfortable seat can help alleviate muscle cramps for the driver. If one likes one's rig, one will be surprised how much time one spends in it. Frequently, drivers use the pulling vehicle for everyday use and trips without the trailer.

## THE HITCH

The appropriate hitch is a heavy-duty one that is used for house trailers. Instead of just attaching to the bumper, the hitch is integrated into a steel frame that is bolted to the frame of the pulling vehicle. The ball of the hitch is fitted into a channel and is removable. The ball unit is also made of steel and very heavy.

The hitch has torsion bars that act as antisway bars. These help prevent jackknifing and loss of control from wind or movement of the horses. In addition, the bars can be adjusted to spread the weight of the trailer from the tongue of the trailer and the rear of the pulling vehicle to the front of the pulling vehicle and the rear wheels of the trailer. The benefit to the horses is that they feel two bumps instead of two bumps, a dip, and two more bumps. The benefit to the rig is that the driver can level the entire rig, making it safer.

The hitch will also have emergency chains to guide the trailer it if accidentally comes unhitched. This is a short-term measure that allows time to stop the rig.

There is also a cable to activate the emergency brakes of the trailer. Normally, the brakes are activated by a special braking-control unit wired into the driver's dashboard. A second cable provides power for the tail and brake lights.

### The Gooseneck Hitch

The gooseneck hitch is used only for gooseneck trailers. This hitch is mounted in the bed of a truck. The attachments connect the bottom of the gooseneck pivot to the ball. It is similar to the hitch of a commercial semitruck and trailer. These are usually seen on four-horse or larger trailers.

## THE TRAILER

Trailers come in many shapes and sizes. Because there is no engine, they depreciate very slowly. Occasionally, they increase in value when sold because the new ones cost more. Many trailer owners have been able to get their original purchase price out of the trailer when they decide to sell. Given good care, trailers last longer, with fewer problems, than cars.

Trailers can be made of steel, which rusts, or aluminum, which does not. Other options include fiberglass and lightweight alloys. Aluminum trailers are more expensive, but are lightweight and hold their value better. In general, saddles and trailers have much in common. Quality is more expensive but makes a better investment.

A trailer should have:

| | |
|---|---|
| • Aerodynamic shape and ease of pulling | There are large differences in pulling ease. A quality trailer will stay stable and balanced in the wind. There are also large differences in gas consumption as a result. Since trailer manufacturers frequently change ownership, one needs to closely inspect the new trailer and ask for references from other buyers. Quality can deteriorate from one year to the next. |
| • Tandem wheels and compensation adjustment | If there is a flat tire or blowout, the trailer maintains position. |
| • Reinforced tailgate | Whether or not the tailgate is used as a ramp, the tailgate takes a lot of abuse from the horses. |
| • Safety doors, both sides of trailer | These are always helpful in everyday situations. They are critical in emergencies, especially in an overturned trailer. |
| • Windows in the safety doors | These provide a view for the horse and ventilation with less exhaust. The horse will be happier when he is in the trailer, and is less likely to start bouncing around. In an emergency, the windows are another access point. |
| • Extra height | Most standard trailers are too short for a sixteen-hand or larger horse. |
| • Extra width | Most standard trailers are too narrow for a sixteen-hand or larger horse. In addition, many horses will panic and scramble in a narrow stall. Given more space to spread their feet, they will ride quietly. |
| • Padding and extra reinforcement along stall walls | Horses kick, paw, and take upper body balance from the sides of the stall. |
| • A divider rail rather than full partition | This gives the horse room to spread his feet while supporting his upper body. Many horses who previously thrashed and kicked in a trailer will ride quietly with a divider rail. This works especially well for large horses. |

| | |
|---|---|
| • Safety release chest bars | These remove easily for loading, unloading and emergencies. They should be designed to be removed under great pressure. Horses can be thrown or climb over them and get stuck. |
| • No sharp edges | Nothing to cut or snag. |
| • Undercoating | To retard rust. |
| • Light-color interior and exterior | The use of white gives the trailer an airy, bright feeling. The horse can see what he is going into and is less nervous as a result. The exterior light color reflects heat, keeping the trailer cooler. It is also more visible to other motorists. In addition, certain shades do not show dust. |
| • Windows | The brighter the interior of the trailer, the more comfortable the horse is about loading. |
| • Sun-roof hatch | The hatch allows enormous heat relief in the summer. It helps tremendously during all-day activities when the horse has to spend a lot of time in the trailer. Properly fitted, a hatch does not leak. |
| • Floorboards | Check carefully under the mats. The floorboards should be pressure-treated, clear, heavy, knot-free oak. These are set into a reinforced frame and should be supported underneath. Test for rot frequently. The frame should be arranged to allow drainage and washing with broom and hose. |
| • Rubber mats | These protect the floor from the horse's hooves and act as cushioning. |
| • Fastener rings | Conveniently located and carefully welded in place. |

In addition, a dressing room is wonderful if one plans to compete or take longer trips. They also make resale of the trailer easier. Locking doors on the dressing room gives you a safer place to put your equipment.

If the rider plans to compete or use one horse at a time, the two-horse straight forward stall trailer works best. If the rider fox hunts or expects to take all the horses off and on the trailer at the same time, the two- or three-horse slant stall trailer is more comfortable for the horse. This configuration makes it difficult to reach the interior stalls without going through the outside stall. The slant stall configuration should be carefully individually adjusted for width by the dealer. Most horses require a seven-foot-wide trailer.

There are several loading options. Some trailers have step-down access. The trailer is low to the ground without a ramp. This is more difficult to use in undulating terrain such as a field.

Another option is a ramp. This is usually spring-loaded to help the rider raise the ramp. Ideally, the springs are set in such a way that a horse cannot get his hoof caught in them.

Another option is a short ramp with small swing doors above it. This combination works well for riders who are not interested in weight lifting. The short doors act as a second barrier to the tail strap and allow the rider to more safely raise the ramp from an easier angle.

Frequently, trailer manufacturers have a choice of doors or canvas covers for the top of the trailer tailgate. The canvas shrinks and cracks, quickly losing the stretch it needs to reach all the grommets that hold it on. The doors need to be carefully aligned so that they stay close to the trailer when open and close properly. They need very strong hardware for fasteners.

A few trailers are insulated, which is nice for extreme climates or competition use.

When matching the towing vehicle to the trailer, make sure that the specifications of trailer tongue weight and gross weight *plus the horses* are within the factory designated capabilities of the vehicle.

Drivers may want to add extra-large mirrors to the towing vehicle since the regular rearview mirror becomes useless.

## MAINTENANCE

In addition to state-required safety inspection, the owner will need to make his own frequent inspections. Never assume that the rig is going to work smoothly if it has been out of use for a few days.

Maintenance of the ground for the electrical system tends to be an every-time affair. Frequently, the ball and socket conjunction and the torsion bar sockets need to have the rust removed with emery cloth. The junction points should be well greased with a heavy-grade grease. This helps retard rust and resultant short-circuiting of the electrical system. Grease is also frequently used for the same reason on the connecting surfaces of the ball to the vehicle.

Lighting systems are often designed so that if one light goes out, all the lights go out. Owners need to add spare bulbs to their emergency kits if they are unfortunate enough to have this system. The wiring needs to be checked for looseness. As there is a lot of vibration in a trailer, wiring shakes loose. If the owner can purchase an owner's repair manual with the trailer, he can make emergency repairs on his own. Trailers never break down at a convenient place or time.

The owner should plan on having the axles and wheel bearings checked and packed with grease on a regular basis. Because of the rough terrain and bad roads, trailers occasionally break axles and develop bearings problems.

Ideally, the trailer is washed every time out. It is especially important that the stalls are cleaned of manure. The mats should be washed with a pressure attachment on the hose and scrubbed. Then the mats are raised and the floorboards given the same treatment. Urine and manure will quickly rot the flooring and rust the metal supporting structures. Some trailers are painted with airplane paint, which is less fragile. Most trailers do better with a protective sealer applied over the paint.

## HITCHING THE RIG

Hitching the trailer to the vehicle can be a frustrating experience. The dealer should explain and take the new owner through all of the steps several times. A checklist is helpful, as each rig is different. The same person should always be in charge of hitching. Someone else, even if he has lots of experience with other rigs, does not know the important peculiarities of this particular rig.

A second person to signal the driver as he approaches the hitch is an immense help. A driver, by himself, can cue off a mark on the trailer set directly above the hitch. He will still need to get out of the vehicle to visually check his progress.

Another point to remember is that the steering wheel is moved in the opposite direction when one is in reverse. An easy way to compensate for this is to look out the rear of the vehicle and concentrate on the movement of the rear of the vehicle rather than using a mirror or looking straight ahead.

Plan on fifteen minutes or longer to hitch. If one is short of time and feeling pressured, inevitably there are more mistakes. If the driver can hitch the night before the time of use, the lighting system can be checked and fixed if necessary. Never load horses into an unhitched trailer. It can turn over, roll away, or collapse.

## LOADING THE HORSES

Before loading the horses, plan on loading everything else. Hay nets should be filled and waiting beside the trailer or already in the front of the trailer where they do not obstruct the horses' vision and space. Horses hate to wait. They bounce in place like bored children.

If the horse does not like to load, there are a few enticements that might work. Grain for the greedy usually helps. Try feeding the horse his meals in the parked, hitched-up trailer.

Some horses load more easily from the entrance to their stall or stable. Back the trailer as close as possible to the entrance to limit the choices a horse has.

Load a horse comfortable with trailers first. The horse who is worried will take courage from his friend.

Problem loading: when leading a horse onto the trailer or van, face the direction that you want to go, as if you are leading the horse anywhere else. If you turn and face the horse, the horse will normally refuse to go forward, having noticed your body language.

Generally speaking, one tries not to escalate resistance into an all-out fight. Horses do not think when they are very upset. Before one loses one's patience and temper, ask for help. Other horsemen are quick to understand and respond. If the horse is regularly difficult to load, the owner should consider professional help to solve the problem.

- Open all the doors and the chest bars

  The more light, the happier the horse is, as well as making the groom's movement easier.

- Adjust the ramp

  Make sure it is sturdily supported and does not wobble when the horse puts weight on it.

- Bucket of grain

  Have a small bucket of grain handy, easy to reach halfway in the stall.

- Load the biggest, heaviest horse in the left stall

  If only one horse is traveling, use the left stall. This helps to keep the trailer upright on narrow roads where a wheel can drop off the pavement or shoulder.

- Open the left stall divider

  Open all the way to the right to give the horse a large space to enter and get his balance.

- Lead the horse on the trailer

  To lead the horse on the trailer, first make a small circle a short distance from the trailer. Walk beside the horse facing forward as normal. The idea is to reinforce the horse's obeying the groom's command.

- Approach the trailer in a straight line

  Make sure the horse is lined up with the stall. He will find it easier to understand what is expected of him. Keep walking beside him, facing where he is to go. One's body language tells the horse to continue forward.

- Walk into the stall a little ahead of the horse

  Face forward and do not turn until you want him to stop.

- When in stall

  Have a second person quickly close the partition and latch the tail strap. This second person needs to be careful not to stand behind the horse. Horses have been known to change their minds and come flying backward out of the stall.

- Tail strap fastened

  Once the tail strap is fastened, the groom can fasten the halter to a safety-release tie and remove the lead shank.

- Process repeated

  The process is repeated for the second horse.

- Raising the ramp

  When raising the ramp, one must be very careful to stand to the side of the ramp and not lower one's head over the ramp. If a horse kicks, it can be lethal. If the tail strap breaks, the horse can push over on top of the people raising the ramp, causing injury to all concerned.

- Praise

  Place hay nets and give treats for good behavior. Praise the horse and make it a pleasant association.

- Double-check

  Double-check, close doors, and be on your way.

## DRIVING THE RIG

Before driving a rig loaded with horses, one should experience what being in the moving trailer is like. While it is illegal to be in the trailer on public highways, a trip down the driveway and back will give an understanding of the horse's dilemmas. It is hard to keep one's balance in a moving trailer. It is even harder on turns. There is not much shock absorption. The process of stopping throws one forward and the final stop throws one again. Starting tosses one backward. No wonder so many horses hate to load and travel. They scramble and kick to keep their balance and register a complaint to the driver.

As the driver, one can vastly improve the horse's outlook. First, by giving him surroundings that make keeping his balance easier, a view out the safety door window so he is not bored, and some hay to give him something else to think about. The hay also helps to keep his digestive system working so he does not colic.

Second, one can change one's driving style for the occasion. By anticipating the horse's needs ahead of time, one can make smoother transitions.

Horses prefer the start of movement of the trailer to be slow, without lurches. This means warming the engine up ahead of time and using lower gears to start the rig in motion.

Slowing down takes more time and usually requires more space than ordinary driving. The rig pushes itself forward and the momentum takes more time to break. Drivers frequently flash their brake lights to warn regular car drivers that a decrease in speed has started.

Turns are made very, very slowly. In a 5-mph turn, it is much easier for the horse to keep his balance. One can use flashers to keep the drivers behind the rig from becoming belligerent. A horse is most likely to scramble on a turn, so consider the investment in the horse when the fellow behind starts to signal irritation. One can also pull over later in a safe spot and let traffic pass.

Horses prefer smooth, straight roads. It is worth the extra mileage to pick the better roads. One ends up making better time, since one can pick up the speed from a crawl.

Travel time elapsed is greater when using the rig than a car. One cannot

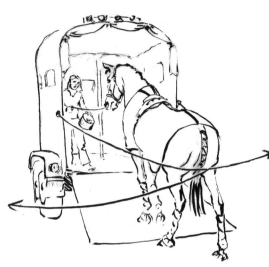

Problem loading: one alternative in loading a recalcitrant horse is to attach lunge lines to the trailer tailgate fasteners. The lunge lines are then crossed behind the horse and pulled snug by helpers. A person stands in front of the trailer with a bucket of grain to entice the horse forward. Move the breast bar out of the way so that you can move back and forth in the trailer without having to duck. Make sure the trailer ramp does not wobble when the horse puts weight on it. Open the front trailer doors to give more light, so the horse can see that there are no dragons in the gloom. Hay net can be hung in the front of the trailer as an incentive. Sometimes putting bedding or hay on the ramp will disguise it. The dividing portion should be pulled all the way over or removed to give the horse lots of space. If a horse is panicky in shipping, frequently cutting out the bottom of the divider or using a divider pole will give more space for him to keep his balance and end the panic.

Problem loading: another alternative, if you do not have lunge lines, is to have two people join hands behind the horse's rump and push him up the ramp. The people stand on either side of the horse so that if he reverses, they will not get hurt.

go as fast as the speed limit except on a highway because of control problems. Always add extra time when moving horses.

Transporting horses is different from any other driving because the horses wiggle, move, bounce, and paw. Every move affects the way the trailer moves and the steering. The driver is keenly aware that it is very live cargo. Some horses develop an ongoing dialogue with the driver to signal discomfort. When the horse's movement is rapid or strong, one needs to stop and check the horse. Little moves many mean "Don't go so fast!" or other problems. Horses sweat when they are worried.

When changing lanes, signal well ahead and look out the window in addition to the mirrors. There are enormous blind spots on both sides of the rig.

Many drivers like having a CB radio. They can communicate with the truckers to find gas stations, signal for help, or call the police. Frequently, truckers are willing to observe the horse in the trailer if they are behind one and tell on the CB what the horse is doing. In an accident, they are often willing to help until the emergency squad arrives.

Traveling longer distances with a rig requires extra planning. One wants to arrive before 4:00 P.M. so that one can find the stabling in the daylight while the stable staff is still at work. Inevitably, one has trouble locating the stable and then the stable is not properly prepared. As a result, plan on leaving very early, even before dawn, to arrive in the afternoon. Gas stations usually open by 7:00 A.M., and interstate gas stations are open all night, so one can plan fuel stops. It is much harder to position for filling a vehicle with a trailer attached.

Backing a trailer takes a lot of experience. A novice driver may want to start practice in a large, empty parking lot to make attempts within the lines. If one looks directly at the trailer, it is easier to coordinate the steering. If the trailer starts to turn in the wrong direction, pull forward until it is straight, then try again. If one continues to back after a trailer starts to turn and does not follow it with the steering, the angle of the two vehicles becomes too great and the hitch breaks or the vehicles are damaged. Many drivers concoct schemes to avoid backing.

If one is parking in a field, plan on staying on the high ground aimed downhill or toward the exit. It is much harder to get out of a field from a standing start than to enter. If the ground is wet or frozen and expected to thaw when you plan to leave, be especially careful to stay to high ground or hard surfaces along the shoulder of the road.

If one cannot get out of a field with the horses in the trailer, enlist help. Unload the horses and try again. If no tractor is available, a number of strong men can usually push an unhitched trailer to a better location. Usually, though, someone has a tow chain. Always plan to leave before or with everyone else in case of trouble.

Never plan to drive a rig in snow or ice. The chances of jackknifing or overturning are high, as the trailer takes on a life of its own.

# VANS

Horse vans are trucks designed to transport horses. Because of their nature, they do not lend themselves easily to a comfortable secondary use. Since the engine is built in, they depreciate at the same rate as a normal truck. Usually, they are more difficult to drive than the trailer rig since they are stiff and very heavy. The heaviness is an asset in snowy, icy climates because they tend to stay on the road.

When one is traveling in a van, one has to take the whole van everywhere instead of being able to park the trailer and use the vehicle separately. The interior of a van is usually very adjustable, so one can make changes to suit the particular animals being shipped. Because of the long wheelbase, the ride can be smoother than the rig. Since the horses can be faced to the rear of the van, they can absorb the shock on different muscles, which gives them a rest on long trips.

Because vans are trucks, the state government treats them the same way. This means special licensing for the driver and van. One has to obey all special truck instructions, such as weight scales, detours, height and weight restrictions. Some interstates have special lanes or ban trucks altogether.

A CB radio is a necessity with a van. The driver needs all the truck information available.

# COMMERCIAL HORSE TRANSPORTATION

Commercial horse transportation becomes useful for long trips. The commercial van lines use very large semitrucks and trailers that can hold twelve horses at a time. As large as a household moving van, these vans have an extremely long wheelbase and an excellent shock absorption system. As a result, the horses are more comfortable and less exhausted by the trip.

### Choosing a Commercial Horse Carrier

The names of commercial horse carriers can be found through horse magazines, breed or competition organizations, veterinarians, blood stock agents, and saddleries. When one is choosing a commercial van line, in addition to price, one also needs to ask about care and length of time on the van. Each company gives different service.

The best companies usually send two drivers who are quite knowledgeable about horses. They frequently check the horses and make stops to hay and water them. On a very long trip, horses may be unloaded and hand walked for a few minutes to stretch their muscles. If a horse is being difficult, one of the drivers or a groom will stay with him until the horse settles down and relaxes.

A twelve-hour trip can easily turn into a nineteen-hour trip because the van stops at other stables en route to load or unload horses.

One also needs to confirm that the same drivers and rig stay with the horse throughout the trip. Some companies may change these several times en route and the horse and his needs can get lost in the shuffle.

Always ask for references and call them. The previous clients can give you a wealth of useful information.

Since commercial van lines fall under federal interstate regulations, they require the horse owner to provide:

| | |
|---|---|
| • Inoculation records | Showing current dates provided by the horse's veterinarian. |
| • Health certificate | Within one week previous to shipment to show horse is free of infectious diseases. |
| • Feed schedule | Including type of feed, supplements, etc. Many carriers will ask for feed to travel with the horse. |
| • Insurance information | Along with emergency telephone numbers. It is a wise idea to insure for the shipping even if one does not normally choose to do so. Shipping is a higher-risk situation. |
| • Peculiarities of the horse | The carrier will need to know if the horse needs extra space during shipping or has other special needs. They especially need to know if the horse requires a groom to stay with him. |

Since the business is built upon compiling a vanload of horses from different stables, the carriers need a long time frame to put a trip together. "Carrier's convenience" means that the horse is shipped when the carrier can organize the trip. There frequently is a month or two wait while the carrier locates enough horses. Once the load is organized, the carrier will notify the horse owner when to expect the van. Since vans travel on a twenty-four-hour schedule, the pickup and delivery times can be in the middle of the night. If a group of riders decide to charter a van, then a more precise time schedule can be adhered to.

## AIR TRANSPORTATION

For very long trips, when the horse needs to stay at the peak of condition, airplane travel becomes a consideration. This very expensive option should only be considered if the horse is a good traveler. If the horse goes into a frenzy on a plane, the crew has authority to destroy him to save the plane.

Horses are shipped in narrow plane-shaped stalls on rollers. These have a bumper guard over the horse's head to prevent him from rearing. The hay nets are tied at the level of the horse's chest to encourage him to keep his head down. Once the horse is in the stall, the whole stall is lifted into the plane, rolled and locked into place. A groom stays with the horses during the flight.

The same paperwork is required as for land commercial travel for inside the United States. For international flights, a passport and customs paperwork are required as well. The United States Equestrian Team headquarters can help with suggestions of carriers, blood stock agents, and appropriate authorities to contact. They also frequently know of charter flights that are being formed for specific competitions. One can expect quarantine at both ends of the international trip.

# PREPARATION OF THE HORSE FOR TRAVEL

How much bandaging, wrapping, and blanketing one does prior to shipping is in direct relationship to the length, type of travel, and the horse's attitude toward it. Some meticulous horsemen always bandage for every trip. Others find that the bandages annoy the horse and he spends the entire trip trying to kick or rub them off. In general, all horses find shipping bandages on their legs uncomfortable at first. They walk oddly and may kick for the first steps.

Shipping bandages vary from standing stall wraps in that they cover the pastern and upper part of the hoof as well as extend above the knee or hock joint. In theory, the wrap protects against minor injury or lessens the damage of major injury. They do not always help. Borium will slice through the padding with the greatest of ease. A horse who is intent on hurting himself can still accomplish it. If one has a bad shipper, one needs to seriously consider professional help to eliminate the causes of the problem.

## Commercial Bandages

There are commercially made shipping bandages that are made of cordura nylon and a washable liner. These usually have Velcro fasteners. They are easy to put on and off and very easy to keep clean. Their drawback is that they do not support the horse's legs for long trips.

## Flannel and Cotton Wraps

For long trips, horsemen frequently use the old-fashioned method of making their own wraps. They buy sheets of brushed flannel from saddleries, tear the flannel into strips that are approximately six inches by seven or eight feet and roll the strips, brushed side out, so they look the same as regular standing wraps. The important difference is that flannel wraps do not stretch or sag.

The horseman also purchases sheet cottons. These are folded to make a two-inch-thick pad and then rolled the same as standing cottons so that the smooth side is against the horse's leg. They and the flannel wraps are placed on the horse the same way that standing wraps are. One does not try to cover the knee or hock joint with flannel and cotton bandages because there is not enough flexibility.

The advantage of this method is that the cotton breathes while supporting the leg. The horse is, as a result, less likely to complain.

## Blankets

If one is shipping a horse in a trailer that is open at the top of the tailgate, the horse will need more protection from the wind unless it is a hot day. Coolers and sheets work well in the cool months or on short trips. Longer trips in cold weather necessitate windproof turnout-type blankets. Many quality trailers are insulated, so one may need less. Horses give off a lot of heat. When the trailer is closed at the top of the tailgate, it is important to open the safety door windows to allow fresh air in with a minimum of exhaust fumes.

Closed trailers, insulated trailers, and vans all provide less air flow so the horse rarely needs more than a sheet.

## Tail Wraps

Tail wraps are used if the horse likes to rub his tail on the rear of the stall. This usually happens if he loses his balance and sits on the tail strap of the trailer. If one can move the strap forward a few inches, there may be enough space so that the rubbing stops. In vans, there are no straps, so one has to continue wrapping. Sometimes, if a horse has more room lengthwise, he may stop. If the rubbing is serious, one may consider a larger slant-load trailer.

## Shipping Attire for Fox Hunting

Shipping attire for fox hunting differs from other endeavors. Frequently, the trailers park on the shoulder of the road and the horses are excited in anticipation of the hunt. It is usually dangerous to tack up the horse at the location. Fox hunters groom, saddle, and bridle the horse at the stable. All the equipment that the horse needs is put on including galloping boots. The girth of the saddle is left moderately loose and the bridle reins are twisted and looped around one stirrup.

A halter is placed over the bridle, and a lead shank for loading is clipped to it. Over the whole assemblage is placed the cooler or sheet with a surcingle to hold it in place. Upon arrival at the hunt, all one has to do is take off the halter and sheet, adjust the tack and mount. There is more information in detail in the fox hunting chapter.

Developing horse transportation skills is an important part of the growth of the rider into a horseman. It takes a long time to do this, but the confidence that comes from the ability makes it worthwhile.

# 6

# Working on the Flat: The Basics

---

$\mathbf{W}$HEN TALKING TO HORSES and giving commands, if you have a relatively high voice naturally, you would try to go to your deepest voice register so it doesn't sound like a normal pattern. It has an entirely different sound to him and he recognizes lower sound as a command. Horses can be growled at and the sound of the growling is taken to mean that this is an important thing, they should listen. In growling to the horse, one gets his attention. You are to be feared and respected. It is more important that he listen than do whatever it was that he was planning on doing instead. Likewise, praising the horse is done in a slightly higher sound than your normal voice pattern and is caressing. The horse responds just the same as a person would to voice patterns. He understands when you're angry and he understands how far he can push you.

A horse will test you a little at a time to see where your barriers are. It's a lot like working with a small child. In teaching a horse anything new, you need to recognize that your steps of progress are very small at the beginning. A wise horseman's expression is, that if you can get one stride of whatever it is you want, you praise the horse. You can build from that one stride to make two strides or three strides. Don't expect a horse to be able to understand and assimilate immediately what it is you're asking him to do if it's something new. He has to learn from your body language, as well as your voice and your hands, what it is you want versus the static of the other body movement that you make.

When working with a horse that is new to you, first try to gain his respect and his affection. This can be done by grooming him and bringing him carrots or apples or whatever food treats he's fond of. You become the person who brings him his meals and he looks forward to this. Also, you provide him pleasure by scratching his ears while grooming him.

In the process, you develop control because you ask him to stand still for you. You ask him to lift his feet or move over or tap him. Each time he does it right, you praise him. Each time he does it wrong, you give a voice reprimand and get his attention. Gradually, over the period of a week or so, he will learn how far he is allowed to go without getting a reprimand.

In testing you, he may move his body a little closer to you than you had in mind, so you have to push him back. Or he may be difficult to bridle or halter even though he was amenable before you brought him to his new environment. He also might be difficult to mount or come up with some other small resistance.

## OVERCOMING RESISTANCE

Usually, he'll start with a small resistance to see what you're going to do about it. If you make too strong a reprimand, he will get upset and lose his composure. Part of the art form of being a horseman is to know how much is enough and not allowing yourself to get angry when the horse tries you. You learn to use what would normally be anger in a positive way.

Compose a step-by-step methodology to break down the horse's resistance. As he accomplishes each step, you can praise him for the part he did right or reprimand him in a small fashion for the part he did wrong. Ideally, the reprimands will place him in a position where he ends up having to do what you want.

## GROOMING A DIFFICULT HORSE

For example, a horse won't stand still for grooming, and you have him in the crossties with the safety latches. You first will release his safety latches to keep him from rearing back and injuring himself or going crazy from the panic of having his head confined. Then you would move him to his stall instead of working in the crossties. Groom him with the chain of the lead shank laced through the front of the halter and hooked to the opposite side. Then, if you tug on the lead shank, it has an effect over his nose.

If that doesn't work to get his attention, you can switch to a lunge line. Thread the halter the same way. Run the lunge line through a breakable wall loop, such as bailer twine or clothesline, then back to your hand so that his head is kept in position at the point of the loop. Ideally, you place him alongside a wall so he can't swing away from you. As you groom him, you can

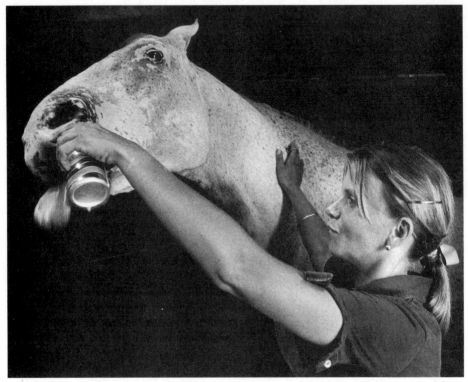
Horses like soft drinks, beer, and junk food, too. Torrance Watkins and "Red's Door" enjoying a soda.

move up and down his body using the lunge line to hold his body in alignment. The movement of the lunge line through the loop provides resistance, but not so much resistance that the horse panics and tries to back. It provides sufficient base for you to work, yet allows the horse to settle into place. You might try putting some hay in front of him—or, if worse comes to worst, apples, carrots, or a handful of hay pellets to give him a positive treat to look forward to when he's getting groomed.

## TACKING UP

You can use the same methodology for tacking him up. Put on the saddle and slowly tighten the girth, taking breaks to allow him to adjust. For putting the bridle over his head, if he's head-shy, you swing your arm around behind his head and cradle his nose in the crook of your right arm. Hold the head stall of the bridle about half way down its length, in your right hand. Hold the bit in your left hand and then gently press it to his lips. Horses do not like having the bit clanked against their teeth. Slip your thumb into the corner of his mouth, since there are no teeth there. Your thumb tastes rather terrible to your horse so he will open his mouth to avoid the taste of your thumb. If this is not sufficient, wriggle your thumb. The movement is enough for him to open his mouth, so you can slip the bit in without banging his teeth. As he gradually learns to trust you, he will be more willing to help.

Frequently, a horse will put his head up in the air to avoid being bridled. If you pinch his nostrils shut with your right hand, the lack of air will persuade him to lower his head. He will also try to back away from you. Just place him into the corner of the stall, so he has to come forward. Continue talking to him soothingly so he doesn't panic. Eventually, he will give in and lower his head sufficiently, allowing you to put the bridle on. It helps considerably if you can arrange to be on something tall when he is being bridled so he won't be able to take advantage of the height difference between you and him. When grooming a head-shy horse, spend extra time rubbing around his ears so that he becomes accustomed to the prospect of being handled in this way and gradually decides that it's acceptable to have his bridle put on. Occasionally, at the beginning, you may have to dismantle the bridle to put it on him, but this should only be for a couple of days.

As with anything else you do with horses, it's the consistency for short periods of time that counts, rather than trying to do a lot in one day. You're well ahead of the game if you spend fifteen to thirty minutes with a horse each day rather than four hours once a week.

## LUNGING

For lunging, one can use either a lunging cavesson or take the lunge line, run it through the ring of the bit closest to the rider, over the top of the

Lunging cavesson: a heavy specially made leather and metal bridle with three rings on the nose-band. The center ring is for the lunge line and the two side rings are used for side reins. There is no bit.

Clip →

Alternate method: the horse wears a bridle, reins twisted together and run through the throat latch. The lunge line is run through the ring of the bit, over the top of the horse's head along the poll, and clipped to the bit ring on the far side of the horse's head. The side reins are also attached to the bit rings.

horse's head and down the other side, clipping it to the ring on the horse's bit. This way, the force of the lunge line acts the same as that of the bit. For lunging, one can use ready-made side reins that have elastic inserts or any other rope or tape that has elasticity to it, for example, twine or clothesline. The use of sliding or side reins helps stabilize the horse and acts as an aid to develop the use of his back and haunches. He will then carry himself in the proper frame.

## The Sliding Rein

The sliding rein bends the whole topline of the horse. It is particularly useful for low-level trained horses as it strengthens the back muscles. It also encourages a correct training level frame for dressage.

To make a sliding rein, take a very long strand of clothesline or baling twine and make a loop in one end. Run the girth through the loop, adjusting the loop to rest on a horizontal line to the bit of the horse. Next, slip the line through the bit ring on the same side of the horse. Then loop the clothesline through the girth, between the horse's front legs. Up comes the clothesline to slide through the opposite bit ring. Then make an adjustable loop and attach the remainder in a straight horizontal line to the girth at the billet straps.

Adjusted loosely, the sliding rein allows the horse to put his head up in the alert position but places pressure on the bit if he tries to rise farther. It rewards him for putting his head down with his neck outstretched. It also adjusts itself to the curve of the circle and allows the horse to feel that he can turn his head. It asks rather than forces. Since the horse decides his choices, he usually doesn't panic.

## The Side Rein

The side rein is designed for higher-level horses who have already achieved collection. It fixes more powerfully the horse's head and does not allow for stretching the topline. Used for collection, it requires a more powerful input from the haunches for the horse to be able to balance itself.

If used too soon in the horse's training, it will give the horse an artificial carriage. It encourages him to lean on the bit, not arch and swing his back and trail his haunches. This defeats the whole purpose of the exercise.

Side reins have an elastic insert or rubber doughnut to provide flexibility. They attach with loops to the girth, running in a horizontal line to the bit. Most snap on the bit to facilitate removing them when the horse is allowed to stretch between collections. Ideally, you want the horse to work with his head low and with his body curved on the arc of the circle toward you.

When beginning to use the lunge equipment, the side or sliding reins are very loose so the horse isn't afraid. If you tighten them up too quickly, the horse will panic, may throw himself over backward and break his neck. When working with the side or sliding reins, each day you gradually tighten the reins

Lunging chambon: this variety of side rein encourages a training-level frame. It allows the horse to correct himself and automatically rewards the horse when he is in the right frame. It is attached to a surcingle, although a saddle could have been used instead.

Side reins: side reins are adjusted for a horse in a higher level of training. His frame is elevated and compact, with high head carriage and his hindquarters coming farther behind him. There is usually elastic in the side rein to allow for the movement of the horse.

just a bit after the horse has gotten used to the loose rein, so on day three you would make perhaps three adjustments rather than starting with the tightest you finished with the day before. Gradually, the horse develops his balance, confidence, and gets used to shifting his weight to his hindquarters. Then, one can tighten the side rein slightly to the point of having him in a vertical face with his head in the proper position so that the vertebrae behind the ears constitute the tallest part of his neck and head. If the reins are too tight, he will tip his head in and tuck his chin to his chest or he'll start fighting them, in which case he might flip over backward. You don't lose anything by taking the extra length of rein to make the horse comfortable and build his confidence.

When lunging the horse, the idea is to work his hind quarters to keep them moving up under his body and his feet overtracking the footprints of the front hooves. When lunging, alternate the direction every five minutes or so to prevent the horse from becoming dizzy.

Ideally, you would work up to between fifteen and thirty minutes on the lunge. Because you're working the horse in a small sixty-feet-in-diameter circle, there is stress on the horse's joints and muscles. It makes it more difficult for him to continue for very long. Check with your veterinarian before you start lunging your horse to make sure he has no underlying joint problems that the lunging would exacerbate.

When starting a horse on the lunge, you have him make a small circle around you while holding the lunge line in your leading hand. You stand even with the point of his shoulder. Your body, in relationship to his mouth, is approximately where it would be if you were riding. You hold your whip in your following hand to flick toward his haunches to take the place of your leg. If the circle is very small as you start, the whip will actually touch the horse. Later on, you let him spiral his way out to almost the end of the lunge line, keeping a reserve for yourself in case you need it for his own oscillations. The whip will have its action from the noise of the crack.

Work your horse through the different speeds of walk, trot, and canter by voice commands. Your hand works the same as it would if the lunge line were a rein, so you ask for half halts and halts with your leading hand. You ask him to go forward with your following hand and the whip.

If the horse is out on a circle and doesn't pay attention to the down transition commands, then you tighten up on the lunge line and allow him to spiral into a small circle. The smaller the circle, the harder it is for him to go forward and the more likely he is to pay attention to you. You keep the horse from turning in and diving across the center of the circle by use of the whip. If he turns in toward you, you quickly move your whip in front of his face to urge him to turn his face away from you and back into the circle. When he does what you want, you praise him. If he comes in and you can't stop him, then step out of the way and use the lunge line behind your body to act as a brake. The longer the lunge line, the greater the braking effect on a horse if he is moving away from you. If you snap the lunge line taut when he has his legs off the ground, it will have an extremely powerful effect on him.

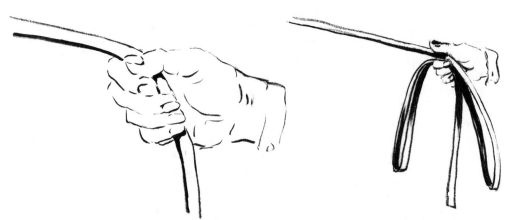

*Above left.* Holding the lunge line: the line can be held in one hand and the rest of the line looped in the whip hand. *Above right.* Holding the lunge line: if the horse is very quiet, you may hold some of the extra line in your guiding hand. Note: the line is looped in such a way that if the horse rapidly widens his circle, or becomes difficult, the line will play out without trapping the rider's hand.

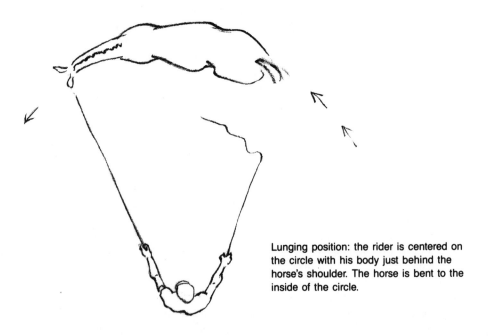

Lunging position: the rider is centered on the circle with his body just behind the horse's shoulder. The horse is bent to the inside of the circle.

When giving the voice commands for the upward transitions, use upward inflections on the words "walk," "trot," or "canter" so that he thinks of going up the scale of notes in your voice. When you want a down transition, you say the same words, but you use a downward inflection and run the word down the scale of notes. You can drag the word out and make it sound very soft on the down transitions and quite sharp on the up transitions. Frequently, the horse will go by the sound of your voice more than the actual word. If he can't understand exactly what the word is, at least he knows what the idea is by your voice tone. Try to make each word that you use be a different sound from the other words. For example, "trot" should have a sharp staccato sound for an upward transition. "Canter" would have an inflection that reflects the sound of the canter stride. "Walk" would be long and soothing, and "whoa" would be very precise.

## A BASIC PROGRAM

The basic program for exercising your new horse is based on his fitness. For example, if you have bought a horse that is out at grass for over a month, you will have to bring him back slowly into work. An example of a gentle conditioning program will follow the same theory as for a human adult who has been sitting at a desk job too long. You would start with lunging, working your way up from ten minutes to thirty minutes a day on the lunge line. You could add to that riding the horse at a walk up and down hills, starting with thirty minutes and working up to an hour. This hacking-out time allows him to strengthen his back muscles and stretch out his legs so he does not pull or bang a tendon.

When working on hills, ideally the horse will be starting his hacking-out program, walking on a loose rein, encouraging him to keep his head and neck long. After about fifteen minutes of long and low, and being very relaxed, you gradually vibrate the bit and bring him onto it. At this point, you are also nudging him with your legs to develop his hindquarters coming up under him. In this frame, the horse will exercise the muscles you're trying to strengthen and will develop more strength through his back. The hill work of going up and down a long steep hill stretches the tendons out in the backs of the legs more than working on the flat. It tests his cardiac and breathing system without injuring him by the pounding of faster work before he's ready.

Then the work shifts again. One starts out with fifteen minutes of hacking on a loose rein to loosen the horse up. Then some hill work, say thirty minutes' worth of that at a walk, then three five-minute trots, which is the beginning of interval training. These trots are separated by three-minute intervals. In other words, you have five-minute trots, three minutes of walk, or get off the horse and walk beside him. Anything to get him to relax for those three minutes. Another five-minute trot and then another three-minute rest, another five-minute trot, another three-minute rest. The rests are active rests: the horse is not standing unless you need to settle him by having him graze.

Balancing uphill: the rider carries his weight in his legs, keeping his seat to allow the horse to round underneath him. Going up and down hills, the rider is perpendicular to the fall line of the hill, similar to skiing. The horse goes straight up the hill, not on a diagonal. He is more likely to fall and not recover if he goes across the hill.

Balancing downhill: the rider carries his weight in his legs but sits deep and close to the horse. He keeps his weight back to free the horse's forehand and help the horse balance. The rider is perpendicular to the fall line of the hill and guides the horse straight down the hill. A series of half halts will help to keep the horse rocked back on his hindquarters.

During the three-minute rests, you can kick your feet out of the stirrups and stretch your muscles through your arms and back. The horse will understand you are going to put no new input in and it is time to relax. It takes awhile for the horse to learn the ritual of the five-minute trots. The first few times that you do them, if he is underconditioned, his breathing and heart rate will go up and he'll be stressed too much. But if you've done your hills, your lunging, and then go to this, it should be very easy for him. After you do your trot work, you can cool him out for another fifteen-to-twenty-minute hack. In other words, you're having a lot of time relaxing and getting to know him and the country before you ask him to do difficult things.

Then the program will change again as he gets fitter: you'll go to fifteen minutes of stretching out, your three five-minute trots, and then you can add, depending on the day, a half hour of dressage, a half hour of jumping, a half hour of cross-country work, or a half hour of hills. Then the last part of the schedule is another hacking-out period as a cool-down. Similar to aerobics, you have stretching, then some aerobic work, then some precise conditioning work, and then stretching out and cooling down.

You can get a lot accomplished in an hour and a half with this program. Ideally, you would be able to visit your horse and work with him every day. As far as the scheduling, riding three times a week can maintain his balance and you can hold your own. With four days a week, you start gaining ground. With five days a week, you start having major breakthroughs. At six days a week, you may start to get a little tired of the whole thing. If you're going for eventing or getting ready for fox hunting, you may need this six-day-a-week program. Ideally, the horse has at least one day off a week to rest and recuperate. You'll find you want a day off, too, otherwise riding ends up being more like work than a joy, which is the whole reason for doing it.

# 7

# Dressage: The Basics

---

**"D**RESSAGE" is derived from the French verb *dresser,* meaning "to train." It is just that—an integrated system of rider movements and cues intended to develop a comfortable, reliable, and—most important—responsive well-trained mount. Although the term is commonly associated with formal demonstrations and horse shows, basic dressage techniques are invaluable for any form of competitive or recreational riding. With proper dressage training, a lumbering tractor of a horse can be turned into a zippy little equestrian sports car, responsive to the lightest touch.

As with most horse-handling techniques, dressage was developed to facilitate the earliest and most basic equestrian employment—hunting and warfare. For these activities, the rider must have one or both hands free to manipulate his sword, lance, or bow. Therefore, balance, leg control, and a system of "body language" was critical.

The date when man first domesticated wild horses and started training them for his own purposes is lost in the mists of prehistory. However, it was most likely among the nomadic tribes roaming the plains of southern Russia, and what is today the Kirghiz steppes, where the embryonic skill first developed.

Early mounted warriors had a distinct advantage over their pedestrian counterparts, being able to stand off and propel projectiles at immobilized adversaries. Various Iranian tribal groups, such as the Sacae, Massagetae, Medes, and Parsis (ancestors of the imperial Persians), brought these techniques to a high tactical level. Such skilled warriors, directing their mounts solely through knee pressure, could swivel in the saddle and fire off a salvo of arrows in any direction, accurate up to several hundred yards.

However, despite the imposing power of these hordes, when the classical world developed body armor and disciplined infantry formations, the mounted warrior's threat was reduced to harassment and hit-and-run tactics. For all his balance and control, the rider's seat was precarious and could not withstand the impact of heavy contact. Although employing light cavalry for scouting, flanking, and pursuit, most classical armies were essentially heavy infantry establishments.

Introduction of the stirrup changed all that. Again probably originating in the Trans-Caspian steppe corridor, this device was successfully adopted by Arab and eastern Germanic tribesmen, and soon by their late Roman and Byzantine adversaries. With the stirrup dawned the first heavy cavalry. It provided the rider with a stable platform from which he could have a close-in go at his enemy with lance or sword without danger of being unhorsed by the impact.

Stirrups were probably introduced into Western Europe by invading Arabs, and were quickly adopted by the Teutonic warrior aristocracy. Mounted on heavy chargers, which were little more than converted draft horses, the early European knight became a formidable, if ponderous, military instrument.

However, the sheer bulk of these chargers, combined with many pounds of heavily armored rider, made them, once in motion, little more than a crowd of runaway locomotives. Faced with elusive Arab and Turkish armies, mounted on their fleet and maneuverable breeds, the Frankish kings had to make modifications. They crossed agile Arab horses with rugged northern strains to create the ancestors of the Percheron breed. Other modifications were made to saddle, stirrup, and armor.

The Percheron was much more responsive to the rider's aids, so bits were lighter and not as much spur was used. By the time Charles Martel fought at Poitiers, he was able to match the Arab mobility and stem the invasion.

As warfare changed, the demand for armor lessened and the cavalry preferred officers' chargers, who had mostly Arab blood with a trace of northern cold (draft). The ideal combination would be intelligent and fast, able to jump, but quiet and responsive in battle. With this swing in emphasis from weight to agility, dressage in the modern sense came into its own. Nations set up schools for both rider and mounts, and valued their breeding stock highly.

Two of the most highly developed studs and schools are still in existence. The Cadre Noir of Saumur, France, and the Spanish Riding School of Vienna, Austria, are considered national treasures. They still perform regularly in public the cavalry movements, including the spectacular airs above ground. These movements were originally choreographed to music as a horse ballet to amuse and delight the king. In them, the horse appears to dance on his own volition and the rider is quiet and still in the saddle with no perceptible movement. This is the highest form of dressage still practiced today.

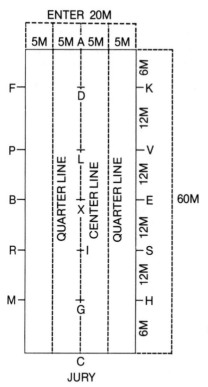

Standard dressage arena:
20 meters by 60 meters.

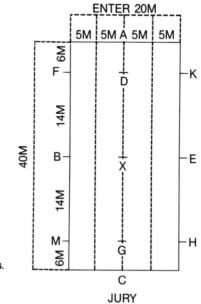

Small dressage arena:
20 meters by 40 meters.

## The Dressage Arena

The basic training is done in a small enclosed arena usually twenty meters by forty or sixty meters. This is divided into sections that are marked by points along the sides and imaginary points in the center (see illustration). The sides of the arena are very low—usually about ten inches tall and painted white so the horse and rider notice them.

In this known measured environment, the rider can concentrate on the precision of the horse's movement and develop accuracy. In connecting the points (marked with letters), the rider creates geometric figures. The shapes themselves create balancing and transition questions to which the horse has to respond. Likewise, the rider must prepare the horse ahead of time for the next section of the movement. For example, if you were driving and your navigator suddenly told you to turn left immediately, you would check traffic, signal, change gears, lurch left, hoping that the road had not been overshot—altogether not an enjoyable experience and dangerous, too. So a horse has to change the center of his balance and compact his gait and frame before he turns, and if he doesn't, he will probably fall.

## Head Positions

Head position is critical to dressage, and indeed all forms of equestrian control. If a ridden horse throws up his head, the shape of his back and spine becomes U-shaped and rigid. The concussion of his feet hitting the ground is sent as shock waves through his body and transmitted to the rider's seat. The shock jars the rider's back, his posterior can become bruised, and he may feel as if all his dental work will be falling out shortly. Also, while the horse has his head up, he can place the bit in his teeth, ignoring the rider's frantic signals to stop or turn. Most runaways follow this course, and the rider feels as if he is supporting the weight of the entire horse in his hands. With his head so high, the horse can't see where he is going and, if really provoked, can rear, or fall over backward.

On the other extreme, if a ridden horse tucks his chin in, he can place the bit against his teeth, also ignoring the rider's command. The rider will feel nothing—no pressure at all in his hands, as if the steering wheel and brakes are no longer attached to a car. The horse will be able to round his back and tip his weight on his forehand. This way he is in position to buck, run away, or anything else perverse that crosses his mind. The rider has lost his steering wheel and his brakes.

The ideal head position for control is when the horse's face in profile appears vertical. Then the bit lies softly on the bars of his gums, not against his teeth, hence the term "on the bit." The resulting arch in his neck causes the activation of the salivary glands and keeps his mouth moist. There frequently will be some froth around the bit and muzzle when this happens.

This way, the back is rounded, suspended, and swings freely, absorbing

Above the bit.

Below the bit.

the shock. Also the horse can compact and expand his frame like a spring. He can easily bend sideways through his barrel, enabling him to curve around corners. Thus, it becomes possible to change his center of balance toward his haunches, lifting the forehand, freeing it for jumping, turns, collection, and extension. With his weight on his hindquarters, a horse can stop quickly and accurately, ready to move off again immediately in any direction.

## Rider Position

To guide and propel the horse, the rider makes contact with the horse's mouth by shortening the reins to the point that he feels any movement of the mouth. His hands are in front of him, over the withers about two and a half inches up and separate from each other about the same distance. His upper arm relaxes from the shoulder a little ahead of his body. There should be a straight line from the elbow to the horse's mouth. The rider is very erect, with weight in the seat. His spine is straight, like pearls dangling on a string. Wrapping softly around the horse's barrel, his legs have steady contact down through the inside rear of the calf and ankle.

The feel of the contact is similar to having a steady hand on a distraught child's shoulder. The hand is constantly on the skin with pressure added occasionally for emphasis. This would be more settling than taking the hand away and then returning it with pressure. A leg should guide quietly with taps only used for occasional emphasis. A tap too often done leads the horse to ignore it altogether.

By keeping contact with the legs, seat, and hands the rider establishes a corridor for the horse. The aids act as walls, leaving the horse only one desirable outlet for movement.

The knee is relaxed and turned outward at about a 45 degree angle, allowing ease of rotating the leg. The knee is relaxed to the point of being horizontally floppy. A person on the ground can see daylight through the gap between the knee and the saddle. The ankle is relaxed with the heel dropped below the ball of the foot. This way, the ankle will be free to move to absorb shock. The stirrup leather lies vertical to the ball of the foot.

One of the most critical elements is ankle position. It should be relaxed with the heel down. As long as this one part moves freely, the rest of the body will follow and the horse will stay soft. Whenever anything goes wrong, first check the position of the ankle. You will soon mentally develop a list in order from bottom to top. Then you can then test your mental agility by adding the horse's checklist to it. No wonder the first few attempts at steering feel like a one-man band playing a symphony while riding a greased watermelon in a pool. Except that the watermelon doesn't have the mind of a three-year-old child, which your horse frequently does.

If the first basic tenet of riding is "Keep your ankle soft," then the second is "Look where you want to go." By looking, you are literally using your head. Your body very subtly shifts weight and balance when you turn your head.

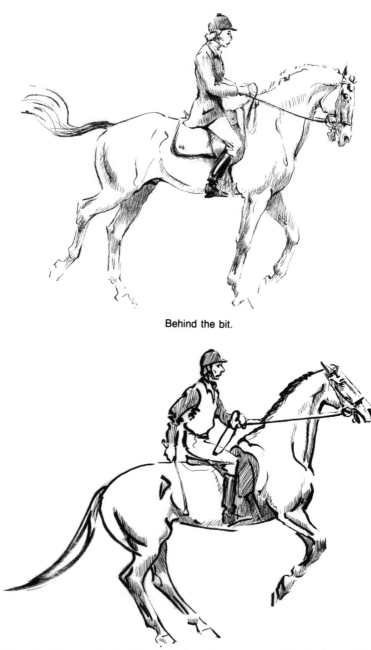

Behind the bit.

Above the bit and not going forward: the horse is resisting and starting to rear. The rider is vigorously using the bat to urge the horse forward. He will bring his weight forward, if necessary. If the horse rears, he will grab the bridle close to the head and turn the horse's head sideways and down. Speedy reprimand with the bat and forward motion are keys to stopping a rear before it gets started.

Frame of the horse from on the bit to FEI (Olympic level): as the horse becomes more trained, his musculature allows him to compress his frame, shifting his weight more and more to the hindquarters. His forehand becomes more elevated and his hindquarters come farther under him to compensate.

### Establishing the Direction

Now you are ready for dressage. For a dressage halt, you look at a distant point, about eye level. For example, in the arena, you are entering at A and planning to halt exactly above the imaginary point X in the center. You look and aim about five strides before entering the arena down the sight line of AXC. By continuing to look at C, you will find it easier to correct the straightness of your approach. As the horse wobbles, correct by increasing briefly the pressure of your leg to nudge him back to center. Then stop the sidewise movement with your other leg. A horse moves away from pressure. If he wiggles left, use your left leg to push him back to center. Meanwhile, because you were concentrating on your left leg, your right leg lightened pressure, allowing him a direction to move. When he is centered, then release the left leg. Since you are looking straight ahead, your balance moves back to center and your right leg regains the usual amount of pressure against his side.

### Half Halt

To cue the horse to expect a change, use a "half halt." Briefly increase your erect back to *very* erect, chin in, shoulders farther back. Think: heavy, through your seat, as if a military hero on horseback surveying the battlefield. Make your back a reversed C. Increase slightly the pressure in both legs equally, while stopping the forward movement of your hand. Vibrate the reins toward you with your ring fingers, or think of closing them repeatedly. All these things happen together for about half a stride—then relax. You are still aiming down the center line using B and E as cross hairs. You will feel the horse slowing down and his body becoming more compacted. You should feel more distinctly the swell of his rib cage as his legs gather farther under him. Your weight changes flow through his back, and force him to tighten the muscles of his croup.

Tucking his hindquarters under him, his hind legs are further pushed under his body. At the same time, the forward flow of movement is retarded by the closing of your hand, so the back end of the spring catches up with the front end. It usually takes about three half halts to prepare for a halt.

### The Halt

As you approach X, about three strides away (thirty-six feet), use the signals for the half halt. Then increase their emphasis and maintain them until the horse is completely still. Now relax! Think: wet noodle, limp, neutral, no new pressure. This is the horse's reward. Give him a big pat on the neck and tell him he's marvelous.

The horse should have stopped with his legs squarely under his body, even front and back. His head should stay in the vertical frame until you release the pressure on the reins. Here is how to correct bad halts.

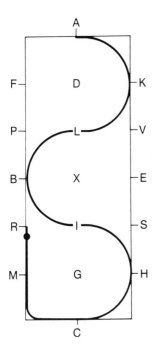

Dressage figures: serpentine.

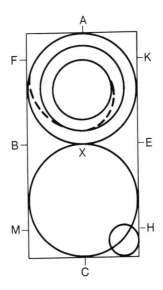

Dressage figures: concentric circles, spiral, figure eight (20 meters), circle (20 meters) (10 meters).

Moving into the correct halt.

The half halt: vibrating fingers in a give/take rhythm.

If:

- His front feet are uneven, the hindquarters behind him, and his nose up, he stopped on the forehand. To correct, try using more half halts to gather him in preparation, and more back and seat in the halt.
- He stops with the hindquarters under him, but one hind foot ahead of the other, your weight and pressure in the back and seat are uneven.
- The hind legs are even, under him, and the front legs are uneven, your hands had uneven pressure. Check to see if one rein is longer than the other.
- He isn't straight, your weight wasn't even through your legs. His hindquarters will move toward the released leg.
- He bore into your hands, during the exercise, use a give-take vibrato with your fingers to keep the bit moving in his mouth. It's similar to the vibrato movement when playing a flute or violin.
- He completely throws his weight on your hands, try giving and taking quickly with one hand and then the other. He can't lean against the bit if you take away the supporting rein. He will be forced into supporting himself.
- He tucks his chin in and drops the pressure on the bit, relax the pressure on the rein, lengthen the rein a little either by giving with your hand and elbow or lengthening the rein itself. Then tease him into playing with the bit by vibrato. If that is insufficient, give one sharp kick with both legs in the ribs. This should result in a loud thud, an equally loud gasp as the air in his lungs rapidly exits and his head comes up in bewilderment. He will also hustle forward. You have just applied a punishment designed to correct the problem and let him know that that particular behavior isn't going to be tolerated. Now that his head is up, you can start repositioning it with vibrato into the vertical. Keep the hindquarters coming up under him.

## Straight Line

To move off in a straight line, gather your reins subtly, by inching them through your fingers. A horse quickly learns that the pressure of contact means he is going to be asked something. Frequently, he will move forward as soon as he feels your movement through the reins.

Now give him a little vibrato to ask him to place his head in the vertical position. Aim your sight line through C to a point beyond, relax your hands through the elbow, and gently squeeze with your legs. The horse will push off from his hindquarters and go directly into the required gait. In practice, make sure that the halt is square before asking him to move. These transitions are easiest to learn at a trot. Keep working on trot/halt/trot sequences when you want to sharpen the horse's responses, slow down his pace at a trot, develop carrying his hindquarters under him, or square the halt.

The hollow halt: incorrect.

The correct halt.

Over the bit halt: incorrect.

## Curves and Arcs

As you reach the end of the arena, about even with the MGH crossline, half halt, vibrate the ring finger of the direction you want to go, look where you want to go and start to curve the horse's body around your inside leg. You should be able to see the horse's inside eye. The turn is really a segment of a circle, with the horse's head and body following the imaginary curve. A green horse cannot make right-angle turns. He is like a boat or train that needs anticipation and space. The half halts are necessary to collect him and cue a change coming up. The arc at C is about a horse's length. That arc is connected to a straight line, then another similarly sized arc in the corner. Try to stay deep in the turns without burying the horse in the fence. Always let him know at least three strides ahead what's coming up next.

## Circle

A perfect circle is ridden by connecting with arcs four points of the arena. For example, an easy trotting circle for an untrained horse is twenty meters in diameter.

For this, C, the midpoints between one end of the arena, and B or E, and X are frequently used. The rider curves the horse onto the circle using the signals for the arc. The line is then maintained with the outside rein and strong inside leg. You should be able to feel the horse curve under you. If the hindquarters move too far to the outside, your outside leg can block them with stronger pressure. If you can practice on sand, wood shavings, or damp grass, your horse will leave a trail of hoofprints. It becomes much easier to tell when the circle is more or less accurate.

This is one of those exercises that looks easy on the ground but isn't when you try to do it. Be persistent! Do three or four circles and then change to the other side and do three or four. You'll find that the horse will try to speed up in some sections (usually headed toward the barn) and slow down in others. He may try to flirt with another horse or misbehave. He finds dressage boring and demanding, using muscles that he would rather not stretch. But the circles settle a horse into obedience very quickly. You'll find that they help whenever you need a quick tranquilizer and a reminder of your authority. You can use them on trail rides, or almost any other situation.

## Ten-Meter Circle

As the horse progresses in balancing himself, the circles can be made gradually smaller. You can work easily on a ten-meter circle in a corner of the arena using midpoints to mentally construct the "corners." For example, to make a ten-meter square, you could use the letter A to the corner of the arena (a ten-meter distance). The next side would extend four meters beyond the letter K. On the opposite side, the square would extend from A through the imaginary letter D four meters toward the center of the arena. The last side connects the midline D to sideline K.

Many riders place markers to define the corners of the square. At the same time, they also place markers at the five-meter midpoints of the square. These midpoints are touched as the horse and rider curve along each segment of the circle. The smaller the circle, the slower the horse has to go to maintain his balance and the more compression or "collection" of the spring of the horse's body is needed to bring his hindquarters under him. If your horse has a tendency to rush, the ten-meter circle will force him to slow down to a normal rhythm.

### Figure Eight

The natural accompaniment to the circle is the figure eight. Think of the figure eight as two adjoining circles. To make the transition from one circle to the other, use the half halt to signal a change coming up. Maintain the curve of the first circle to one stride before the meeting point of the two circles. The next stride is straight, giving you a chance to change diagonals in your posting. (Just sit one bounce.) Look in the new direction, change the bend, so you can see the horse's eye on the inside of the new circle, and reverse the rein and leg pressure. This transition is known as a "change of rein." Now you are ready to complete the new circle.

The figure eight is a wonderful exercise. Starting with twenty-meter circles, it is somewhat relaxing for the horse while keeping his interest up.

### Smaller Circles

The ten-meter circle figure is demanding for the horse and rider. It forces both to make definite changes at precise moments. The ten-meter figure eight forces a horse to balance himself on his hindquarters and develop alertness to the rider's cues. Frequently, the horse will carry you farther out of the path. If you find that you can't make the turn, don't jump the fence or he'll do it later in public and embarrass you. He also won't respect the fence as a psychological boundary.

Try making a proper halt, rein back a few steps, then ask for the resumption of the trot in the proper direction. Another alternative is to change rein and circle back to a starting point and try again.

If you can make the turn, then stick with it and push him into a tighter circle. Remember, the smaller the circle, the stronger the aids. Do only a few ten-meter figure eights at a time, then go to some stretching exercises to reward the horse and give you both a break.

### Coffee Breaks

The exercises so far are designed to develop balance, compression, regularity of gait, and a free-swinging back. They slow a horse down and are used with the vertical head position. Normally, they are done at a trot. As with any muscle-training program for people, the breaks and the stretching exercises are just as important as the building exercises. It is also important that both sides of the horse are equally exercised. To let a horse have a break, you can transition to a square halt, maintain it to a count of ten, then relax and loosen the reins. Encourage the horse to stretch his neck and drop his neck down by feeding him rein a little at a time. If he has been working his neck and back muscles, he will gratefully stretch down until his muzzle is just a few inches off the ground. He may try to nibble some grass, but as an afterthought. Give him lots of praise and use this time as a reward. You can, of course, verbally praise him when he is working; he appreciates that, too.

## Walking Stretch

Another break is to transition to the walk. Establish a good, regular walk, then allow him to stretch out his head as described above. He can walk and stretch easily. Usually, the walk, stretching walk, and walk exercise are done using the short segments of the arena for regular walk, and either the diagonals or the long sides of arena for the stretching.

To bring him back to a working walk, make a small circle or use a corner of the arena to bring his head up and start the shift in balance to the hindquarters. As his head comes up, it is easy to take in the slack in the reins until you are riding on contact again. Once the working walk is established, you can go forward to whatever exercise you choose.

## Concentric Circles

Concentric circles are used for adding variety to circle work. They compact the horse as the circle diameter gets smaller and develop the rider's eye. You start with a large circle of twenty meters, and establish it with two or three trips around. Then tighten the curve to establish a smaller fifteen-meter circle within the first circle, and tighten again to ten meters. What makes these different is each circle is established within the rings of the previous one. Then reverse the procedure to come out of the circles. They are normally done with the horse's head in the vertical position.

## Spirals

Spirals can be done either with the vertical head position or can be used as stretching and balancing exercises on a more fully trained horse. A spiral is a fluid movement from the large outer circle to ever-smaller circles ending with a ten-meter circle. Visually, the path on the ground looks like the geometric figure. These are fun to do both at the trot and the canter.

The aids are the same as concentric circles, but everything happens continuously. Once at the center of the spiral, stay only a few rounds of the ten-meter circle and spiral out again. This exercise can be done with the stretching exercise of the head and neck, using the rider's back and legs to keep the horse balanced on his hindquarters. You'll find it may remind you of the zippy circular amusement park rides you had as a kid—there's quite a wonderful tingling of suspense.

### Serpentines

Serpentines are more easily done in the larger arena (twenty by sixty meters). A serpentine consists of three equal loops. It actually is ridden as three connecting half twenty-meter circles. Each circle segment is round and the connecting change of rein stride is straight, just like a figure eight. You should have a stride touching each of your guiding points (see diagram on page 95). On a green horse, the serpentine is best done at a trot. In later, higher-level work, it is used to introduce the "countercanter." The sneaky part of the serpentine is that your inclination is to have lots of straight lines between the loops. Resist this reflex. Check your steps, and if the path looks straight, the snake just got you.

### Diagonals

The longest straight line in the arena is the diagonal. Diagonals are used for lengthenings and extensions in stride because they give the maximum opportunity to develop the change of stride and bring the horse back down to the working stride. One of the most torturous trials devised is a long "free" (stretching) walk across the diagonal. It feels as if several centuries pass as you try not to anticipate the next movement. Your horse, meanwhile, is much more interested in wiggling, eating grass, daydreaming, or finding something at which to shy.

As usual, consistency counts. Your only hope of a decent crossing is in using the previous corner well. Coming around the short side of the arena, make as deep a corner as you can without burying the horse in the fence. This should buy you some space before the take-off letter. Use that space to organize a clean departure with half halts. Sight down the line through X to the far point and don't waver with your eyes. Three strides before the end of the diagonal, start your preparatory half halts and cue a transition. Always give the horse lots of notice of what he is supposed to do next.

### Combination Programs

These geometric figures can be used in any combination. Generally speaking, use the halts, circles, rein-backs, and short segments to collect and rock the horse back on his hindquarters. They also develop the neck and back muscles—and vertical head. The diagonals, big circles, long straight lines, and spirals are used for stretchings. The more transitions, the more difficult the combinations become, and the more the horse has to listen. Plan on a program of fifteen minutes of relaxed hacking before dressage, fifteen to thirty minutes of dressage, and at least another fifteen minutes of relaxed hacking. Horses and you can become bored, sour, and cranky if pushed with too much arena work. Once you learn how to do the figures accurately, you can practice them here and there on trail rides. It's much more interesting to both of you and you stay more relaxed. It also pays off when you go to a competition or gathering of other horses and riders. If you want the stimulation, pick up some copies of low-level dressage tests. You and your big friend will both enjoy the variety.

## Collection and Extension

The concept of compression or "collection" and "extension" in a horse body is like a spring. You push it together to develop energy and then when you release, it flies forward in the air. Compression is done by collecting the horse to develop the energy and move his haunches under him. The forehand, when released, floats in the air and the stride becomes very long. The feeling of being on a horse collected is of tremendous power, and when he extends, the float is so long that you wonder if you will ever come down. It's addictive and exhilarating!

The exercises work to develop the muscles a horse needs to collect and extend. At the beginning, our goal is just to complete accurately the figures. Gradually, as the muscles develop, it becomes easier to place the horse "on the bit" in the vertical head position and keep him there for longer periods of time. When he can do this comfortably, he has moved to the first level in dressage and the start of lengthening of stride.

## Working Walk

The "walk" is much like the walk exercise. The horse is on the bit, moving at his regular four-beat walk. If when you feel the swell of his ribs against your leg you increase briefly the pressure in your lower leg against him, this will increase the stride of his hind leg. By alternating your legs as the ribs swell against them, you develop longer strides. At the same time, you are holding him lightly in front. It's important that the rhythm doesn't increase or change. You should feel the compression in his body build. His stride will become more elevated. Do this for short periods of time—the short side of the arena coming around to the diagonal starting point. At the starting point, aim him either down the long side or across the diagonal. Now gently soften your hands, allowing your elbows to come forward. His neck and head will stretch forward and low and you will feel his whole frame lengthen. As his body extends, so does his stride.

Concentrate on not changing the rhythm. At the working and extended gait, it is always the same. If the horse feels faster, he has tipped on the

Developing power and surging into an extended trot.

forehand and isn't lengthening. He is just rushing. Bring him back to the working gait and prepare more next time.

At the walk, you can use the stretching movement to increase a walk-lengthening as well. There should be a distinct change in frame and stride. Gather him together with half halts three strides before the end point, so that, as your body passes the end point, he is back in the working walk.

## Working Trot

In the regular working trot, the horse should be quietly, consistently, and freely moving along with a free-swinging back. To develop the power for a lengthening, you must work on compression. With the horse on the bit, you intensify each rhythmic squeeze of your legs as you sit each posting step. If the back is relaxed enough, you can sit the trot. Then you can squeeze with each step—a kind of double time. Remember to be rhythmic and relax between each stroke of your legs. Also remember to breathe—many is the struggling rider who feels dizzy and turns a colorful shade of blue from lack of oxygen. Another way to get the feel of the rhythm is listen to some bouncy Bach or other lively composer. You and the horse will quickly pick the rhythm of the music.

Work in circles to bring the hindquarters farther under his body. When you feel a lot of elevation in his stride, take him along the short side of the arena. Using lots of half halts and leg to cue and build pressure, bring him deeply around the corner and aim him down the diagonal. While intensifying each stroke of your legs, relax your hands forward, allowing the whole arm to come forward.

Be careful not to rush your hands and drop contact with the mouth. If the horse loses contact with you, he will drop on the forehand and rush. Correctly done, you will feel the hindquarters drop underneath you as the forehand rises and lifts off. If the horse is brilliant in his movement, you may even see his forelegs flashing out ahead of you. The power surge is frequently so great that you feel thrown out of the saddle with each thrust of a hind leg. Stay relaxed and maintain the driving strokes of your legs each time you are deep in the saddle. About two strides after X, start half halting to collect him into a regular working trot at the end of the diagonal. *A horse at an extended or lengthened trot or canter cannot go around corners and stay up. He will fall.*

Another method of developing lengthening is to ride with a friend. The friend's horse can act as a pace-setter. Find a large field or straight open expanse and have the friend's horse trot alongside while you collect your horse. When you are ready, the friend can push his mount faster at the trot or slow canter. Your horse will want to keep up, providing his own impulsion. Signal a lengthening with your hands, and you should have a nice long one.

The rider's up-and-down movement at the posting trot. The rider only moves as far out of the saddle as the horse throws him, staying in balance over his feet.

The movement of the horse at the canter.

## Problem Corrections for the Trot

A horse and rider just starting lengthenings usually can only maintain them a short time. Don't be discouraged. If you can get one stride you can build more onto it. In fine tuning, the horse may either rush or lag at the trot. In either case, he doesn't have his balance shifted to the hindquarters. Use a short canter to make him move forward again and then back to the working trot, using more leg this time.

If he does a few lengthening strides and then breaks to the canter, he can't maintain the trot. You need to support him more with your hand and lighten just a touch with your legs. Don't do too many lengthenings at a time. They are very hard to do successfully. Both you and the horse will need great quantities of praise and breathers.

## Canter

For some reason, canter collection in preparation of lengthening, and the lengthening itself, usually come much more easily to the horse and rider team than the trot. Like the trot, work in a circle to bring the hindquarters under the horse. Check that you have the correct lead within the first few strides. Using your regular sitting canter position, bring the horse on the bit with half halts. Meanwhile, maintain the rhythmic pulse of pressure of your legs and seat every time you are down deep in the saddle. If you feel as if you are getting thrown out of the saddle each stride, try bringing your shoulders farther back so you are sitting more vertically. Frequently, the change in balance is something that is more felt than observed. You merely appear more glued to the horse, like a "general on horseback" statue in the park. Intensify your leg pressure until you feel the elevation and compaction in the stride.

When you feel he is ready, take him along the short side of the arena. Using half halts to cue, take him deep in the corner and use either MBF or KGH lines for the lengthening. He will soar along, feeling as if he's floating. Your legs maintain the same steady rhythm of the working canter, only with greater intensity. Think of the same music being played louder.

Reaching three strides from the end point, bring your hands back to the normal position with half halts. Soften your leg pressure, but maintain working canter levels. The rhythm never changes. Keep collecting with half halts through the corner and make a circle at either A or C to organize. Don't try a lengthening or regular canter on the diagonal until the horse is schooled to the point of coming down to a trot at the end of the diagonal. Usually, the diagonal is reserved for higher-level work, since this is a difficult maneuver.

Horses like to lengthen at the canter but don't like to come down to a working canter afterward. You will need to be very strong in your aids to insist on obedience.

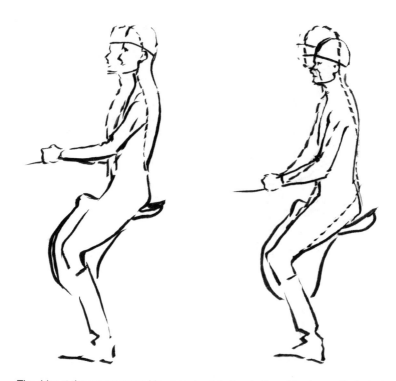

The rider at the canter sways his upper back to the rhythm of the horse. At the trot, the rider's movement is up and down.

The rider swaying at the canter on the horse.

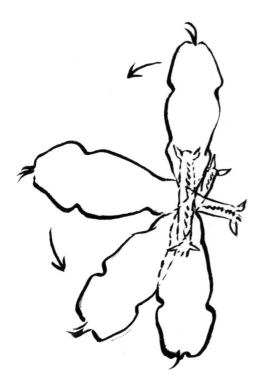

Lateral work, the turn of the forehand: the rider maintains the rein position of the halt while urging the horse with the seat. At the same time, the rider pressures with one leg and releases pressure with the other. The horse will shift his hindquarters away from the driving leg, making a large circle around his still front legs. This exercise is best done against a wall to give the horse a barrier.

Lateral work, the turn on the haunches: the rider holds the haunches of the horse still with the halt aids of back, seat, and legs. At the same time, the rider moves the reins sideways while giving the rein cues to turn. The horse will move his forehand in a circle around the haunches. This exercise is best done against a wall.

110

Lateral work, shoulder-in: the exercise is started off of a circle along a wall. As the horse moves straight, parallel to the wall, the rider pushes with his leg the haunches off the track, so that the hoofprint of the interior hind leg overtracks the hoofprint of the ouside front leg. The horse's head is bent slightly to the inside, showing the eye.

Lateral work, half pass: this more advanced exercise is started off a circle. The horse is bent in the direction of movement. The rider, with a series of taps, pushes the horse sideways, while urging him forward with the seat. While the horse is aimed straight, he is actually moving on a diagonal. He does this by crossing his legs in front of each other. The haunches should neither lead nor trail, but move evenly with the forehand.

Lateral work, half pass: Linda Oliver performing the half pass at a trot. Note the parallel movement of front and back legs, indicating the correct engagement and power from the hindquarters.

## Problem Corrections for the Canter

If, when down-transitioning from lengthening to working canter, the horse abruptly falls into a trot, he lost his balance and landed on his front end. Next time, use more leg and seat in preparation with the half halts to keep his hindquarters under him.

If he is also inclined to run off with you, try lengthening for only three strides and then bring him back to a working canter. Still, use the twenty-meter circle immediately afterward to keep control and the hindquarters under. Make a series of twenty-meter circles down the arena, connecting them with the few strides of lengthening. Don't try lengthening outside the arena until you can maintain comfortable control inside.

## Transitions

If he is really obnoxiously pigheaded, work him in rapid fire up and down transitions: halt—walk—trot—canter; then trot—halt—trot—halt—rein-back four steps; walk—trot—halt—trot—canter—trot—halt. This should rattle his brain enough to confuse him into paying attention. It also forces him on to his haunches, so when you slip a lengthening in, he's ready to go. The rapid-fire exercise is like playing the scales—boring to you but necessary at times for precision.

Make each transition well prepared. He has to be cued to know what is expected of him. If you are sloppy, he is more likely to become confused and angry, compounding problems. When he does the transition well, praise him lavishly with your voice, so he knows he's done what you want.

If he is trying to please you, but just can't get the hang of lengthening at either trot or canter, consider how long he has had to develop the muscle tone. If you have been working six months or longer on his exercises and he is a mature horse, you should consider having a more advanced rider, who already can easily perform extensions, teach him. Once the "buttons" are in place, it will be easier for you to hit them.

When he finally does something well, especially a new step, give him a long break, lots of affection, and take him for a relaxed trail ride. The pleasure you will both have is the reward.

Cavalletti: the rails usually lie on the ground, although this form works well, too. The horse learns to relax while placing one foot between each rail. Ideally, the rider would be looking up at a point straight ahead while giving the horse free rein to make decisions.

Cavalletti: after the horse has mastered cavalletti, a low cross rail can be set up 9'6" from the last cavalletti pole. Note the groundline pole in front of the jump. This helps the horse develop the takeoff point. *(See page 118.)*

# 8

# Jumping on the Flat

---

JUMPING, as a concept, is really dressage with some bumps in it. How you get the horse to the fence is what is going to make the difference as to whether or not the horse will be able to get over the fence. If you do your dressage homework, which is also known as "flat work" in hunter parlance, the more supple the horse is side to side and the more responsive and obedient he is. You are going to be better able to make the adjustments to get over a course of fences successfully.

For example, in eventing stadium jumping, most of the lines, or the ways that you get to a fence, are set on segments of the dressage circle. A turn to a fence may be a twenty-meter circle if that is what is called for in your dressage test. Or you may have a ten-meter circle or a pirouette with a 180-degree turn if that is in your test. You may be asked for distances between fences that require you to extend the horse's frame and then immediately contract it, similar to what you would do for a collected canter from an extended canter. The multiple fences will require that you be able to rock the horse back onto his hocks as you would in dressage to keep his weight balanced throughout the entire combination.

## SAFETY PRECAUTIONS

When practicing for jumping, first of all, you need to have a person on the ground to observe you, to help you with picking up rails and also to pick up the pieces if the horse makes a mistake. It is unsafe to practice jumping without having an observer nearby in case you have a bad fall and need an ambulance. It is also dangerous to jump without using a safety helmet. The combination of the horse's force going forward plus the height can give you a very nasty fall. In actual practice, you are more likely to make many little falls, which may not be serious problems if you have your safety equipment, but could be very damaging if you do not. The AHSA requires safety helmets for all of their jumping competitions since several Olympic riders have been severely injured when their helmets flew off in a fall.

## RIDER CONCENTRATION

For a new rider building up to a course of fences, it is difficult to develop the mental concentration to deal with all the unfamiliar elements coming so quickly. It is very confusing and it takes a tremendous amount of mental as well as physical energy. Frequently, the new rider has an adrenaline attack just looking at the size of the massive one-foot or two-foot jump in front of him, and the whole idea of jumping can become intimidating. It may help to bring the horse to a halt; take several deep breaths and concentrate on an image of something pleasant, let your body relax, and the adrenaline level drop.

Adrenaline can be an extremely effective, helpful aid to a rider in competition. But it is a natural drug that the body produces that the rider needs to learn to control. It gives you much greater strength than you would have normally. It increases your breathing and makes it shallower. It also increases the tendency to hyperventilate and it gives your movement a quick, jerky effect. If you learn to work with adrenaline, all of those things can come in handy. A cross-country course where you are pushing the horse over a variety of difficult fences is a good example.

But when you are just learning to ride, you do not want to tap into your adrenaline reserve until you have absorbed all of the basics, because your horse will respond to the adrenaline. He will become more frantic as you tighten your body, your squeeze, and your balance. He is going to feel that he needs to escape from all of the increased pressure that he is not used to. Therefore, he will tend to flatten and rush to his fences. If he rushes to his fences and he realizes that he cannot get over the fence because he is now off balance, he will either crash through it or duck out to the side.

One of the images that frequently work for people is to think of a Caribbean vacation, where they are bored to tears, or they think of palm trees. Any serene scene that you can put in your mental eye will relax you immediately. You can practice this when you are at work in the office and you need to reduce your stress factor as well.

Likewise, if you need to increase your strength, you can either use your whip and spurs to help your leg or you can visualize something stressful. The problem with this particular methodology is dealing with the other side effects of the adrenaline kick which immediately go into effect.

# CAVALLETTI AND GYMNASTICS

When starting to jump, many riders find cavalletti and gymnastics grids useful as preparation for jumping individual fences.

Cavalletti are rails placed on the ground at regular intervals. For this exercise, four or five rails are placed four feet, six inches apart. From cavalletti the horse learns to space his strides so that each foot goes between each rail. The next step includes a crossrail at the end of the cavalletti, nine feet, six inches away. The horse balances himself all the way through the poles on the ground and then has a low jump at the end. As he gets better, you can reduce the number of rails from the first rail before the fence and add standards behind that fence to gradually build a gymnastic. The gymnastic teaches the horse to be balanced and learn how to get off of the ground safely so that his bascule is centered over each fence in question. Eventually, you will end up with up to five or six gymnastic fences set in a long line with different distances between them that encourage the horse to collect himself or extend as he goes through the grid.

When you first look down a cavalletti, it looks like a jumble on the ground. When you first look down a gymnastic, it looks like an impossible maze. But you and the horse will figure it out very quickly if you start with just the one fence and add to it a little at a time.

# LUNGING

When you first start cavalletti, you can either start to trot the horse under saddle or lunge him over cavalletti, depending on how agile he is on the ground. If your horse is not particularly catlike on the ground, it might be better to start him on the lunging first, without the weight of the rider to confuse the issue, as he is learning what to do with his own body. The same thing is true with going through the beginning of the gymnastic. Once the horse is accustomed to the concept of the grid, he then can be ridden over the grid.

# DISTANCES IN CONTAINED AREAS

For work in a contained area or a gymnastic grid, the distances between fences are short because the horse feels confined. There again will be some variation in this depending on whether you are using a small horse or pony or an oversized warm blood. After trotting cavalletti and crossrails, one can then add an in-and-out one-stride that will require eighteen feet. If you want two strides to the next fence, you will need thirty-three feet.

The basic distances that are used for an enclosed area for setting small

Cavalletti: the next step is adding a back rail to the cross rail. It is placed just high enough that the horse can easily see it. Then spread it as small as possible.

Cavalletti: now the cross rail is changed to a very low horizontal rail. This gives a miniature spread.

118

A small spread made from cavalletti.

Gymnastics small bounce: here the horse learns to center himself in the space between cavalletti. He will take off as soon as his hind legs hit the ground, not taking a stride.

Gymnastics: the next element of the bounce has been raised. The horse is too close to take off comfortably and has hung his legs.

The first time you look down a gymnastics grid, it looks like an ocean of rails. This one is a cross rail to a vertical, to a spread, to a vertical. All of the fences have groundlines.

After the initial view, the rider can distinguish the different elements.

Gymnastics, jumping without reins: after the horse has learned the grid, a jumping lane can be built to school the rider. The fences are very small. Optical walls have been made using the bushes on one side and extra cavalletti on the other. The reins are knotted so they do not flop around. After the horse is aimed at the start of the lane, the rider removes her hands while she legs the horse on. Still focusing on the up and straight ahead focal point, she has time to grin. This really is fun!

# Gymnastic Grids

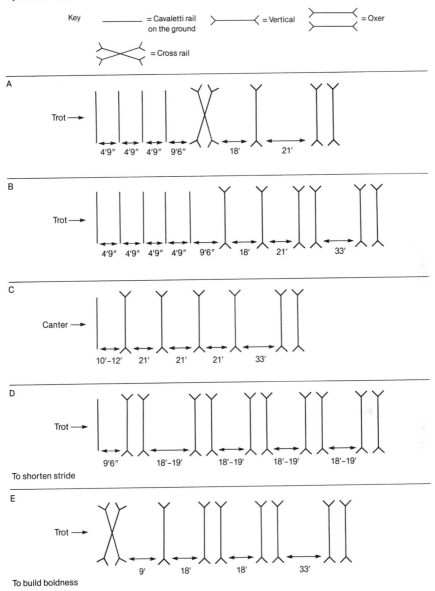

**Key**
_____ = Cavaletti rail on the ground
>———< = Vertical
>——< = Oxer
>✕< = Cross rail

**A**

Trot →

4'9"  4'9"  4'9"  9'6"  18'  21'

**B**

Trot →

4'9"  4'9"  4'9"  4'9"  9'6"  18'  21'  33'

**C**

Canter →

10'–12'  21'  21'  21'  33'

**D**

Trot →

9'6"  18'–19'  18'–19'  18'–19'  18'–19'

To shorten stride

**E**

Trot →

9'  18'  18'  33'

To build boldness

Gymnastic grids: these examples are meant to be built with low fences, three feet or less. By keeping the height low, you can jump more often, since it is easier on the horse's legs. When raising rails of an oxer, always raise the back rail first, let the horse jump, then raise the front rail. Parallel rails are much harder to jump. Use enough rails to make the face of the fence look solid and formidable. Airy fences are hard to jump, and many horses do not respect them. Note that the "C" grid is taken at a canter, unlike the rest. The "D" grid must be slowly trotted, as it is designed to shorten the horse's stride. The "E" grid encourages boldness in a horse in preparation for cross-country obstacles.

A) Vertical: the horse has a steep-sided bascule with a short horizontal of the apex of the jump.
B) Oxer (spread): the horse has more speed coming to the jump, which gives him a sloping-sided bascule with a long horizontal at the apex of the jump.

The bounce: the bounce consists of two jump elements spaced so that the horse does not take a stride in between them. He lands, reshuffles his feet, and immediately leaves the ground again.

courses are multiples of nine, ten, or eleven feet depending on what you are trying to accomplish in the schooling exercise. You can keep, for instance, the fences small and the distances short, which will help a horse that is starting to get careless. This is assuming you are jumping from a trot. When you switch to jumping to a canter, then you need to increase the distance to multiples of ten and then eleven feet. This is all assuming that you are schooling. Another thing that you can do is to keep the distances short and raise the fences slightly to force the horse to arch more in the air. This is useful as your horse is starting to drag legs and isn't really working over the fence.

With the grid work, it is important to realize that the horse cannot be expected to jump complete grids all in one day. You work slowly on this particular project and it will take months to go through all of the different grid exercises at different points in the horse's training. You want the horse to accept and be comfortable with each step before you add on to the next. Ideally, you never overface the horse by giving too much information too fast and destroying his self-confidence. The purpose of the schooling exercises is to increase his self-confidence and therefore his boldness, because he understands what is expected of him in each of the particular situations.

When you have worked your way through the grid of crossrails, then you can slowly work your way through by changing the crossrails to verticals and then verticals ending with an oxer. Eventually, you can work from crossrail to vertical to oxers. Oxers do take more space and you need to adjust the distances for them.

If a horse jumps in too big at the first fence, he will have trouble with all the other fences. If he does, try taking him through the gymnastic again. If he has figured out how to adjust his stride, he will back himself off and get himself organized.

## LANDING POLES

If your horse has not learned how to adjust his stride, you may want to help him by laying a pole about ten or twelve feet away from the landing side of the fence. Since the horse doesn't want to land on the pole, he will change the shape of his bascule shorter or higher so that he lands where he can take a stride over the landing pole.

The landing pole is not appropriate with high-spirited horses. In their anxiety, they may try to fly the landing pole. Use instead closer striding between the elements of the in-and-out one-stride. Frequent use of bounces is also helpful.

If the horse starts to twist or has trouble getting his knees up in time, the distance is too short. Lengthen the distance so the horse can establish his self-confidence again. When shortening distances, only move the standards four inches to six inches at a time.

Only use one or two "short" distances, then immediately allow the

The perfect bascule: this is the shape of the horse in flight. He is on the rising side of the fence, tucking his knees up and balancing with his head and neck. He looks "round."

Jumping hollow, a fault, versus round: if the horse jumps with his head high and hollows his back (dotted-line horse), he is both more uncomfortable and more unstable in the air. He is likely to stall and hit the fence.

Jumping with hanging legs, a fault, versus with knees up: if the horse leaves his knees down instead of at the horizontal or above, he is quite likely to hook the top of the fence and cartwheel. A horse with his knees up can still slide over a hit obstacle, whereas a horse with his legs down cannot.

Twisting, a fault: on the landing side of the bascule, if the horse is worried about hitting a fence with his hind legs, he can twist his hindquarters and legs up and out. This movement is very unsettling to the rider and can cause a fall.

horse to lengthen stride. Just as dressage requires lengthening after collection, so do the muscles used for jumping. You can also roll the ground line of the second fence a little toward the horse to make the horse rock back on his hocks sooner.

If a horse stops or swerves halfway through a gymnastic grid, you may have taken him too fast for him to absorb all the knowledge, the grid may be set incorrectly, or he has run out of gas. Again, you take him back to the beginning. Reduce the number of fences to where he is comfortable, making this an easier, longer-distance grid. Then you encourage and support him more going through the grid to build his self-confidence up again. Using your legs and voice and clucking to him will help a great deal. Make sure that you are using your hands in the horse's mane for your balance rather than balancing off of the bridle, which can cause a stop. If the horse starts to drift out again, you can use a drift pole to keep him in the grid. A drift pole is a rail set with one end on the ground and the other on the top of the standard. It forms a wing to funnel the horse toward the jump.

Another use of the gymnastic grid is to help a horse build boldness that can be useful later for cross-country work. An example of this would be to start with a trotted crossrail and have a nine foot, six inch to twelve inch space to a vertical, which would mean that the horse would be bouncing that. When the horse can bounce through that with confidence, then, at eighteen feet out, you can add an oxer. This would give you a bounce to a one-stride. Once that works out well, then you can add a second one-stride, that is another twenty-one feet to another oxer. When that is accomplished thirty-three feet out, you can place one more oxer. If your horse gets upset or confused at any point through this, stop and take down one of the jumps and start over again so that he builds his confidence back up again.

## GYMNASTICS ON A HILL

Another variation of the gymnastic is to set it on the side of a hill. By the placement of the one rail up off the ground just a touch, you can turn a small hill into a drop fence or a bank without having to go to the expense of building one. The placement rails before and after the miniature jump help the horse get himself organized and a placement rail after the jump will help him if he needs to adjust his bascule.

## FIGURE EIGHT

When one has a horse that rushes through cavalletti and gymnastics and seems to get more upset and nervous, there is an alternate schooling method. You put one rail on the ground and concentrate on making a circle with the edge of the circle crossing the rail. As the horse gets used to concen-

Leaving the ground too soon: if the horse leaves out a stride, he will jump flat and is likely to come down in the obstacle. This movement surprises the rider and throws him backward in the saddle—known as "getting left." Frequently, even if the horse makes it over the fence, the rider does not.

Jumping too late: the horse does not want to leave the ground and takes off too close to the fence. There is no room for him to bring his front legs up, so he hits the top rail of the fence, knocking it off. The sudden impact of hitting the fence catapults the rider forward and may result in a fall.

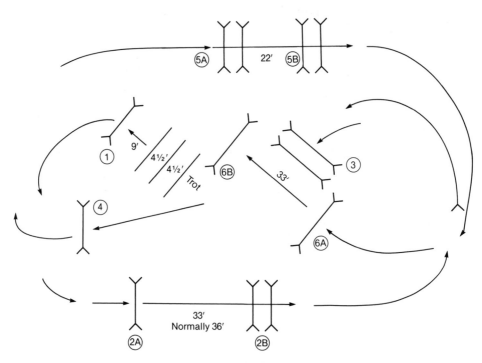

Very basic schooling course.

trating on the circle, and then there is a little rail that he just happens to have to go over, he relaxes about the rail and feels more comfortable about his body organization.

Then one can make a figure eight with the rail as the transition of the figure eight. When the horse gets bored with that, he can do it at a canter with your transition strides being over the rail. Again, the ideal is to lull the horse into thinking he is doing dressage that has a little bump in it. Gradually, you can slightly raise the little fence to a crossrail and then to a regular horizontal.

How do you get the horse to the fence? When you are riding, you have to think about where you are going. If you are making a circle and you want the horse to jump off that circle, you have to be looking ahead to where you are going—the horse follows your eyes.

## RIDING INDIVIDUAL FENCES

When one can comfortably do the gymnastic lines, bounces, one-strides, two-stride verticals to oxers and back again, then one can start riding individual fences. When you first start riding an individual fence, use a placement rail to a crossrail and work on your canter circle going over the fence, similar to what you did in the beginning as the rusher exercise. From that, you can go to your next fence, which would be a small vertical. As that becomes comfortable, you can add another fence. The second fence should be set at least three to four strides away so that the horse has plenty of time to become adjusted after the previous fence.

When schooling over fences, you want to keep the fences small so there is less concussion, because the horse is learning and it is important for both of you to keep your balance. You can jump many more fences if you keep the fences small than you can if you take large ones. In addition, your success rate goes up. Most schools, begin with a crossrail to a vertical that is about one foot, eight inches to about two feet, six inches. You do not want to get any higher than two feet six inches to three feet because your horse has to be more confirmed in his jumping as do you. As the jump gets larger, the push of the horse to get off the ground is greater. The trajectory is more powerful and it unsettles the rider.

In judging how many fences you can take in a day, ideally the maximum number of fences that the rider would take in one day of jump schooling would be about fifteen. It is a lot of effort for the horse and for the rider.

When adding more fences at a time, one does it slowly. It is quite difficult for a novice rider and horse combination to work up to the ten or twelve fences that are required for a novice competition because of the energy involved. Frequently, the rider will take breaks. You do three fences and then pull the horse up and give him a pat and tell him he is wonderful and relax for a little bit. When the horse is calm, pick him up again and ask him to go forward and do another set of three fences. Gradually, you will be able to do more than three at a time, but do not plan on doing fifteen fences as soon as you walk out of the barn. It is very much like dressage in that you practice different segments of the test, but you don't put the whole test together until the end of the session, if then. The whole test is actually ridden very little because otherwise the test does not ride as well. Horses become bored with jumping courses just as they can become bored with anything else. You need to interject a fresh outlook by changing directions or taking the fences in a different order, or reversing the entire order. Try anything that will, after three times over the same fence, make it a different fence.

## FALSE GROUNDLINES

Riders have to watch for false groundlines. These can be either mechanical or from the change of the sunlight across the face of the fence. As the sun goes through the heavens, the shadow line changes across the front of the fence. The shadow makes a black space in front of the fence, which appears to the horse to be a ditch or a bottomless hole. As a result, a horse will time his takeoff point for a different spot than he would if he had sunlight all the way to the bottom of the fence. This can make the fence quite dangerous if he takes off too far back. He may also spook or refuse because he is unsure of what he is dealing with.

The mechanical problem of a false groundline is if the bottom of the fence does not have a ground rail in front of the fence that marks the takeoff point but instead the rail is placed behind the fence. The horse sees an optical illusion and cannot place where the fence is. He tends to take off too late, thereby hitting his front legs, and can flip in the air. For this reason, when one is setting up a fence, it is important to make sure that all of your groundlines are in the direction you wish to jump. It is a very bad idea to jump a fence backward because the horse cannot adjust for the optical illusion and you are more likely to have a fall.

## SHAPE OF SPREAD FENCES

A proper spread or oxer fence ascends away from the horse so it follows the line of the trajectory of his bascule. The groundline is the first thing that your horse gets to, then the lower part of the fence, and then the back rail of the fence is farthest away from him. The square oxer, which is two verticals that are exactly the same height, is difficult for him to jump and should be left until you become a more experienced rider and he becomes a more experienced jumper.

The straight vertical should have the groundline in front of it. It isn't until one gets much further advanced that the groundline is omitted and there is space under a fence. This kind of fence is quite difficult for a horse to judge

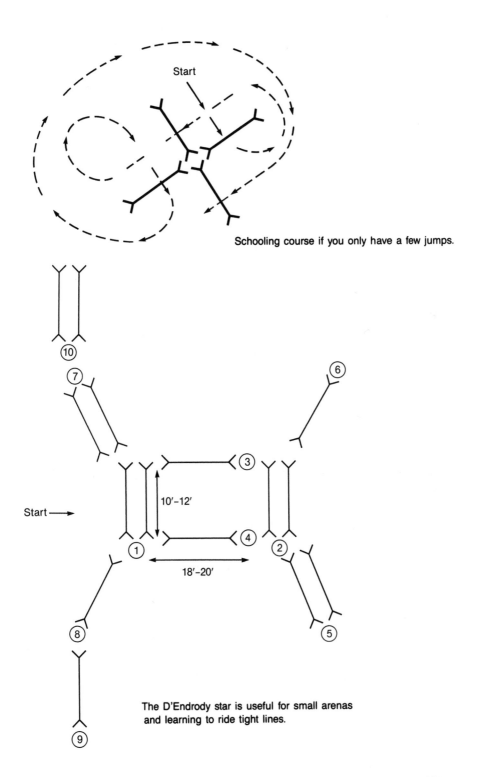

Start

Schooling course if you only have a few jumps.

10′–12′

Start →

18′–20′

The D'Endrody star is useful for small arenas and learning to ride tight lines.

and is a more advanced exercise. In eventing, this kind of fence is known as a Trakehner. Frequently, there is a ditch in open space under the fence. These are some of the most difficult fences for horses to jump.

In stadium, you will rarely find a fence that is constructed without a groundline until you reach higher levels. Even if you watch a Grand Prix show jumping course, there will be groundlines for even the most experienced of jumpers on the most difficult of courses.

## OUTSIDE DISTANCES

The classic distances that are used for placing courses outside are twelve feet for the bounce, twenty-four feet for a one-stride, thirty-six feet for a two-stride, forty-eight feet for a three-stride, sixty feet for a four-stride, and seventy-two feet for a five-stride. You will notice that the strides open up as you get more of them to compensate in the changes of terrain and the horse becomes bolder, moving with a more extended frame. The carry of a horse's jump extends from six feet in front of a fence to six feet after the fence. So when you are setting distances, you will have twelve feet that will be eaten up from takeoff and landing.

## WALKING DISTANCES

You compensate for this when you are walking the distances between the fences. While you are learning to walk distances, it is advisable to use a tape measure at home and mark off each of the distances and learn to adjust your gait so that you can walk accurately. There is a big difference between jumping an eighteen-foot distance and a twenty-one-foot distance. If your own stride is off then it makes it difficult for you to help the horse. The cavalletti can be worked over regularly as part of your flat work. You use them as a part of breaking up the horse's boredom and relaxing him at the same time.

## THE TURNS

Horses do not do well with being quickly turned and they lose their balance very easily. You need to organize your approach to the fence from either the previous fence or from your starting point. Ideally, you want to have a number of straight strides before the fence so the horse has time to analyze what he is expected to do. If you are working on a fence that requires a turn, if you look ahead to where the fence is when you need to do the turn, you can make the curve a segment of the circle.

# RHYTHM AND CONTROL

During the whole time of working over fences, you want to maintain the same rhythm that you worked on in dressage. The rhythm of the trot and the canter stay continuously at the same tempo that you had on the flat. Many horses get a little panic-stricken and want to increase their speed when they come to a fence. It is the responsibility of the rider to maintain the same metronome-like cadence to the fence and from the fence.

A green horse, in figuring out how to get to the fence, may suck back. When this happens, it feels as if there is nothing in your hand as he drops the bit and releases the pressure. You can feel his weight shift as he is going to halt, which you do not particularly want him to do. So you need to keep your leg going at the same rhythm and encourage him to maintain himself in the frame he would use for his dressage.

If you are coming to the fence and your horse is too fast, is not paying attention to you, or has slowed down sufficiently so that you do not feel that you have complete control, turn the horse out of the fence, make a circle, maintain your circle until you have reestablished your control, rhythm, and balance. At that point, sight for your fence, giving the horse the maximum amount of approach to the fence off of your circle. In other words, if you are working on a thirty-meter circle after a fence that has not worked out for you, use most of that thirty-meter circle to get yourself turned around and headed into the fence properly. It is a variation of the earlier rusher's exercise of working with the one pole on the ground.

# RIDING COMBINATIONS

Many horses will rush between fences in combinations of close stridings. They are in a hurry over their first fence and then jump too far out, eating up the amount of distance allowed between the fences. As a result, the rider needs to steady the horse as he lands, getting back into balance, and then ask him to go forward again.

If the horse is rushing between fences, the rider does not have to take the second fence. If the horse is unbalanced, instead, the rider pulls the horse out and makes a circle, gets the horse under control, and then brings him back into the combination again. Eventually, the horse will decide that this is a boring exercise and will relax over it.

# DRIFTING

Occasionally, a horse will drift coming into his second fence. This can be a bid to open up more space between the fences because he has not shortened his frame sufficiently to be able to jump the fence comfortably. You can correct this by using the drift pole that you used for the gymnastic and working on having more cadence and more rhythm to your pace coming into the fence.

Since getting to the fence is a major part of the battle with these low fences, you ride the lines as if you were following a roadway in your mind. You want curves as smooth as possible to make your turns into your fences. You can make a large circle and fit the fence in question on the edge of the circle, and if you are positive that the rhythm of the horse is correct, go ahead and take the fence. Then, as you get ready for the next fence, you look to the fence until about three strides out and then look up.

If your fences are placed so that it is not a straight line from one to the other, you need to look ahead to where you are going to give your horse the maximum amount of comfortable turn into the fence, leaving him with three or four straight strides before the fence.

## CHANGING CANTER LEADS IN THE AIR

Ideally, you will be signaling to him which direction you want to go to at the apex of the first fence by looking to your second fence. Turning your head to look to the second fence does a very subtle weight shift in your body and if the horse is going to land at the canter, will help him free the correct lead when he lands. Frequently, event horses are not trained to do flying changes of the canter until they are fairly old. This is because the way the stadium courses are set up, the lead changes happen in the air at the apex of a jump. The horse actually changes his lead as he is going over the fence and then lands on the correct lead.

Every horse jumps a little bit differently, and all of them need the help of the gymnastic grid to get themselves organized and to have the apex of their bascule over the fence rather than a little before, or a little after. Smaller horses or those that have a bit of a straight shoulder may feel as if they are struggling through the gymnastic grid and may need to be ridden more forward to help them develop their balance. They instinctively know that they can't bluff their way through the grid and must be precise and workmanlike to get their spots for takeoff in exactly the right place. Another horse may go through very flat and get strung out, and the grids will help him readjust himself and reshape his bascule. Every one in a while you will find a horse that is so athletic and so catlike that the grids are a piece of cake. With these horses, you use variations of the grid to remind them that they have to think about their jumping and not get lazy, careless, and strung out.

Another reason for use of the grid is that it helps the horse work his way through a sea of rails. He has learned to follow the instructions of his rider with great precision. Ideally, the horse, through the grid system, will learn to rock back on his hocks and project himself up over the jump rather than throwing himself at the fence.

134

Always ride your horse forward through your jumping grid and on course work or individual fences. You can't take a half halt if the horse is not coming up from behind. You will stall out instead.

The art of jumping is the marriage between the impulsion and the balance of the horse. You can get the impulsion by sending the horse forward, but then half halt to keep the horse in balance so he can lift off. If the horse will not accept the half halt, then he is on his forehand and has lost his balance. The gymnastics grid will help you with developing the impulsion and balance as a goal that can then be used for all of your other jumping efforts.

## CORRECTING STICKINESS

If your horse is sticky and unenthusiastic, gallop him around the ring a bit to get him going forward, to add more zest to his outlook, then you can go back to the technicalities of the jumping. This is similar to the work in the dressage when you extend the trot or use the straight lines to get the horse to move forward after doing your lateral work or working on circles.

## NOVICE JUMP POSITION

The novice jump rider needs always to think of looking up with his eyes, ahead to where he is going. He also needs to place his hands in the mane about halfway up so that he doesn't hit the horse in the mouth over the fence with his unbalanced movements as he is learning.

The lower leg of the rider needs to be pressed against the horse with his weight in his heel below the stirrup. If the rider's heel is not pressed down with his full weight, the lower leg will swing back over every fence. Occasionally, shortening the stirrup leathers a couple of holes will help put more flexion into the ankle and help with lowering his heel. Riding without stirrups on the flat work also helps develop a stronger seat, bringing the weight down and around the horse. After jumping the fence or the gymnastic grid, the rider should halt the horse on a straight line away from the fence. These are basic exercises that are the cornerstone of jumping technique.

When using the "grab the mane" technique, the rider holds the mane about halfway up the neck. If the rider grabs too far up the neck, he unbalances himself and in effect stands in his stirrups with his crotch almost above the pommel rather than having his body be a series of angles at each of the joints. If he grabs the mane too close to the saddle, then his upper body will tip over and become unbalanced. If you have trouble with keeping your horse going to the fence in a straight line, you can grab the mane with one hand and steer with the other when you get close to the fence. This allows the horse to make mistakes and adjustments on his own without the interference of the rider's weight tipping him forward or backward. It also helps the rider in that, without the contact of the reins, the rider will concentrate on the feel of the jumping and centering his own balance on the horse.

## REGAINING POSITION

One of the rider's problems to work on is regaining position and getting reorganized between fences. It requires the rider to move forward in the bascule and then quickly bring his body back up to the vertical, close the leg and seat, and push the balanced horse forward to the next fence. The whole time the rider needs to be looking up and out at a point even with his eyes so his body doesn't tip forward. This will help to keep the horse's forehand free for the jumping and also keep the horse straight.

## CREST RELEASE

Once the rider has stabilized his form, he can then go to the more advanced step of having his hands on either side of the horse's neck, sliding his hands up as the horse jumps and pressing them on the side of the neck to keep his balance. This is called a crest release. Again, if the rider's hands are too far forward, they cannot support the rider's body and he ends up standing in the stirrups with his upper body slung along the horse's neck, out of balance. If his hands are too far back, again he will tip his upper body. The crest release, like the mane release, is used from about two to three strides before the fence. The rider learns to ride his turns and the lines to his jumps, thinking the whole time about how to get to the fence. He is still worried about keeping his eyes up but is beginning to influence the movement of his mount more. He will gradually be able to develop the lengthening and shortening of the horse's stride to suit the distances between the fences. By developing his seat, he is learning not to tip in or out on his turns, but to wait for the turn and let the horse carry him around, staying centered over the horse's back, the same as he would for a dressage turn.

## THE BRIDGE

Eventually, as the rider gets better balanced and more centered in his jump he can use the option of a bridge release. Take the extra leftover part of the rein, literally drape it over the horse's neck, and hold a small part of it with the other hand. The rein forms a bridge over the top of the horse's neck, with the rider's hands supporting the pylons of the bridge on either side.

If the horse is jumping a drop fence, or the rider feels that he is going to need help on a particular fence, this is another alternative way of keeping his balance to grabbing the mane. It is less steady than grabbing the mane—the mane is attached to the horse and therefore is not going anywhere. But the bridge has its advantages in that you never release contact with the horse's mouth and your body and arms will flow with the horse's bascule.

If one carefully looks at the photographs of the Olympic riders on a difficult three-day event fence, frequently you will find them using the bridge. Occasionally, if it is a particularly bad fence, you will see a hand in the mane. In event riding, your skill in getting over the fence is aimed purely at survival. So instead of looking pretty, you want to remain in the saddle. The methodology used by three-day riders on cross-country is quite different from the show ring hunter rider who wants to present the perfect picture at all times and is on level ground. Each is difficult in its own way.

## FOLLOWING THROUGH THE AIR

Eventually, when the riding legs and seat are very strong, the rider can use an independent hand. This follows the motion of the horse's head and neck through the air. Hands are close to the sides of the horse's neck but not touching it. An advanced technique, it is used only for jumps on level ground.

## PREJUMPING

A common characteristic of the intermediate rider is to be so enthusiastic that he overanticipates getting to the jump and tends to get there before the horse does. He leaves for the fence before the horse does, and they end up jarring each other. The rider appears to stand in the stirrups with his upper body forward, long before the horse has even left the ground. An exercise for this problem would be to canter over small fences, making the rider wait for the fence, and letting the horse lift him and allowing the movement of the horse to close the angles. He needs to concentrate on closing the angles of his body, rather than getting to the fence. Sometimes even the thought of this angle is too potent and the rider just has to sit and wait to let the horse make the movement instead.

## DUCKING

Another problem that intermediate riders frequently have is to duck over their fences. This can be avoided by looking at a focal point somewhere beyond the fence and using a two-point position to keep the rider in motion with the horse. Always the rider's eyes are looking up and forward as he approaches his fence, goes over, and lands on the other side. He is always looking for the point he wants to reach. Ideally, the rider's body is fluid and is always in motion. If his arms are rigid, his eye is rigid as well, looking for only one spot.

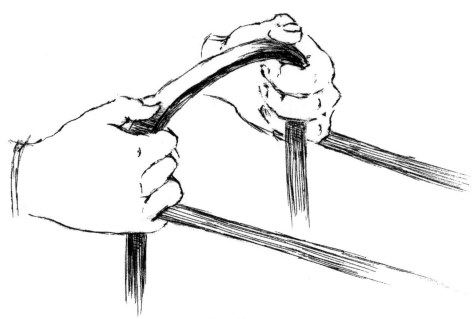

The bridge.

If he allows his arm to relax and move with the flow of the horse, he will discover there is a variety of spots from which he can take off.

Building a repertoire of spots to leave the ground comes from riding hundreds and thousands of fences. The more you do it, the better you will get. It is sheer practice. Ideally, you will end up riding each fence smoothly and fluidly, so you feel you are just gliding over, softly landing, and moving in balance to your next fence. It is the stuff of which dreams are made.

Coop set into a fence line.

# 9

# Cross-Country Jumping

$O$NCE THE RIDER is comfortable and established in his form over fences that fall down, such as the gymnastics or the stadium type, he can then move on to his education over cross-country types of fences. Cross-country fences are not only difficult because of the type they are, but also because they are placed out in the open and in natural terrain. Where the fence is placed is frequently as important, if not more so, than the actual fence.

## FENCES AND OBSTACLES

### Coops

The fences that are most common both for fox hunting and the eventing course include things like "coops," which are triangular solid fences set into a fence line. They are usually sixteen feet wide across the face, with fox hunting models about three feet, three inches in height and about six feet deep at the base. They are designed to keep cattle in while allowing the horses to cross from field to field. A coop is one of the most inviting fences and good for starting out your cross-country career. It ascends easily, helps to center the horse in the bascule, and is sufficiently solid that he does not want to hit it. A horse, generally speaking, will jump better over a solid obstacle than he will over an airy one. It is respect for being stung by a solid obstacle that brings to the fore his sense of self-preservation. Coops can be ridden anywhere from a trot to an ongoing balanced hand gallop, which is one reason they are so successful in the hunt field.

### Approaching Fences

As with all obstacles, you want to have as straight an approach as possible to the fence to give the horse the maximum amount of time to see what it is that he is doing. With fox hunting, this usually translates into three or four lengths of clear space in front of you before you go to the fence. When jumping in company, make sure the horse in front of you has cleared the fence before you start your approach. In a fox hunting situation, people tend to forget that rule and can jump on top of the rider who has just gone before them and then had a fall one stride out. As long as you keep the four strides or horse lengths between you and the rider in front of you, there is enough time to stop your horse or circle away from the fence in an emergency. It is also safer for you and your horse in that he has more time to judge the fence and understand what is being asked of him.

In any jump situation, you want to avoid surprising your horse, which will cause a hesitancy and therefore perhaps a fall or a refusal.

### Ditches

Ditches, especially cross-country course ditches, are revetted on the sides and usually have a groundline of a log on their takeoff. A beginner ditch may be revetted on the takeoff side, quite narrow and fairly shallow. It may have a sloping backside so the horse does not sting his feet if he lands a little short.

The key to jumping obstacles successfully without height is to lengthen the stride going into the fence. You want to lengthen the horse's stride out and get his nose in front of him a bit so that he does not really look into the ditch. Ditches are a psychological horror show for a horse. He is quite positive that there are alligators in it just waiting to attack him. If you start on a small ditch that he can get his confidence over, he will be more confident as you move to the larger ones. It is better to gallop on a lengthening stride to the takeoff of a ditch. He then knows what is expected of him. If you ride to the edge of the ditch in a trot, he does not know whether he is supposed to jump down into the ditch and then back out of it or look for alligators. Whereas, if you come in with enough speed and balance, his very speed will push him over the fence and give him the extra length that he needs to jump the ditch. *You never want to take back or adjust the stride by shortening, or fiddle with the horse's mouth going into a ditch.* It will throw him into a shorter stride onto his forehand and he will either refuse or fall into the ditch.

### Trakehners

For ditches that have a rail over the top, which is the type of fence known as a Trakehner, you meet on a lengthening stride also, but with not as much

Oxer: this higher-level-size jump is part of a three-day event course. Note the rider, Torrance Watkins, has a weight pad under her saddle to bring her weight up to the required 165 pounds.

The maze fence requires careful measuring to ensure that striding is right. This intermediate-level one set downhill makes a horse take larger strides just when he needs to take small ones. The horse has taken off from the wrong spot and now is twisting to clear the fence.

speed. You focus your and the horse's attention on the top rail and ride for it, ignoring the ditch underneath. Again, because you have an obstacle with width, you need to hand gallop to get comfortably over the Trakehner.

Another kind of gallop fence is the tiger trap. A tiger trap looks like an openwork side of a coop. It is usually poled and is quite airy. Behind it is a ditch that the ascended side covers. You ride it as if you were riding for a coop, sighting off the top rail. They are very easy to ride. It just takes a hand gallop and being steady in your sight line going into it.

### Oxers

Oxers require more speed than verticals. Again, when we talk of a gallop fence, what we mean is that a horse is galloping on, in balance, at a hand gallop. You do not need to take back and come down to a short, bouncy canter, nor do you want to go as fast as you would for, say, steeplechase. These fences can be taken at cross-country speeds that are appropriate to the level you are riding. For example, 450 meters per minute for training and 520 meters per minute for preliminary.

### Verticals

Vertical fences, maze-type fences, and stadium jumping are all met on a short, bouncy, impulsive canter stride. The short impulsive striding gives the horse a short, close takeoff spot. This tightens his frame, resulting in a higher arc to his bascule. When you talk of a short, bouncy stride, you want lots of impulsion, with the horse's weight to his hind end, thus freeing his front end. It is a lot of leg and enough hand to contain him, so his energy does not run out the front through his nose. You have compressed your spring so that when you release it over the jump, it has the power to make it over the fence. Since you have given lots of short, bouncy strides, it gives him more time and more adjustment spots to pick his own spot at the takeoff. The feeling that you want as a rider would be similar to that of riding a motorcycle and revving the motor up to do wheelies. It is the same maneuver that you sometimes run across with hot-rodders sitting at traffic lights looking for a drag race. Again, you have the energy up, the horse's zest up, and he is looking for a place to go.

### Maze Fences

Maze fences need to be walked before they are ridden. They usually have very tight lines through them of the different ways the horse can go. Normally, course designers will build in at least three options. An easy option, which takes more time, will probably require some weaving but gets you safely over the fence. A second option, which is pretty straightforward, and a third for time. The third option is always the most difficult and requires the most experience. At the lower levels, courses are designed to encourage the horse and make him bold so you will not find traps on the courses.

When jumping maze fences, the first consideration is taking it apart by its elements and then making your line of attack from each of the alternatives presented. So you may have a chance to take a corner, you may have a bounce to a one-stride, you may have a combination of the two, or if you look carefully, you may discover that there is a chute that you can swing your horse through and miss the first face of the obstacle and still be legal. You closely look at where all of the mandatory signs are to be sure that there is not an alternative that you might have missed.

The "Ledyard Coffin" is famous for being a difficult, advanced-level fence. The horses gallop up the side of the hill to what they think is a vertical, discover that there is a drop afterward, and then a large, revetted coffin that looks a bit like a double Trakehner. They then jump into the side of the hill and out over another vertical. What makes this such a difficult fence is the element of surprise. The horse does not know what he is getting until he is into it. There is an option that very few riders have recognized, of going down a chute on the side, which gives the horse enough time to see what it is expected to do with the coffin and the exit vertical. Very few riders who used that alternative had problems. But it took a number of eliminations before the riders realized there was another alternative they had not considered.

Maze fences almost always require short, bouncy strides in order to provide enough space to get out. The best method of preparing for a maze fence is to practice your gymnastic lines until the horse goes exactly where you want him to go. Your lines are true all the way through individual fences that are set in combination, like a bounce to a one-stride. By practicing jumping your horse over slight angles over a simple vertical, you will gradually learn to jump at an angle on the cross-country course. This does come in handy for fox hunting as well, where the horse can effectively turn in the air to follow the rest of the horses in the hunt.

### Water Jumps

Water jumps are some of the most difficult obstacles for horses. Psychologically, a horse looks at a water jump and he does not know how deep it is. He is not going to know until he sticks his foot in it—and he has to make the decision of whether or not to do it at quite a distance. Horses are worried that they will be swallowed up by the water, and that it will be too deep for them. They have no way of knowing that it is only two inches deep unless they can see the bottom.

They also worry that the resistance of the water will knock them off balance and make them fall. This is a very real concern, because if the horse comes into water too fast, his legs are stopped by the resistance of the water while the motion of his body continues on at its previous speed. So if you come into a water fence at a canter or a gallop, you will most likely fall, because your horse cannot free his feet fast enough to keep his balance. In addition, the spray from his movement through the water is sufficient to blind both horse and rider.

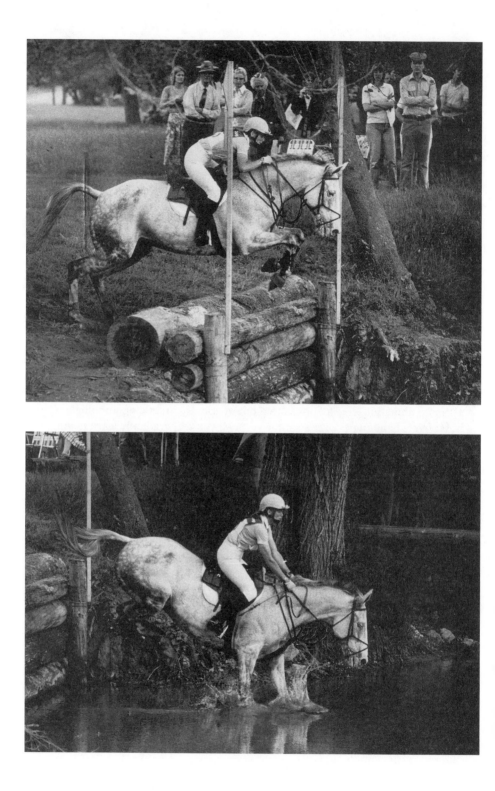

Water jump: Torrance Watkins and "Red's Door" in correct form. She keeps her weight back and deep for the drop, immediately kicks on for the next bank. Her contact with the horse's mouth is constant and supportive even when the reins slip. Her eyes never waver from the chosen line.

147

Water fences should be approached with caution. They are usually best ridden at a trot or short, bouncy canter when in competition. The rider gets pulled out of position by the concussion of the horse's being stopped by the water and there is always a shock. First of all, you have a drop fence, in effect, plus the resistance, which makes it worse.

Most riders will use the double bridge, that is, taking the excess of the rein into both hands so it makes a bridge over the crest of the horse's neck. That way, the rider can keep contact, keep supporting the horse's front end while getting support for himself by pressing his hands into the sides of the horse's neck. It is very easy to get unsettled going into a water fence. In addition, if a rider has tipped his weight too far forward, the shock is enough to unseat him and send him swimming. Ideally, when riding a water fence, if there is no vertical before it, use a very encouraging trot with a lot of leg and keep your weight back. Keep your seat close to the horse throughout the jump.

If you are faced with a vertical before the fence, similar to what is found at training level, you need to stay with the horse's motion over the vertical, and as he lands the angle of your upper body will come back to absorb the shock. It is important not to slip the reins, if at all possible, to help the horse support himself.

### Introducing the Water Jump

Introducing water fences is best done on a daily basis. If there is a stream near you that has a gravelly bottom that can hold the weight of the horse, crossing it on a regular basis encourages the horse and sends the signal that he has nothing to worry about. Eventually, you can place a crossrail about a stride away from the water. Hop him over the crossrail and then the one-stride to the water. Once that is old hat, you can add a crossrail on the far side of the stream one stride out. Eventually, you can place a groundline rail at the edge of the stream to give him the feeling of a small drop fence.

Sometimes horses are very afraid to try water for the first time. You may find that it is easier to turn the horse around and back him into the water if he is being difficult. Some horses are encouraged if they see another horse go into the water first. If you have a friend with an old campaigner that can quiet a novice horse and encourage him, it will make it much easier for you.

Horses like to be ridden into a stream where the water is about a foot or so deep and be allowed to relax for a while. They learn that the water feels good on their legs. The catch with this is that some horses will lie down and roll with you. If your horse feels as if he is starting to buckle, urge him vigorously forward with your stick, leg, whip, voice, anything and everything you have available.

Stream crossing is one of the things that fox hunting helps a horse develop. He learns from watching the other horses cross that it is safe for him to cross, too. Fox hunting also helps develop his boldness on the other cross-country types of obstacles.

The amount of water that gets splashed up on the rider when the water fence is ridden properly is really rather minimal. It is very similar to the amount of sweat you have on the horse at the same time. Using rubber reins and rubber strips on your gloves will help you keep contact as you ride through a water fence and afterward. They are very useful for any cross-country endeavor.

## Falls in Water

If you are unfortunate enough to have a fall in water, you will discover that you have a whole new ball game to deal with. The rider is soaked to the skin, the horse is soaked. The rider's boots have now filled up with water and are now sloshing around and stretching out so that when you put pressure on your boots they will not support you. The saddle has become slippery, because all of the saddle soap and oil that you use on the saddle has floated up to the surface. Staying on the saddle is a bit like staying on a greased basketball.

If you have rubbed a little extra sand into your saddle or your boots to make them a little tackier, that will have washed off, so it is not going to help you either. The saddle itself slips around because the girth has gotten soaked as well. So there you are, your horse unnerved, you are miserable and cannot stay on very well. You are no longer in a position where you can help your horse perform to his best advantage and the game turns into just surviving. All you can do is try hard to keep your balance, keep your weight in your heels, kick on and use the mane. You can get into the same predicament if you are unfortunate enough to be caught in a severe downpour. Unless you are going for a major championship, you may decide after this experience that it is better to retire all in one piece and try again on another day than it is to continue on. Events are never called because of weather conditions. It is up to the rider to decide what is safe for him, and that rule applies also to a fall at a water fence.

The more time you spend wisely schooling your horse in water at home, the less likely you are to have a disaster in competition. Once you have judiciously ridden your horse through water, he will become bold and accept it and will treat it like just another obstacle. Never, ever, go to a competition with a water fence and do your first crossing at such. You are asking for a major setback in your training. Horses that have had bad falls in water rarely will continue to jump water.

## Drop Fences

Drop fences are very similar to water fences in that there is a change in elevation. The American style of riding a drop fence is a little different from the English style. The American style is to ride forward at an energetic trot or bouncy canter. As the horse's bascule drops, you keep your weight forward

On hot days, most horses love trips to the swimming hole. This pond has a very good bottom and gently sloping sides.

This is what happens if your horse hits a hole or you go too fast.

until his hindquarters have cleared the top of the fence. At that point, you allow your upper body to open your angle and come back. This way, the horse does not drag his stifles over the top of the fence, if there is a vertical in front of the drop, and he will continue to jump willingly time after time. You need to use a double bridge in order to support yourself in the concussion of the landing because there is quite a bit of shock when his front feet hit. Drop fences are not taken at great speed because the horse can cartwheel. If you feel you need to make time on the course, you can make your adjustment down to a strong trot or bouncy canter three or four strides before the fence. You can do this farther out in the lower-level courses because the time restraints are more generous.

A horse that gets sat back on prior to clearing the vertical before the drop quickly gets a bad attitude. He is anticipating getting hooked in the mouth by the rider and dragging his stifles, which can really hurt him over the top of the fence. And if the rider thumps the horse's back hard enough, he can make him fall. If you do lean back, you need to keep a strong control of your reins to be ready to rebalance the horse as soon as possible. If the horse is going to land awkwardly, you need to make your corrections as quickly as possible— ideally, before he lands. You have to get the horse rebalanced and put together by the next stride after landing or he will buckle because he is so out of balance himself.

### Bounces

Jumping a bounce on a cross-country is done the same way as jumping a bounce in stadium. The way you get in is what is going to make the difference on how you get out. You want to come in on a short, bouncy stride with lots of rpms, power, and impulsion, and bascule the horse over the first vertical. That way, he will land in the middle space and have space for his front end to curve up and over the out. If you come in too large and too flat, then there is no space for him to lift his front end and he will breast the second element. If he does not land close enough to breast the second element, he is likely to hang his knees because his forehand has gotten trapped.

## CHOOSING OPTIONS

Any time one walks a cross-country course, one has to look at all the available options because a horse may feel differently by the time he gets to that fence. While the fence may ride as a big galloping fence on one option, your horse may have tired out a bit, and will need to take the more moderate middle road. He may be very weary or unsure about that fence. Then he will need to take the slowest option, which is the easiest.

The drop fence: drop fences are usually ridden slowly with impulsion. While a trot is preferred at the lower levels, a canter can be used. The important points for the rider are to look up, focus on where you are going, keep your weight back, and do not let the horse stall out. Use of the bridge will help with the shock of landing.

## Refusals

If you have a refusal and there is an easier option available in that fence, take it. Do not take the same spot that he refused the first time or you are likely to have him refuse with you again. After you have had a refusal, his momentum is stopped and you are motoring from ground zero. In addition to which he is backing off your leg the whole way up to the fence. If you give him an easy option on the obstacle that is a different presentation, he is less likely to resist again, successfully get through the obstacle, and build up speed to your next fence.

Once a horse has had one refusal on cross-country, you need to guard against having another farther down the course. You do this by making sure that you have him between leg and hand and you are keeping his haunches up underneath him and he is not allowed to tilt onto his forehand. When galloping cross-country, try to keep the horse in balance but allow him to lengthen his stride.

## Rider's Galloping Position

The rider's position will be forward, balanced over his feet to give the most direct air-flow pattern. If the rider is standing straight up in his irons, he is telling the horse to slow down. Likewise, if he sits on the horse's back, he is constantly giving a half halt to ask the horse to come to a halt. If he sits on the horse's back at a gallop, he is also going to be very out of balance from push of the horse's hindquarters against him. If you keep your horse in balance at the gallop, you get ready to adjust your stride five or six strides out from the fence. To lower your speed for that particular fence, such as a vertical, it is easy to bring your shoulders back and be a little more upright, then transition to sitting deep in the saddle a stride or so before the fence so that you drive the horse forward. Then it is easier to stay in the middle of the horse over the fence. This way, you will be able to make time around the course. The idea is to maintain the horse's rhythm and breathing and allow him to be fluid. If the horse is too compressed in his galloping style, his stride will shorten, his knees will come out, and he will look as if he is climbing the air. This will slow your time down also.

## BANKS AND STEEPLECHASE FENCES

### Simple Banks

Simple banks are easy for horses to jump, although they sometimes can be intimidating to the rider. A horse quickly learns to jump up on a bank. It is most comfortable for him with some forward momentum. But once he jumps on, he has to get his landing gear down quickly in order to steady himself, because his legs do not have as much space as he is used to. The rider also needs

The galloping position: at the gallop, the rider shortens his stirrup leathers to allow him to float above the saddle. This adjustment may be as much as four holes from the long dressage length. Usually, the stirrups are shorter for just galloping than for galloping and jumping. Generally, the faster you go, the shorter the stirrup leather. The rider balances over his feet with his heels dropped below the stirrup irons to absorb the shock of the horse's movement. The upper body opens and closes the hip angle as the horse surges forward. If the rider brings his shoulders back to the vertical, the weight shift acts as a powerful half halt.

Gallop position.

to keep his leg on the horse to push the horse's hindquarters up and on to the fence so the horse does not get stuck halfway up the side of the bank. On jumping off the bank, the width of the bank lets you know how much space you have to deal with. If it is a one-stride, the horse will reshuffle his feet, organize the one-stride and then pop off and it will feel much the same way as it does for a drop fence.

## Normandy Bank

When going over a Normandy bank, which is a bank with a ditch in front of it and an obstacle on the far side of the bank, you need to consider getting close enough to the edge of the ditch when you take off. You want to have enough rpms to clear the ditch, but like any ditch fence, you want to be close as possible to the groundline so that you do not make the abyss wider than absolutely necessary. If the distance on the top of the bank to the obstacle is, for example, a bounce, then you cannot come barreling into the bank or your horse will not have enough space to take off. If it is a one-stride, you can come in with more speed. Usually, a good galloping stride is your best bet on coming in on these fences.

*You never, never want to adjust for the takeoff to a ditch or a bank.* You always let the horse make the decisions. This is another fence where the double bridge comes in very handy. It is very important that the rider urge the horse forward as he is coming on to the bank, so that his hindquarters do not drop down into the ditch. If necessary, the rider may have to go to bat if his voice and his legs do not give sufficient encouragement.

## Irish Banks

With the Irish banks, which are unrevetted but may have ditches, one rides the horse the same way. The horse will jump into the side of the bank and scramble his way up to the top, peer over the top, decide what to do and then scramble his way off, usually popping on the takeoff. A horse who flies an Irish bank will only do it once because it is such a shock to him. Like any bank, the rider needs to support the horse all the way through the jumping effort to make sure that his hind legs do not drop. Horses are usually fairly enthusiastic about bank fences.

## Helsinki

Helsinki, which is a vertical fence set on the side of a hill, is an obstacle that looks much more difficult than it is to ride. To jump a Helsinki, one brings the horse up to the level of the panel far ahead of time, so the horse is cantering alongside the hill. You jump the Helsinki as close as possible to the side of the hill, so that it is a small fence. These are usually first seen at the preliminary level and they are ridden the same way you would for a show jumping fence. A very bouncy canter will do the job nicely.

Jumping uphill, and banks: come to a bank or uphill fence at a hand gallop. The obstacle will act as a brake, so you need to keep kicking on. There is a large surge of torque as the horse thrusts up into the air. It is easy to get left, so consider grabbing the mane or at least using a bridge.

Steeplechase: the horse jumps flat and fast. This rider has chosen to ride a little behind the motion with his foot forward in anticipation of the concussion of landing or a possible bobble—Jim Day of the Canadian 3-Day Team.

## Bullfinch

Occasionally on cross-country, you will run across a brush fence that may be airier and quite tall called a bullfinch. Pick an airy spot and jump through the fence. By using cross-country speed, the horse knows what you are expecting of him. If you come into a brush fence at 520 meters per minute, he is going to take it in an entirely different form than he would the steeplechase fence.

## Steeplechase

Steeplechase fences are unique because for all the previous fences one needs to have the bascule over the fence. A steeplechase fence is ridden at greater speeds than any of the others and the horse jumps fast and flat rather than arching over.

A steeplechase fence needs to be much larger and more imposing to be safe for the horse to learn to jump it properly. It needs to be at least four feet, eight inches high and lean away from the takeoff. In addition, it should have a takeoff board and be very densely packed with evergreens so that it presents a solid, inviting front. It usually has wings and is trimmed. The horse needs to be going at least 600 meters per minute to be able to pick up enough speed to fly the fence properly. *For steeplechase, the rider never takes back or half halt.* You make what minor adjustments you are going to make many, many, strides back. Ideally, you keep the horse galloping and moving forward the whole trip around. You want him to gallop on after the fence as well as before. It will take the horse a few tries to be able to learn what you want. If a horse sucks back and gets sticky, you may not have had enough speed coming into the fence. In any case, you need to go to bat after the fence to encourage him to move on. Before your next fence, you need to go to bat again to remind him to keep his speed up. Never make any moves close to a fence because the effect of any movement you make is magnified by the speed that you are traveling. Once a horse learns to jump steeplechase, he will be smooth, fast, and flat. And they jump farther away from the takeoff rail than they would for a regular fence. They can cover twenty-two feet when they are at full steeplechase speed, so the momentum is sufficient to carry you the extra width. You only have to school over two or three steeplechase fences to give the horse the idea of what you want him to do.

It is not necessary either to construct an entire course or to ride an entire course. One does not school at the high speeds of steeplechase until the horse is extremely fit, as is the rider. It is usually done just before a major three-day competition, in which you will have a steeplechase phase, or if you are going in one of the fast time hunter paces and you think you might possibly have a steeplechase fence on the course. Most hunter paces are run at a lower speed than steeplechase speed. They are usually around 520 meters per minute and are ridden more like a cross-country course.

When a horse is going at steeplechase speed, his frame is different in that he is more of a racehorse frame. It is longer and lower with a longer stride and his nose is a little farther out in front of him and his balance is farther forward. As the horse comes up to the steeplechase fence, he will raise his head slightly to look at the top of the fence and shift his weight back and the rider will have less weight in his hand. The rider then encourages with his leg to keep the momentum and to keep the drive going on so that the horse does not shorten his stride. You do not want the horse to get too close, throw his head up in the air, and then jump hollow-backed. It breaks all of his breathing, it breaks his momentum, and it is very hard on horse and rider. You, in addition to all of that, lose time—and time in competition is extremely expensive.

When schooling just for the pace of 600 or more meters per minute, the rider only needs to do a short amount of it. A short interval training program can be used where he slides up to the speed from 560 meters per minute, touches the 600 briefly to become accustomed to riding at that speed, and then drops back down again. It is not maintained for a long time. The greater the speed, the greater the chance your horse will break down and be injured. Steeplechase in three-day eventing is one of the safer versions of the sport in that horse and rider go one by one and the speeds are lower than they are in a true racing situation. It gives the rider a chance to have the thrill without the combat.

# 10

# Fox Hunting

---

**D**AWN. The pink-gold light of autumn sifts through the shadows of the copse of trees. The light turns the early-morning mist rising from the ponds and lowlands the pearly-pink of a seashell. As the sun comes higher, the pink light fires the trees' brilliant reds and golds with the mist changing colors in between.

At the edge of the grove stands a quiet line of horses and riders, their tweed coats blending into the autumn colors. They are fox hunters. They are watching the huntsman as he casts his hounds into the grove of trees. They are very quiet. The only sound is the jingling of the horses' bits, occasional rustle from the hounds' pads on the leaves. There is a hush as they all tune their ears, horses and people alike, to the music of the hounds.

The huntsman will direct the hounds with his voice. The melody that his voice line takes tells the hounds what to do. The melody rises in one direction. The hounds will swing as if they are a fan, to the left. If the melody goes in a different way, they will move to the right or straight ahead. He can call them forward. He can call them back. They now eddy and circle around his horse's legs, waiting for the next direction.

The huntsman's voice follows a melody that has been in use since medieval times. The words really are not that important. It is more the flow of the line that makes the difference. The hounds listen to that flow and occasionally the huntsman will use a very small horn to direct them if they get a bit too far away from him to use his voice.

The huntsman says as little as possible, though, allowing the hounds to concentrate on the work at hand. He does not want them distracted, trying to listen to him and concentrate on their noses at the same time.

The huntsman sounds his horn, playing the ancient melody of a hunting call to the foxhounds.

The foxhounds respond to the huntsman's call.

160

Outside the covert, on the opposite side, the whips—the huntsman's helpers—keep a wary eye for the fox or a deer. They will tell the huntsman if a fox has been seen or reprimand the hounds if they mistakenly chase the deer, running riot. They will show by pointing their whips and by verbal descriptions to the huntsman what is happening around the copse.

Foxhounds are allowed to hunt fox. They are not allowed to hunt any other game, especially deer. As a matter of fact, it is illegal to hunt deer in most states with hounds. It is considered to be an unfair advantage. The fox is *not* hunted to be killed. He is merely hunted to be chased and he is wary enough and cunning enough and interested enough in the chase so that he participates.

In most hunting country, there are lots and lots of holes, usually made by groundhogs—occasionally made by other animals as well—that the fox can pop into any time he decides he does not want to play the game. This is especially true along the edges of fence lines and in cornfields. And he is also quite good at locating piles of brush and climbing trees and hopping into barns and other evasive maneuvers, if he feels the need to.

The odd part of chasing foxes is that half the time, when you are sitting on a hill surveying the scene, watching, you will find the fox sitting on another hill, watching you and watching the hounds to see what they are going to do. He will only run as far as he thinks is necessary to be able to keep his lead. Then he will sit and he will watch and he will enjoy himself. Most of the time he does not even bother to take shelter to watch them.

If the huntsman's hounds pick up the line of the fox's scent in the early morning, they will have their noses to the ground. One hound will pick it up and another hound will hear him as he speaks. The huntsman will recognize that hound's voice and then tell the other hounds to hark to him, to pay attention.

The hounds then can converge on the line and soon it is like a string of pearls, the hounds are following the line, which is quite close to the ground, early in the morning.

The master of the field, of the fox hunters—that is the group of people who are watching the huntsman work—will maneuver the field around the copse of trees so they can watch the fox break cover—if they are lucky. If they are not quite so lucky, they can see the hounds work their way through the copse and out the other side where the fox has left.

Usually, the fox is a couple of agricultural fields away by the time the hounds have picked up his scent. It is very rare that the fox and the hounds are even in the same geographical field, much less very close together, as portrayed on a hunting print. Most of the time the fox has a tremendous advantage.

The early-morning hunting sessions are called "cub hunting." They are done in early September before the corn is taken in and they teach the young hounds how the game is played and they also teach the young fox cubs the same thing, so it is a learning session for both. Frequently, the riders will be mounted on their young or new horses, and they all are learning the game as well from the older mounts.

It is one of the few ancient pageants that is still alive. All those joys that were there for medieval times are there for you, too. It is a little like walking into a time warp.

When the hounds pick up the scent of the fox and take off, all of the hounds start singing, and it is called "hound music," as each hound's voice is slightly different from the others and it weaves a harmony. However, they all are very similar in their voices when they are all happily following the line.

A fox will usually pitter-patter across a grassy field or two and then swing into a cornfield. Now, in a cornfield, the hounds have a tough time getting through the rows of crops. The horses and riders have an even tougher time, so, while the corn is standing, the farmers usually have kindly left a one-tractor-width path right against the fence line. The horses and riders will trot down that and if they need to cross to another field, they then have to jump that fence line, and on the other side, there is usually only the same tractor-path-width. This means that the horses must learn to go from almost a standing start, take one step, jump the fence, turn in midair, land, and continue on their way.

But horses like fox hunting, and by watching the horse in front of them, they know what they are supposed to do. All you have to do, basically, is tell the horse to wait his turn in line—which horses do not like to do. They are like unruly children. Everybody wants to be first, and queuing up sometimes gets rather exciting as everyone's horse is quietly bouncing in place waiting for his opportunity to be over the next fence.

The fox will weave his way in and out of a cornfield, totally perplexing the hounds. He may come out and sidewind across an opening or pop over a fence to sit and watch to see what happens next. If he feels the necessity, he will move along to another field or a rocky outcrop. A fox with a particularly perverse sense of humor might weave in and out of a fence line that he knows has very few jumpable spaces and is hard for the hounds to follow.

If he pulls this maneuver, frequently he will do it for almost a football field or so in length and then he will come up to a rise and sit there and watch to see what happens. If he decides that he has had enough of this sport, he will then go to ground—find himself a burrow and pop into it, as the hunt moves on to locate another fox.

In the United States, the fox is never, ever dug out; he is never forced to leave ground once he decides that he has had enough of the game. This is part of the reason why the ASPCA does not get upset about fox hunting in the United States.

The real object of fox hunting is the pleasure of watching the fox outwit the hounds. It is not to kill the fox. As a matter of fact, most hunts get rather upset if one of their foxes is killed inadvertently. They mourn the ones that get hit by cars, which is more frequently the cause of a fox's demise.

Occasionally, one will have a fox that one will hunt for several seasons and you get to know that particular fox's method and the way that he runs.

He will choose his own little pathways, and if he is bored, he will keep to those pathways because they have worked successfully for him. In this way, you get to know that you are running the same fox.

When you are galloping along following the hounds, frequently you are moving up and down hills, and as you crest a hill and look out over, often two hills away you can see the hounds working. Four hills away, you can see the fox watching and, in between, you will see that he has put a herd of cattle in between himself and the hounds. Occasionally, he will do things like jump on top of the back of sheep and, as the sheep are terrified, they run and scatter, with their scent covering that of the fox.

Another thing that he is likely to do, if he decides to take advantage, is running in concentric circles, like a spiral, until he ends up in the center of it, and then he will jump to the outside.

A fox can cut off his scent whenever he wishes. In other words, "If I don't want to play, I can pick up my marbles and go home." So he will jump to the outside of the concentric circle, cut off his scent, trot up to a convenient rise, and sit there to watch the hounds be frustrated as they circle inward on themselves and end up in a great muddle in the center.

Occasionally, a fox will decide that he will use as his refuge a barn. He might run through a feedlot, causing total chaos of the hounds and the cattle. The hounds end up with manure up their noses and cannot smell anything for quite a while.

Another time, a fox might climb the ladder up into the hayloft, stay up there, and watch the whole of the hunt trying to figure out where he is. The fox is also quite likely to use stacks of firewood or brush piles as places to hide if he decides that he has had enough for the day. Every once in a while, particularly in the spring, the fox will be together with his family. He will have a fox condominium! There will be three or four foxes in one den, in which case, one will start the hunt. Then he will decide that he wants to go to ground, and does so. The second fox, who is his buddy, then pops out, runs for a while, and goes back to ground. The third fox will then pop out, and so it goes.

Unless you are very close and can see what has happened, you think you are running the same fox for forty-five minutes to several hours at very high speeds and the hounds are exhausted, as are the riders.

In the fall, though, early fall, the hunts are quite short. The foxes will usually run for about fifteen to twenty minutes, decide they have had enough, and go to ground. As foxes, horses, and hounds become more fit, and the corn is cut, the foxes must go farther to get their meals and so the runs become longer.

The foxes are never dropped arbitrarily into an area, because then they do not know how to get away as they do with their customary holes and their natural terrain. They will just run in a straight line and end up killing themselves off because they do not know where they are going. It is very important for the fox to know his country and to decide what he considers to be his best possible advantages. That is what makes the sport interesting.

One of the other surprises of fox hunting is that the horses absolutely adore it. It is their big social opportunity to be out with other horses all doing their favorite thing, acting as a herd.

Horses like fox hunting so much that, once they are seasoned, if they hear a hunt go by and they are not participating, given the slightest opportunity, they are likely to jump their pasture fence and go run with the hunt. They are always very excited when they hear the hunt horns and they have learned all of the huntsman's calls as well. Frequently, a horse will not settle until the huntsman calls the signal for the end of the day on his horn. Then, all of a sudden, the horse is quiet—and up until then he has been very, very excited.

In many ways, fox hunting is like skiing or sailing. You can do it as a family outing with small children, going in the hilltoppers group; or you can go very fast with the first flight, or anything in between. It is a social interaction in a beautiful setting. If you are single, it is a terrific way of meeting other people. As a single lady, it is one of the very few ways that one can get out and be very comfortable spending an afternoon with a group of people. If one is a gentleman, one is very much appreciated by all the young ladies.

## PREPARATION FOR A HUNT

One never goes hunting without prior permission of the master, which is usually given through the hunt secretary. When you just start fox hunting and feel that's what you want to do, contact the hunt secretary before the season begins in the summer to make arrangements to have someone teach you as you go. If a hunt seems too advanced for you, as a beginner, the hunt secretary may suggest another hunt that would be a better match for you. Pay attention to these suggestions and you'll have a better, safer time in the field.

If you live near a fox hunting area or do not have your own horse but are a good rider, the secretary can frequently tell you, at your request, where you can find horses for hire that are seasoned for that hunting territory. These are called hirelings and they generally cost around $100 a day to rent. Another source of information is the American Masters of Foxhounds Association in New York. If you're planning on hunting in Europe, *Bailey's Fox Hunting Guide* is another source of information.

To learn about the different hunts and their country, whom to contact, what their terrain is like, what days of the week they hunt, how many times they meet, and so forth, the best resource for hunting in the United States is *The Chronicle of the Horse,* a weekly magazine that's published in Middleburg, Virginia. It publishes an annual hunt roster with the names and phone numbers of all of the hunt secretaries to contact if you decide that you want to go out with one of the meets.

Each hunt describes what kind of horse you need. For example, one will even advise horses should be sensible, athletic, and bold. Some hunts are noted for being extremely fast, and those particular hunts will suggest that you use a Thoroughbred. Others will advise that its terrain has deep footing and a horse with a bigger foot will be a better choice. By contacting the secretary before you plan to go hunting, you can arrange to have the right horse and not get yourself in over your head on the terrain.

## CHOOSING A HUNTER

When picking a fox hunter, remember that beauty is not your first criterion. You need a horse that stays sane, stable, and is enthusiastic about the job at hand. If you can possibly get a seasoned hunter rather than making your own horse while you're learning to be a fox hunter yourself, you will enjoy what you're doing a great deal more and it will be safer because your horse will be able to cover your mistakes for you. A seasoned hunter has basically been out for at least two seasons, frequently more. Find an older hunter who still has lots of mileage left. He will take you along, show you the ropes, and will safely jump whatever you put him at even when you make your mistakes of getting him to the fence at the wrong spot. He'll be able to analyze for you until you learn to do it yourself. Also, a seasoned hunter is not going to waste his energy bouncing about when he knows he's going to be out there for a long time. As a result, he will usually stand very quietly at the checks, so you can understand what's going on with the hounds, and he'll be able to moderate his pace so that he can last longer. He won't run himself out. If you're riding a good fox hunter, you'll probably enjoy the sport of fox hunting immensely. If you're riding a horse that is not well trained and you are not familiar with the sport, you may never really learn to enjoy it.

A fox hunter should have a basically quiet temperament because he'll become more excited when he's with other horses. His bone structure will be very substantial, so that he can handle rough terrain and rough jumps. Frequently, a first-time fox hunter is part Thoroughbred or a grade horse such as an Appaloosa, a quarter horse, or a combination of those with Thoroughbred. Some of the nicest ones are half Thoroughbred, half draft. The quarter horses are known for keeping their cool under all circumstances and being very generous to your mistakes. A full Thoroughbred tends to be very excited and isn't a good choice for a first-time hunter.

If you're planning on hilltopping, you don't need a horse that covers a great deal of ground quickly. You can move at a slower pace, and that means you can pick a quieter horse to ride, such as the Appaloosa or the quarter horse. Quarter horses can be appendix registered quarter horses, which means they have a lot of Thoroughbred in them. These are capable of doing faster work, so that you move into the middle flight of the hunting field from the hilltoppers group. These are the horses that like to have a leader and are quite content to maintain their place in line without trying to rush over everyone. They make very comfortable hunting horses.

You need a horse that is capable of safely jumping whatever is in your hunt country. It is a general rule of thumb you'll have fences that run up to three and a half feet in most areas, occasionally you'll have a jump that's four feet because the ground is washed away on one side of the fence or another. Get someone else to jump the horse for you over a measured fence and watch to see if the horse jumps safely. He should keep his knees up when he goes over, not hanging a knee that might possibly get hooked in the fence. You want a horse that is a tidy, safe jumper. He doesn't have to be a spectacular Grand Prix show star but he's got to be safe.

Ideally, pick your fox hunter during the beginning of hunting season and ask to ride him fox hunting. Most people will allow you to take a horse fox hunting if they can ride another of their horses to make sure that you don't abuse their horse. This way, you can see if you and the horse get along well. If you don't, you've got someone with you who knows how to take you home, if you don't want to stay out because you're having such a miserable time. Also, you can learn from the owner the peculiarities of the horse you are considering and what that owner has done to correct for them.

Many horses will come with references. You can get in touch with the secretary on the hunt or the master of the hunt and find out a little more about the horse's background in the hunt field. You will, of course, always need to have the horse vetted, making a point to tell your veterinarian the purpose that you have in mind for the horse. If you are planning on just fox hunting, tell him so. If you are planning on doing more than fox hunting, some other aspect of riding, it's important to give him the whole picture of what you need. Frequently, the horse will pass the veterinarian inspection for one equine endeavor but not be suitable for another. A good veterinarian will be able to distinguish the more likely prospects for you. Your veterinarian will also probably do X rays on the horse's front legs and feet to make sure that they have no bony growth that will cause the horse to go lame and refuse jumps because of the pain in his feet. The veterinarian will also check heart and lungs to make sure he doesn't have a potential for heart attack or other problems. Get an estimate of how much it will cost to have your horse thoroughly vetted before you buy him. If the price of the veterinarian's exam is more than you had in mind, consider the cost of buying an unsound horse and not being able to sell him afterward. You'll find that your veterinarian exam is one of your wisest investments.

A horse used as a fox hunter, that goes out in the field to follow the hounds, is not the same as the show hunter seen in the competition ring. A show horse is usually much finer built and more high-spirited than the horse found fox hunting. Also, the show hunter tends to have better conformation for the aesthetics, but not necessarily conformation that will hold up to the work that a field hunter has to perform.

## HUNTING ATTIRE

Hunting attire has been developed over the centuries into what is the most workmanlike, practical combination of garments for being out in all kinds of weather on horseback. It is very traditional, but the traditions are functional. It is important that when you show up at the hunt, what you wear and what the horse wears are all spotlessly clean and well cared for. Your safety depends on having your equipment in excellent shape. After each hunt, make a point of cleaning your own equipment and frequently oiling it to check that all of the connecting points, such as the billet straps on your saddle and your stirrup leathers, are in good working condition. It is extremely dangerous to have your saddle come off in the middle of a gallop or over a fence.

## CUB HUNTING

The attire that you wear yourself during cub hunting season—that is, from the first of September until the opening meet of the hunt, which is usually around the first weekend of November in celebration of St. Hubert's Day, the patron saint of hunters—consists of tweed jackets in muted tones (never any red), a black riding cap, preferably a safety type with a chin strap.

The American Masters of Foxhounds Association has been encouraging people to change this one particular tradition and use safer helmets. If you go to a hunt where a lot of people have not made the change, do not let that sway you. They just have not bothered to read their rules and regulations lately. The safety helmet is very, very important and may save your life one day. A broken bone will usually heal without incident but head injuries are often more serious.

You will see riders in hunting hats, both the black velvet hunt cap and the bowler. It is not recommended that you follow suit and wear them, as they are not as safe as your safety helmet.

You can use the ratcatcher shirt, which comes with its own neckband, or you can use a plain or a colored stock tie with a plain safety pin. Breeches can be tan or russet or beige. If you have got a blue tweed coat, you can use black boots. Otherwise, you need brown boots. Ladies will need a hairnet.

Some hunts will allow you to use a turtleneck rather than a ratcatcher shirt. It is hard to get ratcatcher shirts for men, so usually it is the men who end up in the turtlenecks. You could also use a collar and a narrow tie, although that is a bit passé.

Frequently, the safety helmets have a fuzz over them, like a skullcap, and you can choose what kind of cover you want. You should plan on getting a black velvet and securing it on your safety helmet with several rubber bands. If you look around a bit, you can find rubber bands that are in dark colors so they're not so obvious.

Occasionally, some masters of foxhounds will give you permission in extreme weather conditions to either wear parkas over your regular coats in cold weather or to skip the jacket altogether in hot weather. You'll need to check with your hunt secretary to find out what the customs are at that particular hunt.

The cub hunting informal outfit is used all the way through cub hunting and, in addition, on informal days by some hunts during the regular season. Again, you need to check with your MFH or hunt secretary to find out which is the preferred pattern of the hunt that you're going to be hunting with.

## FORMAL HUNTING

During formal hunting, the formal attire for a new gentleman member of the field is a black safety helmet with safety chin strap with the harness fastened, or a bowler. He can wear a black wool melton coat with three buttons, or a black frock coat that is cut the same as the scarlet coat. He can wear a top hat if he wears the frock coat. He'll want a white shirt without a collar, which you can tie a stock over so that it's just the stock that shows. Some men prefer using turtlenecks for this purpose and then surreptitiously pinning the stock in place. The stock is fastened with a plain safety pin, designed for the purpose, that is fastened horizontally. He wears beige or canary breeches. Rust breeches are also permissible. The boots are plain black calf with no top and if garters are used, the garters are designed to match the breeches. The buttons on the coat are plain or dark in color until the member has been awarded his colors. A gentleman member may carry a flask or a sandwich case or both on his saddle.

Ladies can carry only the sandwich case, not the flask. The hunting stock is worn by everyone in the field as a safety measure. It is quite long and it's designed to be able to be fashioned into a sling or a tourniquet or a quick bandage, which is why the pin is an oversized safety pin. If you decide after having spent a year or two hunting that you want to wear a more elaborate pin, you still need to keep the safety pin with you for emergencies. The correct gloves are white cotton knit for rain or dark brown leather. In cold weather, deerskin gloves with wool liners are very warm and hold up well.

Everyone's breeches are made of heavy materials that are likely to hold up to hunting, such as wool, corduroy, twill, and synthetic twill. Not appropriate are knits or silks like in racing silks or lightweight synthetic knits.

A lady member of the field, before she has received her colors, also wears a black wool melton coat with three buttons, the buttons being plain. She can wear canary, beige, or rust breeches. She wears the white stock with the stock pin horizontally. Again, she wears the safety helmet with the chin strap fastened. She has a choice of wearing a bowler or a top hat if she's wearing a frock coat instead of the standard black wool melton. Her boots are black. She can have a sandwich case with her flask inside it and she can wear regulation hunting spurs, as can anyone else in the hunt field. There should be no other jewelry visible other than her safety pin. In practical matters, it is difficult to wear most rings when you're working with the horse because the rings cut into your hands from the reins. Earrings are definitely out, as is perfume, and a lady should always have a hairnet.

Lady members of the field may also wear dark blue, gray, or other dark hunting coats in addition to the black. Frequently, one will see a twill that has both black and navy blue in it. Frequently, underneath the coats, ladies and gentlemen wear wool vests that are cut longer than conventional vests so that the lower back of the riders stay warm when jumping and galloping.

Ladies and gentlemen can carry a hunt crop, but it is only used for the hook for opening and closing gates. It is extremely rare that you would be asked to use the thong on it. The crop is not designed for hitting your horse; it's an aid to correct the foxhounds. As a new member, you may decide not to carry it at all and carry instead a longish riding bat just to keep your horse under control. If you do decide to use the hunting crop, you carry the thong wrapped up in your hand rather than hanging loose. It is difficult to manage the hunt crop and maneuver your reins, especially if you're using double reins.

In cold weather, a great deal of creativity is put into ways of keeping warm. You may find visiting your local ski shop is your best bet. Some of the choices have been pantyhose worn by gentlemen members of the field as well as ladies under their breeches, silk long johns, various synthetic fibers that you can get made up in long johns at ski shops, and double layers of socks. Every once in a while some creative soul will have electric socks. The one catch that you have to remember is that periodically you cross streams, and if water gets in your boots, you could electrocute yourself.

## COLORS

The members of the field who have been with the hunt at least two or three years and are capable of leading the field if necessary or to take other positions of responsibility as directed by the master are awarded their colors, which is a great honor. Occasionally, you'll find a hunt that will not give colors for a very long time period. But, usually, if you do a lot of hard work for the hunt, it's about two or three years before you're given them.

A lady at that point is given the color that is the unique shade to that particular hunt and it's registered like a jockey's silk with the Masters of Foxhounds' Association. This is a piece of wool, occasionally velvet, that is sewn onto the collar of the hunting coat. At this time, she's also given the use of the buttons of the hunt, which have the hunt insignia on them. Normally, these are black with a white inscription. Occasionally, they'll be of other materials, such as silver.

She doesn't change really anything else about her dress except that she can wear the patent leather tops if she wants to on her boots. The benefit of the patent leather is that when you cross your legs, you don't end up with smudge marks on your breeches.

Once you're awarded your colors, and you go to visit another hunt, you have to revert back to a plain black melton because you don't have the skills to be able to hunt that particular territory. You only wear your hunt colors when you are with your own hunt.

A gentleman has a much bigger fanfare when he gets his colors. He is allowed to wear the scarlet coat with hunt colors on the collar. His scarlet coat will have rounded corners, whereas the master's coat will have square corners. He has four buttons, with the hunt insignia. These buttons are gold or silver, usually. The coat is a frock coat in shape and is quite long, to give warmth. There are two hunt buttons on the back of the coat, and there are also two or three buttons on the cuff of each sleeve. With the scarlet coat, he can wear a top hat if he wishes, or he can continue wearing the safety helmet or bowler. He uses white breeches of a heavy material.

At this time, he can use the black calf boots with the tan tops. Tan top boots are only used when you've got your colors.

Alternatively, the gentleman member of the field can also wear a black frock coat cut the same way as the scarlet coat. The buttons can be the hunt buttons again, but they can use the black buttons with the white insignia or crest design. He does not wear colors on the collar of his black coat, however, when he wears that.

The master will wear a square-cut, single-breasted frock coat that has no flaps on the outside at the waistline and no pockets on the outside of the coat except an optional whistle pocket. The master who hunts the hounds will have five buttons down the front, a master who doesn't hunt the hounds will have four buttons. These will be in gold or silver with the hunt insignia on them. The master has more buttons down the front than the field does. In addition, he will have lots of pockets on the inside for whatever he needs. The cloth of the coat is a very heavy melton or twill. He normally will wear scarlet, but occasionally the hunt livery will be in a different shade. He'll wear the colors of the hunt on his collar.

The master can wear a hunt cap with the ribbons down the back instead of the ribbons up. He can also wear a safety harness with the chin strap permanently attached as well. Breeches are usually white, but can be rust, depending on the colors of that particular hunt. Again, they're in heavy materials.

The boots are black with tan tops with tabs that are sewn on but not sewn down. The spurs are the heavy hunting pattern and the gloves are the same as the rest of the field.

The master carries a regulation-length hunting crop with the thong. He usually carries his down and out since he will cue the hounds with it. The master's horn can be carried between the buttons of his coat or on a leather case on the front of his saddle along with the wire cutters.

Lady masters frequently will prefer to continue to wear the dark coat with the colors on the collar rather than wear scarlet. When masters are visiting other hunts without their hounds, they don't wear their hunt colors. They change to black melton coats with no markings that a member of the field would wear before they've been awarded their hunt colors.

The colors allow the leaders of the hunt to be seen at greater distances. If one is on one hillside and you've been separated from the hunt, you can find the scarlet coat of the gentlemen quite a bit away from you. It helps you get back on track again.

## FOX HUNTING CALENDAR

Fox hunting is divided into several seasons. The cub hunting lasts from September 1 until roughly November 3 or so, which is St. Hubert's Day, the patron saint of hunting. At this time they have the official opening of hunting and the hounds are blessed by a chaplain. At that point, the field turns from the informal fox hunting clothes of tweeds to the formal black coats and formal hunt colors. In the spring, the masters frequently will relax their formal dress code to the tweeds again because of the weather being too warm for the heavy winter clothes.

## ARRIVAL AT THE HUNT

When you first arrive at the hunt, you make a point of going up to the secretary of the hunt and paying your respects and taking care of your financial obligation—the capping fee if this is one of your first times out. Usually, you can hunt as a guest and pay a capping fee, which is around $50 or so. Each hunt is a little bit different on pricing. This way, you can go with them for two or three times. After that, you can be invited to be a subscriber in order to continue hunting. The hunts are quite happy to have checks. They are also happy to have cash. As long as they get paid in advance, you are always welcome back.

On the matter of arrivals, try to plan on arriving at least thirty minutes before the start of the hunt. If you do not know where you are going, you can lose fifteen minutes or more searching for the location in the wrong pasture. The hunt gets very upset with you if you are late. Also, there is no way for you to follow them.

You need approximately fifteen minutes to back your horse out of the trailer, locate all of your paraphernalia, get mounted, and give the respects to the secretary. You need the time to walk your horse around and do a little trotting and cantering. This will run him through the gears, so to speak, check for brakes, and make sure you have got everything together before the hunt officially moves off.

Once the hunt starts, you will be gone for about five hours, so it is important that you not forget anything that you have to go back for.

When you call the hunt secretary to make arrangements to hunt with them, be sure to get very good directions. If you can possibly drive to the meet the day before the time you actually have to ship horses, it will help you get to the right place on time.

The morning of the meet, most people will tack their horses up before they leave their barn. That is to say, they will have their saddle, bridle, breastplate, protective boots—if they are using them—put on the horse before they put the horse in the trailer. Over this, they will put whatever traveling garment they have decided on for the day. It may be a sheet to keep the dust off the saddle going down gravel roads, or a woolen cooler if it is a bit colder out, or a blanket, if it has gotten very cold.

The halter will be slipped over the bridle, hooking the reins up inside the throat latch and the extra bit of rein will be tucked under a stirrup leather to keep it from sliding around the horse's front onto his chest. The girth is left slightly loose. This way, when you get to the meet, and your horse is extremely excited by the prospect, you have your work done and all you have to do is cinch up and make sure your saddle is in the right place. You are then ready to hop on.

If you can wear a protective jacket up until the last possible moment before you climb on your horse and then switch to your riding coat, your riding coat will survive in much better shape. Frequently, if you try to put on your riding coat and hard hat before you unhitch the horse and back him out, he will leave a large track of slime down your back.

When shipping your horse, plan on enough time that you can drive quite slowly, because you will be driving over mostly very bad roads as you get closer to the meet. Horses much prefer it if you make your turns at five miles an hour, even though it may drive people behind you to distraction.

If you are shipping only one horse, stick him in your left-hand stall. If you end up with one wheel off the road as you are getting passed on narrow country roads, the trailer does not flip.

If you can hitch up your car and trailer—or truck and trailer—the day before so you can double-check your hitch, it is a wise idea. The morning of the meet there will be many things going on and it is harder to make sure that everything is okay with the hitch. Needless to say, you have also checked to make sure you are not out of gas and that you have your car in working order.

## ACCESSORIES

If there is to be a hunt breakfast afterward, you may want a different jacket to put on, usually something lighter-weight, since you will be indoors. Take along a rag to wipe off your boots before you enter the house. You should also remove your spurs before you go in so that you do not hook the furniture or trip yourself as you are walking around the house.

Ladies will find it very handy to have a very large purse that they can stuff long johns in for when they come in after a winter meet. They will also find it important not to wear earrings when fox hunting, especially earrings that go through pierced ears, because the briers will catch your ears and can rip the earrings right out. It is a very painful way of remembering.

Ladies are always expected to wear a hairnet, which usually survives for the first half of the meet. You usually end up with a new one every meet. If you keep a couple of spares in the glove compartment of the car for fox hunting, it will save you a certain amount of grief the morning of the meet as you are on your way and then discover that you do not have it.

## SUSTENANCE

Since you are going to be spending four hours out in the country away from bathrooms, it is wise idea not to drink a great deal the morning of fox hunting—coffee or any other liquid refreshment. While traditionally there is frequently something called a "stirrup cup," which is a small glass of brandy, sherry, or port, frequently served with a bit of cake while you are in the saddle before the hunt leaves, it is wise not to drink very much.

One of the more embarrassing aspects of fox hunting is when one has to heed the call of nature. You need first enlist a friend to hold the horse, so it does not pull away when everybody else leaves. Inevitably, as one is in a compromising position, the hunt will then either circle back—going right by you—or they will immediately have the best run of the day and disappear and you will never find them again. Either one is sufficient motivation to put off drinking until after the hunt is completely over.

What is handy to have along with you, then, is sandwiches or some substantial food that will survive being bounced about on the horse's back. There are exquisite sandwich cases made for this particular purpose, but, frequently, what you can stuff in your pockets is much easier to get to, and if the hunt leaves rapidly, it is easier to put it back than to fool with your sandwich case. Also, since you already bought the riding jacket, you do not have to pay the extra cost of buying the case.

Frequently, people who have sandwich cases fill them up with other wonderful but less frequently used needs, like a first aid kit or medication for bee stings, or, occasionally, candy. Ladies can carry a small flask in their kit. The gentlemen are more generously permitted to use a separate flask that is quite a bit larger and can be carried on the front of their saddles. Again, the idea is to have a little sip of something to wet your lips, not to drink great quantities.

## THE BUDDY SYSTEM

Generally speaking, the hunt secretary will suggest when you first start hunting that you go with the green horse group, unless you have prior experience, and you will be assigned a member of the hunt to be responsible for you. This is a variation of the buddy system used in skiing. Fox hunting is a risky sport. It is an adrenaline sport, but it is also one where you want to make sure

The huntsman takes his foxhounds to the covert to look for a fox. It is early cub-hunting season, so the huntsman, Jim Atkins of the Old Dominion Hounds, is wearing a scarlet turtleneck.

that someone is looking out for you. You then have the responsibility to look out for them, too.

Your assigned host will ease you into the format of that particular hunt's style and will answer any questions that you have. They are quite willing to teach you whatever you would like to learn. Never be afraid to ask questions. Never be afraid to be appreciative of what you have seen or something that really strikes you. Frequently, as everyone is galloping along over the country-side, the pure beauty of it overwhelms the riders and everyone will speak at once or comment on just how spectacularly lucky they are to be out in such a setting.

## FOXES

Officially, on sighting the fox, one is supposed to say "Tally-ho!" and take one's cap off and point to the fox—if one is a gentleman—or, if a lady, leave the hat on and just point to the fox. However, what usually happens is that the field disintegrates into cheerful babbling: "Oh, look, isn't he cute!" "How adorable!" "Look how pretty those eyes are," and other similar endearments.

On rare occasions, the fox may decide to do something spectacular, such as weaving in and out of the horse's legs of the line of fox hunters or swimming in someone's pool or leading the hounds across an ice-covered lake in hopes that they will drown. He might startle a deer and it will run into the line of riders, jumping the horses and riders as they come through. This can lead to occasional saddles of venison in the most literal form as you end up with a deer straddling your horse in front of you. This sort of maneuvering is more likely done by a gray fox than a red fox. The grays tend to prefer staying in the woods and running in smaller circles, from brier patch to brier patch, à la Brer Rabbit.

The red fox tends to run in straight lines and go for longer distances. In the spring, during their courtship season, red foxes are very likely to take you for hour-and-a-half-long runs.

In the early spring, which for hunting purposes is February and March, the males, or dog, foxes will come great distances to find a vixen to mate. Frequently, there will be three or four dog foxes in contention for one vixen's favor. If the hunt happens upon them as they are establishing who wins the lady's hand, whoever is winning at the moment gets to go to ground with the vixen and whoever did not do too well in the outcome then hoofs it for home. These particular runs will go ten or fifteen miles and at high speeds as the fox is unfamiliar with territory until he gets to his own. These are the fastest hunts of the whole season and require an extremely fit horse to be able to stay up with the hounds. Hunting is probably at its fastest in February and March, and hunting comes to a close the first of April.

# DIVISIONS WITHIN THE FIELD

Because new horses and new riders take awhile to learn the game—usually a season or two, and sometimes three—most hunts are divided in the field by groups based on experience. "First flight" is made up of the very experienced hunters and most seasoned horses that have proven that no matter what comes in front of them, they know what to do with it. Those are the leaders and they follow right behind the master of the field.

The master of foxhounds may work alone in close proximity to the huntsman, though he or she may elect also to be master of the field. The master of the field's responsibility is to make sure that those people who are following the hunt have the opportunity to see what is going on without interfering with the work of the huntsman. So one stays close by, but not so close as to cross the line of the fox or interfere with the hounds.

The mid-group of the body of the field are usually hunt members who enjoy being in the center of things, and either they or their horses do not feel comfortable being farther forward. The horses frequently like to have a steady leader in front of them, so they do not have the responsibility of deciding where is the safest place to go in a field, cross a stream, or take a jump.

In addition, there is a separate section for the new horses and the new riders to learn. The new horses are called "green hunters," as opposed to "seasoned hunters" that have been out for three or four years and know the ropes. The new riders usually go with this group.

The hilltoppers are another group that may or may not merge with the green horse group. They frequently have their own separate appointed master of the field and they tend to move at a much slower pace and stand on the tops of hills to watch the fox and the hounds in the field eddy around them at a greater distance. They usually move at a walk or a trot from point to point, rather than at the faster speeds and gallops.

With the green horse group, or the hilltoppers, considerable support is given to teaching the new people in the field and new horses the etiquette of fox hunting. Historically, the reason for this orientation has derived from safety considerations. While fox hunting etiquette may seem a little archaic, when you start, you will find out there is good reason for perpetuating the forms.

# HUNTING SKILLS AND SAFETY

Make sure that your horse's nose stays in the vertical position that you practiced when you were learning galloping, because once the nose is out of that vertical position and forward, the horse can take off and run away with you. You can use the crest of a hill to help you balance your horse. As you come up the hill, you have got the gravity and the leverage working with you to get your horse's nose in and collect him. As you reach the top of the hill, make sure you have got everything organized.

When you go down the hill, bring your weight back as if you were a skier. You want to keep your body perpendicular to the fall line of the hill. In this way, you can break the horse's descent so that he cannot gain speed and go too fast, like children running down a hill.

Another point to consider, going down most hills with horses, is that if you go straight down the hill, if the horse starts to slip, he can recover quite easily by shifting his hind feet underneath him. If you make the mistake of going sideways down the hill and his feet slip out from under him, he can fall sideways into the hill, catching you underneath him.

In the general area of hunting safety, one rides along the edges of fields that are in cultivation, or recently have been, following the exact path that the master has given you. It is only in fields that have been a long time in grass that the hunting field can spread out. If you decide to spread out, be sure to have an excellent person to follow, as there are lots and lots of holes and hidden bogs that an experienced fox hunter will know about and can warn you of. If you hear the term " 'Ware," followed by, for instance, " 'Ware hole," " 'Ware wire," or " 'Ware tree branch," that means you have a hazard coming up.

Occasionally, when you are queued up for a jump, there will be holes on the other side of the fence and the other fox hunters will tell you about it. It is your responsibility to pass the word down the line to the person behind you. It is not necessary to actually shout—you usually are together with other people—but it is important that they know what is coming up.

On jumps, you need to have enough space before you jump—the horse in front of you should have cleared the fence and galloped on two or three strides. You want to be very sure that there is enough stopping room on the other side of the fence so that if you have to come to a complete halt, you can. It is a very uncomfortable experience to have your horse jump on top of another horse and rider.

On crossing water, follow exactly the path of the person in front of you unless someone else has safely gotten across in a different location. When crossing fields with limestone in them, try not to cross the limestone ridges. If you can, always stay on the grass. The limestone will bend your horse's shoes and rip them off and frequently there are crevasses with a thin layer of sod over the top and your horse can suddenly go in them up to his shoulder if the sod gives way.

On groundhog holes, frequently you will see one hole. You can tell that there is a hole coming up if it is an area that has not been under cultivation because the ground cover changes. It is usually rougher-textured leaves. The ground may look bumpy and churned up a little bit more. There may be briers there. Try to stay at least fifty feet away from the groundhog hole. Every groundhog hole has at least two entrances. Most of them are twenty to thirty feet away, occasionally farther, and groundhogs, being sociable animals, have friends who have moved into the same community.

If you do not see the groundhog hole until you are up on top of it, try to stay very quiet in the saddle and let your horse figure out what to do. Frequently, a made fox hunter will be much more observant of the holes than you are and will do his best not to fall in one. He will adjust his stride to compensate, or he may jump the hole if he thinks it is absolutely necessary.

On hard ground, when the temperature is about freezing, particularly if you have had rain and then a hard freeze on top of it, the actual ground itself will be quite slick. The general precaution is to put borium, which is a very hard metal, on your horse's shoes to give him traction. Frequently, hunters will, in any case, put borium on their horses' shoes as a preventive measure when they start fox hunting so that when they are crossing asphalt, the horses do not slip. It is imperative to have it on your horse's shoes if you are going to be hunting during the winter months so that he does not slip and fall with you.

Another point to remember is that when you have frozen ground, try not to go on the muddy or soil-type paths. If you can go on the grass on the side of the mud or the side of the trail, the footing is much, much safer. This is especially true for areas where the groundwater is on top and the soil itself is slippery as a result.

If you pass someone, you always ask for permission to pass, excuse yourself, and thank them afterward. It gives them a chance to maneuver their horse away from your horse and give you more room to pass.

If you have a horse that particularly enjoys passing other horses, try not to get ahead to the first flight people. Every once in a while, the hounds will overrun the line of the fox and everyone will have to stand around and wait while the hounds find the scent again. This is called a "check." While you are at the check, you can circle your horse at a walk and bring him back to the starting spot that you had decided that you wanted to be in. You can do this very surreptitiously by quietly chatting with people, ostensibly moving from one group of people to the other to talk to them, but actually you are just maneuvering your way back to the line point in which you want to be.

Another subtle thing to do if your horse is being totally obnoxious and requires disciplining: drop to the back of the field with the green horse group. There you can quietly make a circle into some bushes, discipline your horse, and then come out when you think he is organized sufficiently to join the group again. No one will be the wiser or know that your horse has been obnoxious and fractious. Suddenly, he is being very nice. That is one way of dealing with temper tantrums in the field.

You can also use the circling maneuver if your horse has been running for a long time so that when you circle at the check, it gives him a chance to get his breathing back down to normal and lessens the chances of a heart attack.

When fox hunting, you try to keep your voice down to a whisper, if possible, and you do not talk all that much because it is distracting for others following the hounds and also for the huntsman.

# HUNTING RULES AND COURTESY

One is riding at the permission of the landowners in your area and you must constantly remember to be very courteous so one's hunting privileges are not suspended. This includes things like:

- If the gate is open when the hunt comes through, it remains open.
- If the gate is shut, make sure that the gate is shut when the last horse goes through.
- If the fence is broken, make attempts to repair it.
- Ride around the edges of seeded or cropland on the tractor verges that are left for you.
- Do not try to jump unnecessarily. You will get enough jumping just in the course of a hunt without adding extra wear and tear to your horse.

    Here are some other caveats to heed:

- Never, ever jump gates. They swing and they can cause your horse to hook his knees and you can have a very bad accident. In addition, it is much harder on a farmer to make a gate work after it has been broken than it is to repair a section of fence line.
- When there are cattle or sheep in the field, if they start to move off or run, you have to come to a walk. Pounds of beef on the hoof can be run off and the owners of the livestock will never let you back again.
- Never ride over someone's lawn. If you have to go up by a house, follow very carefully behind the horse in front of you, staying on the driveway.
- Most hunts prefer that you do not smoke at all, especially in dry weather. If you think about it, the hunt would be extremely unpopular if it caused a forest fire. If you must smoke, be sure to extinguish your cigarette and retain the butt after it has been put out—stick it back in your pocket. Never leave any refuse behind you, no candy or sandwich wrappers. Ideally, the landowner should not know that you have been through the property.
- In addition, when jumping, never cut off the horse in front of you from a fence. It is extremely dangerous. Also, if your horse refuses a fence, clear the right of way immediately and let everyone else go and then try again. Do not monopolize the fence.
- Frequently, someone else will give you a lead over the fence and will make it easier for you to go. Try not to crowd the horse in front of you. Always give yourself at least three lengths so that the horse in front of you has cleared the fence and is away from it so that you do not crowd him on the other side or jump on top of him.
- Do not try squeezing through narrow spaces because you will lose your knees. It also makes the horse in front of you inclined to kick your leg or your horse. Especially, do not try crowding through gates, as the

The opening meet of the Blue Ridge Hunt: this meet is always a celebration day for hunts. There usually is a stirrup cup send-off with many well-wishers on foot, and many guests from other hunts. Afterward, there is a hunt breakfast. In the foreground is James Fisher on "Beauregard," a half shire—half Thoroughbred heavy hunter, and the author on "Orion," a Thoroughbred-standardbred event horse who also hunts. "Orion" is annoyed that "Beauregard" is starting to close the distance between them.

*Photo by Leslie Howells*

180

gatepost is quite a bit more solid than your knee and you can end up with the rest of the season spent in a cast.
- Never let your horse bite the horse in front of you, as you are likely to get kicked into little pieces, while making yourself most unpopular.

## COURTESY TO THE MASTER

- One of the most important points to remember is that you never pass the master. If your horse is running away with you, turn him in a circle so you do not pass the master. If you make the circle smaller and smaller and smaller, the horse will have to slow down his speed and will come to a halt for you. Also, if you are in that predicament, shortening your reins and crossing your reins over the horse's neck and hanging on to the extra bight of the rein with the other hand in a double bridge will give you some leverage to use against the horse's neck. If you then bring your weight up so your shoulders come up to the vertical position, you will be able to leverage the horse into submission.

    Another trick if you do not have enough space to stop is to aim your horse in a totally different direction. He will not want to leave the pack, so he will come to a halt. Frequently, if you are just starting to have a runaway problem, find some nice convenient bushes that will work as a visual block.
- In addition to not wanting to pass the master, you very much want to teach your horse not to kick the hounds. It is hard to say which *faux pas* is worse in the hunting field. Either one is a matter of major disgrace and you are not very popular afterward. If you have a horse that you think is either new to the field and you do not know whether he kicks, or if you have a horse that you know kicks, you need to tie a red ribbon in the top of his tail as a warning so that everyone will stay away from you. Usually, a horse that kicks will kick other horses as well as people and other animals. They are very, very dangerous. If you can possibly manage it, don't buy a kicker. Many hunts will excuse you from the field and not invite you back if your horse clobbers one of the hounds or one of the other horses.
- Frequently, you will be going through gates. The master will ask for a person to get the gate for them. This is a volunteer job. If you want to make some points and you feel that your horse is quiet enough, getting gates is very much appreciated.

    With the green horse group, the group will stay with the person who is getting the gate so that his horse will not go berserk when he sees everyone else running away in pursuit of the fox and he cannot join them. It is very difficult to get back on a horse that is bouncing because he wants to be somewhere else. Waiting for the gate person is an important courtesy. Never leave a green horse and gate person until the gate person is safely mounted.

## MANNERS FOR THE HORSE

It is very important, when working with a horse that has learned to become a fox hunter, to teach him manners. The horses are very, very close together, like cars that are on a freeway at rush hour. They all may be moving fairly quickly and your horse does not want to get left behind. He will try to put his nose over the rump of the horse in front of him, which is quite dangerous for you in that your horse's legs can get tangled up with the other horse's legs and you can both fall. Or the horse in front of you can get annoyed and kick the devil out of your horse. Try to maintain at least one horse length between you and the mount in front of you.

If you are going down a woods trail or you are in single file, frequently you will have very fast stops and there will be little chance to give the horse the kind of warning he is used to in dressage or out on a normal trail ride. There just is not much time. So you need to develop a stronger set of brakes in the bitting.

As the horse learns what is going on in the fox hunting, he will watch the horses in front of him, and if they start to brake, he will do so as well. But while he is still new to it, he is much more likely to be going as fast as he can, in hopes of being able to be right up on top of the horse in front of him and then override when the other horse stops and he cannot. Often, when you are first starting with a green horse and the horse in front of you stops, you just aim to go alongside, as if you were on a freeway and the car in front of you came to a sudden halt. You would use the verge to go around him until you had time to stop.

Since the horses are so enthusiastic at the prospect of fox hunting, when one is preparing to hunt, one changes the bitting on one's bridle as a way of increasing one's brakes. So, for instance, if your horse has been well trained in dressage and normally goes in a snaffle when he is out for trail rides with other horses, you would probably move him up to a Pelham. You might consider moving him up to a full bridle, which would give you the use of a complete snaffle and only occasionally use the brakes of the curb rein.

Sometimes you will see a very young horse, a four-year-old or a five-year-old, in a full bridle for that reason, because they can mouth the broken bit of the snaffle. It is a little softer than using the straight bar or curved part of a Pelham—which is a more severe bit on the horse.

## WEATHER CONDITIONS

The weather conditions affect the scenting for the hounds. If it's very cool and damp, the scent will lie close to the ground. As it warms up, the scent will rise in the air and you'll see the hounds running with their heads up instead of their noses to the ground. Frequently, if you have a mist or a drizzle or a lower barometric pressure—if, for example a storm is coming in—your hunting will be excellent. The foxes, however, do not like going out in heavy rain and are content to stay in their burrows.

Also, it is not usually terribly worthwhile going out when the ice is quite thick. If you get below about 32°F and the ground freezes hard, it's hard for the horses to keep their traction. If there's a snow cover, the hounds are not allowed to go out because it's considered to be an unfair advantage. Also, if the streams freeze over, the hounds can't go either because it's too dangerous. A hound can go through the ice and be trapped. Occasionally, an entire pack can be lost this way.

## RIDER'S CARE

One of the things a fox hunter has to guard against is hypothermia—be aware of being chilled and come in before exhaustion sets in. There's no rule that says that you have to stay out for the entire five hours. If you feel that you're getting tired, stop before you get really tired because usually you have a several-mile ride home and you'll be using all of your energy to get there, to get your horse put away, and to drive home. It's very important not to push your physical strength too far. Many of the accidents that happen in fox hunting happen on the way home when everyone is tired and stiff and sore and there is no extra bit of energy and agility.

Likewise, if there are winds, especially high winds, the hounds can't carry the scent either and you're more likely to have a blank day in addition to your chances of developing hypothermia.

## DRESSAGE EXERCISES FOR FOX HUNTING

One of the useful exercises to know for fox hunting is lateral work. Being able to push the horse with your leg in a lateral direction, that is to say, move him sideways, comes in very handy for opening gates, pushing a horse away from another horse, and for switching the horse's hindquarters around away from the master and other horses that are reversing. In a reversal, the master and whoever is in front of you and the staff have right of way. You're expected to get off the trail with your horse's hindquarters away from the passing horses. Frequently, the easiest way to do this is to apply your leg and push your horse over.

Likewise, another dressage exercise that comes in handy is lengthening the trot. When you're doing a lot of trotting, it's a little softer on you. You have to remember to shorten the trot before you make any of your turns so that the horse is capable of literally making it around the corner. You can also use your lengthening at the walk to avoid a jogging trot. Frequently, when you're teaching the lengthenings at each stride, it's much easier to have the horse do it naturally, out of his own enthusiasm, in the hunt field. You can work on these when things are quiet and everyone is moving along at a sedate pace.

## END OF THE HUNT

If you have to leave early, make it a point that the master knows that you are leaving because he is responsible for you. If you have been separated from the master, tell one of the members of the field who has his colors and who is planning to stay late to be sure and tell the master. Don't try to leave alone. Make sure that you go with someone else who has his colors and who knows the terrain. That way, you get home safely the fastest possible way, which is frequently by going cross-country. Many hunting countries have areas of ground that look very similar and it's quite easy to get totally lost. Alone, you may not be able to get out of the field because you can't find an exit that is safe for a horse to cross.

When you leave the hunt, you want to plan on walking at least the last mile or two miles home so the horse cools out. If your horse is rambunctious and insists on jigging and generally being upset about leaving the hunt, when you get to your trailer, you may end up having to hand walk him. This will help him to calm down enough so that he can go in the trailer. Again, don't put him in the trailer until his nostrils have closed down to their normal position, there's no pink showing, and he's cooled off between his front legs and his chest.

When you get to your trailer, you can put the cooler or the loose-woven cooling blanket over him, take the bridle off, and put on the halter. Loosen the girth but leave the saddle on at first and then walk the horse for about ten minutes. After the horse cools off, you can then take off his saddle and rub his back and put on a warmer blanket to ship him home, something that will cut the wind if you don't have the top back of the trailer closed. When you put the horse in the trailer, be sure that he is fastened in front and the hindquarters strap is connected before you put the tail gate up. Otherwise, he may back out of the trailer and you may be injured as you try to put the tail gate up.

Your horse will appreciate it if you've got a little hay for him to munch on his way home. He'll frequently settle a lot better. Many horses prefer, if you're going to go to a hunt breakfast after the meet, that you leave their side door open so they can look out and see what's going on. Frequently, they'll be a lot quieter and happier if they've got a room with a view. If you do go to the hunt breakfast, don't stay a long time. Your horse is getting sore, stiff, and annoyed standing out in his trailer. If you wait too long, you may come back and discover that he has rearranged the inside of the trailer for you in a configuration you didn't have in mind. When you open the side doors for the horse to look out of, it's a wise idea to tie the doors open so that if he gets bored and starts pushing on the doors with his nose or foot, he can't break the joint and slam the door shut in his face. Some particularly perverse horses will also figure out how to undo the breast bars given the time and opportunity. If you have a friend who will travel with you, perhaps you can put your friend's horse in the trailer and then your horse will be a lot happier having a little company.

## APRÈS HUNT CARE

When you get home, take off all the horse's tack, if you haven't already, reblanket, and let your horse relax in his stall for an hour or so. He'll want to answer the call of nature and stretch and roll and generally relax. If the weather is nice, you can turn him out in a small paddock and let him do his rolling, romping, and stretching outside. If you decide on the latter, you need to keep an eye on him to make sure he's all right.

After the hour is up, he can have his grain feed or a bran mash. You want to make it a fairly light meal at that point, and give him a heavier meal several hours later. If you have a horse who is very, very fond of his stablemate, it can frequently make him calm down and be quieter if his stablemate can be in the stall next to him when he gets back from hunting. He'll want to tell his stablemate everything that happened.

After the horse is relaxed and has had his roll, you can brush him off and then put his night rug on. Be sure when you're doing this grooming to check his legs to make sure he doesn't have any cuts or other problems that you might have missed along the way and his shoes are okay and his feet are clean. Frequently, if it has been a relatively hard day, you'll want to put his legs up in bandages, which your veterinarian can show you how to do. A little liniment does wonders for keeping his legs tight when it's properly applied with bandages over it. Your horse will appreciate a massage and your grooming him will give him that. If you can arrange it the next day, give him very, very light exercise so that he gets a chance to work the stiffness out of the muscles.

## CARE OF THE HUNTER

To prepare for fox hunting, the basic conditioning, as described earlier, will be enough of a base for you to start cub hunting. The horse will build condition each time he goes out fox hunting and you can use a fox hunting day as a heavy-duty cross-country and endurance day. Usually, if a horse hunts one day, he gets the next day off. Most horses can end up hunting one day a week and being hacked two or three days a week other than that. A few horses who are very fit and are in good shape can hunt two days a week without problems, but it depends on their physiology. If you hunt a horse three times a week and you're resting him in between, you are still burning the candle too heavily and he will become tired and more likely to have injury. Occasionally, you can do it three or four times a week, but then you will pay for it the following week. When you go to three or two times a week, it is important that the horse have sufficient time off to recuperate. If you're hunting him twice a week, you only need to hack him once that week to help him stretch his legs, assuming that he is turned out in a pasture during the days.

Make sure the horse is getting enough grain and hay to maintain proper weight. Your veterinarian will be able to help you adjust to the individual needs of your horse. Frequently, a horse needs a vitamin supplement to furnish energy as the hunting progresses and to keep the bloom in the coat. The coat of a fox hunting horse is frequently clipped quite short to keep the long hair from getting soaked and then taking a long time to dry. If you were to participate in an athletic activity dressed in a heavy winter coat and got wringing wet and then cooled down with the cold, wet coat still on, you are likely to catch pneumonia. It works the same with horses and it is for this reason that hunters are clipped.

Several different clips are used. One is the hunter type; another is the hunter type with saddle pattern. Some people feel that this protects the horse's loins. Other people don't like it because that area stays wet. Usually, another one is the trace clip, which is used for horses that spend more time outside with less stabling and blankets. In all of the hunter clips, the legs are left shaggy to protect the horse's legs from briers and thorns and the inescapable mud of the hunting field, going through the rough ground, and also to keep them warm.

If you decide to clip, it is very important to keep the horses blanketed when they're not in use and to check with your vet and learn how many blankets you need to use for what weather conditions. Frequently, a drafty barn will require that you use an undersheet as well as a blanket, perhaps another blanket on top on cold days. Sometimes, you get into the same kind of layering that you do with skiing. The veterinarian is frequently your best bet in knowing what combination of blankets works for your particular area.

As a general rule of thumb, if your horse looks cold, he is cold. If he is shivering, he is cold. If he has got his head down and he looks pretty miserable around the edges and you slip your hand under the blanket and he is shivery, he is cold. He may have a runny nose. If he is overheated, he'll break out in a sweat.

Frequently, when a horse comes in from fox hunting, he should be covered with a lighter cooler. This specially woven blanket quickly draws the moisture out of his coat, and has properties similar to skiing underwear. About an hour after initial blanketing, the horse may break out in a second sweat, so do a blanket change and check the horse. If he is okay, then you can put his heavy blanket on and give him his regular dinner. Never feed a hot horse anything other than a tiny bit of hay. If you can see pink inside the horse's

Fox hunting is a family sport, too.

nostrils, you need to walk him until the nostril closes back to the normal color. A horse should not be given water until he's cooled down, not blowing. Then he can have a little at a time until he seems totally cooled out. When you put your hand on his chest in between his legs and it's cool, then he can have some water and a little hay. Try not to give a grain feed in the first hour of his coming back to his stall from hunting.

A hunting horse needs to have his legs and shoes carefully checked for cuts and other damage. The shoes often will get bent from going over rocks and with the hard wear on the hard ground. Horses used in fox hunting will go a much shorter time between shoeings—anywhere from four to six weeks. If you are hunting and your horse loses a shoe, you should take him in immediately. Otherwise, his feet will break up, you won't be able to get a shoe back on him, and you'll lose several weeks waiting for the foot to grow back out again. If you can manage to have a trailer brought to you, that saves your horse's hoof even more. At the very least, don't walk on pavement or gravel, stay on the grass as much as possible.

During the week, take the horse out for a gentle bit of exercise, whether it's trotting with interval trots, say three five-minute trots with a three-minute interval between trots, a little bit of light canter, 450 meters per minute for two minutes, or you can just stay at a walk and work up and down hills. Anything that gives the horse a chance to stretch his muscles and stay in a quiet, relaxed frame of mind. Fox hunting is a very invigorating, exciting, high energy, fun thing for a horse to do. The rest of the time you try to keep him cool, calm, and relaxed, or he will be like a firecracker looking for a place to explode.

## GROOMING THE HUNTER

When you're fox hunting, make a point of talking to someone whose horse is well turned out consistently and ask if you can learn from them how they go about their stable work to have the horse look so well groomed. There is an art to feeding a horse well and doing the grooming and having the tack look neat and tidy each time you go out. It doesn't take that much time to do the job well; it takes a lot more time to correct the mistakes if you don't do the job well. Especially make a point of cleaning your tack yourself frequently, even if you are paying someone else to do it for you on a regular basis. This way, you'll know if your tack needs oiling, if it's drying out, if it's getting too much saddle soap, if it's being done in water instead of getting the nurturing it needs, or if it just simply isn't getting done. Most importantly, check all the stress points of your equipment for possible breaking. If equipment is going to break, it will do so at the moment of greatest stress, probably while you're jumping a very large fence somewhere, a long way from the trainer and from home.

# SOCIAL ACTIVITIES

## The Hunt Breakfast

After the hunt meet, occasionally one of the members will invite everyone back to a hunt breakfast. Served buffet style, the meal is really more like
a dinner than anything else because the food tends to be hearty. Great fun to
attend, they give you a chance to visit beautiful houses as an invited guest and
the opportunity to meet some of the people you spent the day with.

## Hunt Balls

Another social aspect of fox hunting is the annual fund-raising hunt ball
staged by many hunts. Gentlemen will usually wear white tie to these affairs.
If they have been awarded their colors, instead of wearing the traditional black
tailcoat or tuxedo, they will wear a scarlet tailcoat with the hunt colors and
the hunt buttons on it. They look very, very dashing. Formal footwear such
as patent leather slippers or velvet evening slippers with an embroidered fox
head on them is also very much in evidence. Occasionally, someone wears a
cummerbund and bow tie specially needlepointed in an appropriate design.

The ladies wear either black or white ball gowns, although this has been
considerably relaxed in recent years. The idea is that the ladies are a foil for
the gentlemen for the evening. Fox hunters tend to be a very lively crowd.
Since they are quite fit from all of that hunting, the dance floor is usually
crowded with happy people dancing until the band finally gives up and goes
home. It is rarely an early evening for anyone.

## Steeplechase

Fox hunters also enjoy steeplechase race days, which are held in the
spring and are called point-to-points. Another set is run by the National
Steeplechase Association in the fall. Fall races tend to be more professional and
the spring races have a more amateur character.

At the spring races, there is frequently a wonderful division for fox
hunters, called "hunter pace." The course covers about four miles over natural
terrain in the hunt's own territory and participants go as pairs or teams of
three. You go for optimum time, that is to say, if hounds were running across
that country, it would be the ideal time that you take following the hounds.
This means that there are some areas in which you might possibly come down
to a walk or a trot. In other areas, by contrast, you might be flying along. No
one knows what the optimum time is in advance. It will usually have been set
the previous week or so by a non-competing member of the officiating hunt
such as its huntsman.

Another section of the hunter pairs or the hunter teams is to go for fastest
time, which tends to be a little on the dangerous side in that you're not on a

groomed course, you're going over natural terrain. After the hunter team races in the morning, there may also be an old-fashioned race, which means that you literally go from point-to-point and you have to know your terrain between the points to be able to make the fastest time.

Frequently, people will bring their entire families and spend the day at the steeplechase races. Bringing picnic lunches along with them, they spread out along the hills beside the course. Occasionally, they'll have carriage parades as well, which add to the festivities. The steeplechase races are big money-makers for the hunt. They give everyone a chance to get together after hunting season is closed down in the spring.

### Visiting Other Hunts

One of the other joys of fox hunting is that it is a bit like yachting. Once you have joined one yacht club, you can visit many others, have permission to use their facilities and get to know their members. One of the great joys of fox hunting is that if one lives in a more northerly climate such as New York, Massachusetts, or Wisconsin, when hunting closes down you can visit the southern hunts. Great pilgrimages are made all during hunting season, especially through November for the Virginia hunts. When the Virginia hunts close down in January because of bad weather, then everyone goes down to Southern Pines, North Carolina, or to Georgia to hunt. These are great fun.

If one becomes very adventuresome, there is also fox hunting in Ireland. One needs to be extremely competent before heading across the Atlantic, though. Irish hunts are much more difficult and demanding than their American counterparts.

# 11

# Dressage Competitions

THE LOCATIONS and dates of dressage competitions are available through the United States Dressage Federation *Bulletin.* The *Bulletin* will also give you information, in an omnibus form, of all the shows in the United States, plus information on where all of the local and regional dressage associations are located.

In addition, you can find information from local saddlery and tack shops. They are also a source for who is riding dressage in the area and who might possibly be an instructor that might be able to help you.

## TYPES OF HORSES

Dressage does not require a specific breed of horse. It only requires a well-trained, obedient, supple horse who moves elastically, showing a floating gait. There are types that are currently preferred, much as styles in dressing. European warm bloods tend to be very large movers and big-striding, so they have a more dramatic look to them. But you do not have to own a European warm blood in order to compete. There are Connemara ponies and Arabians who compete, as well as Lippizaners, Andalusians, and a variety of others. As long as the horse is doing a good test, he will still be acceptable.

## UNMOUNTED OBSERVATION

When you first decide that this is something that you think you would like to do, it is a wise idea to plan on going to a show without your horse and watch. Observe the classes, take the time to go around the barns and the trailers and see how people do things.

In short order, you will be able to tell who is doing well in the placings from the results that are posted. Spend some time watching them prepare for their next ride. Where they are located in the barns and how they organize and polish their appearance. How they warm up their horses, and then observe the ride itself.

Frequently, the exhibitors, as long as they are not pressured, do not mind if you come to watch and learn. If they are not pressured, many are quite sociable.

When you are actually watching the test that is going on, you do not make any sound at all, until the very end and the horse has left the arena—at which point you are allowed to applaud, if you wish. Dressage horses are not used to lots of noise and any at all can disturb their concentration to the point that they will blow a figure.

Another way for you to learn is to watch the judging, particularly in one of the lower-level classes. Then, after that class is over, make a point of going over and talking to the judge. Ask first whether this is an opportune time. Explain that you are interested in the sport, that you are thinking about doing it, and you would appreciate any helpful suggestions.

Usually, a judge at the lower levels will be very encouraging to you and will suggest that you join the local federation. He or she will probably ask if you have an instructor already. If you do not, you may want to work with this person, or she may suggest a local person in the area.

## FINDING A TEACHER

You will need a dressage instructor to help you with the nuances. The basics of staying in the arena you can probably do on your own, but when it gets into the fine points that make the difference between a ride at the bottom of the class and the winning ride, you need a more experienced eye to help you.

By talking with people at the dressage show, you will quickly find out who is considered to be an expert and who is considered to be a good teacher. Frequently, the person who is a very good rider is not necessarily a very good teacher and vice versa. Only on rare occasions will you find both.

Most riders who are going for high level will also take students. A lot of them are professional. Occasionally, the professional ones are contracted into working with one barn only.

What you will find as you talk to people at the show is who is available, how much is the going rate for your area, and who are the visiting professors who come in and give clinics. They are a very good source of outside information.

Eventually, as you get further along in your training, you can work with teachers who have worked with the Olympic riders—and the Olympic riders,

The collected trot: this higher-level movement has elevation instead of the usual amount of forward movement. The rhythm and cadence remain the same for collection, regular working, medium, and extension of the gait.

themselves, are always trying to earn money to be able to afford their habit of going for the very best.

Never be afraid to ask for instruction. If you click with a teacher, you will learn an enormous amount in a very short time. If you do not take with a particular instructor, then simply go and find yourself another one.

## RIDING STYLES

There are several different styles of riding dressage. One is the French style that is used for the American Thoroughbred type and is frequently used for eventing, as well as regular dressage. It is a lighter, more going-forward style. The horse is more lightly in hand and tends not to be pushed into shape. He is encouraged to go into a shape and then he is given some freedom within it.

The other style, which wins very, very frequently and has done extremely well in the international circuit, is the German style that has been used for the Olympic riders. This uses a colder-blooded horse that can handle more aggressive riding. You can push the horse into a frame with your back and seat, and hold him in front with your hand. The horse will put up with a great deal more pressure from all of the aids and will also be more willing to take endless repetition.

The German warm bloods, or the European warm bloods, are bred for doing this particular kind of work. They do not mind making the same geometric maneuver over and over again, whereas an American Thoroughbred or an Arabian or hotter-bred horse gets frustrated and wants to have change. Their minds cannot handle the repetition and they will explode if you don't give them more freedom to go from one maneuver to another and then come back.

A major problem with dressage is that the horses will go sour and feel that they have had enough, needing frequent release from the dressage to go do something else. This can be a trail ride, or getting out in the country, or just doing something that is of a totally different mind-set from the endless repetition.

## THE DRESSAGE ARENA

When you are at the dressage show observing, you will notice that there is a wide area around the actual dressage ring that has been roped off for the horses to do their final warm-up near the arena. When you watch them, they will be doing mostly the exercises that they do extremely well—because they are in the judge's eye, even though they have not yet formally started being judged.

It also encourages the horse to do something he likes. It gives him a positive frame of mind before going into the arena to use that last moment in a positive manner.

Before the horses and riders go into the arena, there is a person who inspects the horses' bits and the riders' spurs as a saddlery check. The *Omnibus Rule Book* will tell you what bits are permissible for each test, and there is a monitor who checks to make sure that these requirements have been met. The general idea is that there is not anything that will hurt the horse. In the warm-up area, the rider is allowed to use a dressage whip but has to drop it when he comes into the dressage arena for the actual performance.

### Reading the Test

A dressage rider is allowed to have a reader for reading the test, which can be a big help to keep you from getting confused as to which test you are supposed to be riding, especially if you are doing several the same day. However, if you have not memorized the test at all before you go in, you can still get hopelessly lost. If you forget the test, you can only lose one point. It is not a major disaster and you can actually forget things two or three times before you are eliminated. So, take a deep breath and do not panic if you forget part of your test, and just pick up where you remember on the next section. If the judge sees that the rider has continued on and totally missed the movement, he will ring a bell and stop him in the test to tell him where he needs to start again so he can continue on from there.

In going around the dressage area, one gives the horse the opportunity to become familiar with the arena—where the letters are and whether there are flowers. Many horses are absolutely terrified of the judge's stand, will shy at it, and generally get very upset. This is particularly true if the judge is seated in an empty horse trailer that has been pulled up to provide shelter. Many horses think that this is highly irregular, because they know the trailer is meant for horses. They are very, very afraid of it and will shy.

### Bells and Entrances

Before the rider goes in, there will be permission granted to come into the warm-up area and then there will be a bell or a whistle sounded for that particular arena. The rider then has approximately thirty seconds to get to the end of the arena, get himself turned around, and make a straight entrance into it.

The amount of time that one is given is enough that if he is at the far end of the arena down by the judges when the whistle is blown, he can comfortably get to the other end of the arena. He can then circle and enter without being over the time allowed, so do not let that panic you.

But if there are several dressage rings next to each other, which there frequently are, sometimes they all use bells and whistles that are quite similar, so it is important to know which is the one for you. Many is the rider who has made his grand entrance only to discover that the bell or whistle was for a different arena, he has entered the ring illegally, and technically should be eliminated.

A way of avoiding this particular problem is to ask the gatekeeper to verify that it was your bell or whistle that just went off before you go tripping on into the arena. Usually, there is a gatekeeper at A who will open the arena for you and then close it behind you. This psychologically gives you a little bit of an edge in that your horse looks for the entry gate but it is not quite available to him.

The dressage arena is just the hint of an enclosure. It is only ten or twelve inches off the ground, so the horse can easily step out of it. It is only the discipline of the rider that keeps him within, so you use your psychological input to keep your horse on the straight and narrow.

### Surface of the Arena

Most dressage riders prefer to work on an absolutely flat surface for their tests. As a result, you will find that most of the rings are on either tanbark or sand, or a combination thereof. At the high-level tests, these will be raked between classes so that the judge can see the actual hoofprints to decide whether or not a figure is actually geometrically correct.

One of the arts of riding is finessing movements on grass with variations in terrain. A horse will rush a bit on a downhill section and slow up on an uphill section and may trip if there is a small depression, so the rider watches other riders go before his ride to know where to urge him forward a little bit more and where to support him on the downhill.

### The Warm-up

When warm-up arenas are located near the actual performance arenas, people will use them to ride the various sections of their tests with which they may have problems. Or they may go all the way through the test to warm up a horse. It is always very interesting to watch how people work with different things to make sure their horse is ready to go.

A horse may only need about fifteen minutes to warm up before going into the arena—loose enough to be in tune with the rider. You have gone over the sections of the test that are particularly difficult for you or that are suppling. Then it is a matter of having enough brilliance left to show some pizzazz when you come into the arena. Since you are capable of riding several tests in one day, the horse can get fairly tired, so you need to conserve some of his energy and sparkle.

## RIDER'S ATTIRE

There are three different basic styles of dress for the rider. One is the very formal top hat and tail coat, known as the shadbelly, that is used by the upper-level riders. Anything from about second level on, they will switch into the very formal habit, and will more than likely use a browband on the horse that carries a tiny decoration—black-and-white check, for instance. Very fine bridles are used, giving the hint that the horse is being held by silken threads, rather than by a more conventional bridle. They are also usually working in a double bridle, and the effect of the lightness of the horse in hand is enhanced by the narrower-gauge tack that is used.

Below second level, you will see the traditional black or navy blue melton coat for fox hunting and eventing. This is the universal coat. The black hunt cap or safety helmet is appropriate with this coat. It is worn with white breeches. One still can wear beige or canary, but dressage people tend to gravitate toward white because it is more dramatic. Then there are black boots and a yellow vest, which may show. If it does not show, you do not need to fret about it, unless you want it for the warmth. Finally, there is a white stock with a fairly severe pin, the traditional oversized safety pin of fox hunting. So you have a little more choice for your showmanship than with fox hunting.

If one's hands are not terribly good, the sins are hidden by black or dark brown leather gloves. They disappear as a continuation of the rider's coat or they match the horse. If one's hands are absolutely superb and you are emphasizing them, which you might do at upper levels, then you can use white kid. But you are really asking for observation, so, unless your seat is close to perfection, you may not want to do that. If it is raining, you still can use white string gloves to maintain traction on your reins.

Another choice of riding habit at the lowest levels of novice is the fox hunting ratcatcher outfit. In this case, the horse is braided hunter style—that is, in thread that matches the horse's mane. His tail can be pulled at the top and banged at the bottom or it can be braided hunter style. The rider would wear the informal tweed hunting coat. A ratcatcher shirt is appropriate with either its matching collar or an informal stock. The stock is used with a bar pin similar to a safety pin. You could wear beige breeches with brown boots or if you are wearing a blue/black tweed jacket, you could wear black boots. A black hunt cap or safety helmet is correct.

It is a more informal look and it says, "Look, you know, we just started in this particular area, but we are neat and tidy and workmanlike," and it is quite correct.


## THE HORSE'S ATTIRE

### Saddle Pads

For the horse's attire, frequently, the saddle pad that follows the basic curves of the saddle is not used. An alternative that you will see is a rectangular saddle pad or a square saddle pad that is more ornamental. It follows its own lines rather than the lines of the saddle, leaving a space behind the saddle for putting in a small bit of ornamentation, such as initials. This can be in the stable colors. As something more subdued, frequently you will find a white pad that is trimmed in navy blue or black. It looks very, very elegant with the dressage saddle.

## Dressage Saddles

You will notice a variety of dressage saddles. They all have a straighter, longer skirt than jumping saddles. They are deeper in the seat and are built up more behind so that the rider stays in an almost perfectly straight, vertical column with a much longer leg, with his heel underneath his hip and shoulder. The spring of the rider has been lengthened and the saddle helps to hold him in that one central position so he stays very quiet in the seat.

You will also notice that the saddles come in different widths, not only to suit the rider but also to suit the horse. Horses' withers can be quite different, from the roundness of a European warm blood or Arabian to the relatively sharp and narrow withers of an American Thoroughbred.

## Grooming Manes

While you are observing the dressage competition, you will probably notice several different styles of grooming for the horses. In some cases, the horses will have checkerboard patterns on their rumps, which is more of a horse show or eventing style, rather than pure dressage. Sometimes the horses have their manes braided into tight braids with a little bit of white plastic, about the size of a Band-Aid, taped around it. This is Mystik Tape, which is to emphasize the curve of the neck when the horse is on the bit. Some horses are very quietly turned out with simple braids that are sewn in. Occasionally, you find rubber bands used for the braiding jobs, but the rider is trying to have a very disciplined look and it is impossible to get that with the rubber band approach.

Someone who has been reading a treatise on dressage that goes back several centuries will ride horses with very, very long manes with latticework so that it looks like a fall of lace down the side of the horse's neck. This style is usually seen on Arabians, Andalusians, or Lippizaners—horses that are traditionally shown with a long, flowing mane.

The latticework is held in place by rubber bands with a bit of tape over it to hold in place. Occasionally, it is done with yarn. This is a variety of showing, which you never see in the upper levels, but it is fun for a change of pace at the lower levels.

## Pulled and Banged Tails

You will also notice, when you are in the barn, a variety of different ways of achieving the pulled and banged tail look. The "bang" refers to blunt-cutting the bottom of the tail as far down as possible while still looking thick, rather similar to what a lady's hairdresser does. The upper part of the tail is trimmed

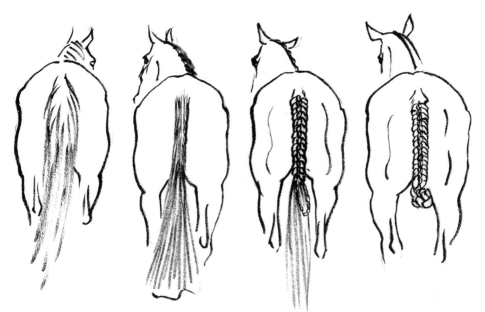

Styles in tail grooming: A) the natural tail; B) the pulled and banged tail for dressage, eventing, and fox hunting; C) the braided tail for show ring hunters; and D) the braided tail with braided mud-knot for show ring hunters.

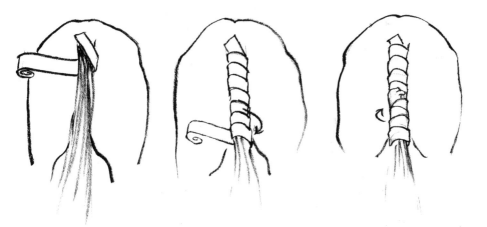

Wrapping a tail: A) start with six inches extra Ace or elastic bandage and wrap around top of tail; B) continue, pulling slightly snug but not tight; overlap the bandage about 50 percent, keeping tension even to end of tailbone; C) continue wrapping, reversing direction and ideally finishing halfway up the tail. Most bandages have Velcro closures. If yours does not, you can use masking tape around the tail to secure.

along the sides and thinned across the top to the point of the hip so that when the horse is engaged, the tail floats behind him, leaving a very clean, open space between it and the horse's hindquarters. This emphasizes the curve and the muscling of the horse's hindquarters and tail.

The traditional way of achieving the pulled part of the tail is to back the horse up to a stall door that is shut. An attendant should hold the front of the horse, drape the tail over the stall door, and then the person who will pull the hairs out one by one at the top of the tail stands outside the door. This way, if the horse kicks because he is uncomfortable, the person doing the pulling is not at risk. Do not attempt to pull the majority of the tail at one session.

Many of the horses that are used for dressage are too high-tempered for you to get away with this maneuver of pulling each hair out, one by one. Frequently, you will find that the riders have resorted to using a terrier stripping knife to, in effect, razor-trim the hair very close to the tailbone. You can buy this device in a pet store, or a similar knife at a tack shop.

After the hair has been pulled or trimmed close to the tailbone at the top, the hair is wetted down until it is soggy and then wrapped with an Ace or a stable bandage and left on long enough for the hair to dry close to the tail. If this is done every time the horse is groomed and left on for fifteen, twenty, or thirty minutes, the hair on the horse's tail will gradually be trained to grow very close to the bone. Be careful not to wrap too snugly or the circulation in the tail will be cut off.

You have to keep a very close eye on the growing out of the tail to make sure that it does not become bushy and ruin the whole effect. If you can pull the tail, it does look much better than if it is just razor-cut because there is no thickness to the covering over the tailbone.

### Care of the Tail

The care of the tail is an art form in its own right. Shampoo the tail occasionally with a dandruff shampoo to remove the dander. Usually, a couple of times a month is adequate unless your horse develops some other problem. The object is to keep it dandruff-free and supple. If you wash it too often, the hair will dry out and break and the horse's skin may become irritated.

Show Sheen is a wonderful silicone product used to keep a horse's tail looking thick and luxurious. It will keep the tail from tangling and will also help to keep manure out of it. One application usually lasts between seven and ten days.

When grooming the tail, ideally you pick each hair knot apart by hand, rather than brushing or, worse yet, currying through it. Show Sheen will help keep the tangles from becoming deeply entrenched and minimize breakage. Never use a currycomb on a tail. It pulls the tail hairs out at the root and breaks off the pieces of those it hasn't pulled out at the root. It gives a horse a very thin, scrawny-looking tail. Many times, fox hunters will do up the horse's tail in a mud knot to keep it from getting caught in briers so that when competition season comes around, he will still have a full tail.

## HEAT EXHAUSTION

Since the dressage show season often tends to be in the summer, it is helpful to notice how the competitors are handling their horses to keep them from having heat exhaustion. Most of the time, the riders have started the horses on electrolytes in their water before they have left home, to get the horses used to drinking the water with that particular taste. When they bring the horses to the competition, they also bring large jugs of water so that the horses do not have a change of taste of water when they are at the competition and they are more likely to drink.

If the horse becomes overheated, he needs to be cooled out as quickly as possible with water. You can check to see how badly dehydrated he is by pinching the skin on his neck. If the skin stays in the shape of the pinch rather than snapping back immediately to his skin, he is dehydrated. If you are having problems, ask the person next to you or near you to help you with your horse. Horses do have heat stroke and they can die from heat exhaustion, so what you are dealing with is a serious problem that should not be considered lightly. You can ice the horse along the veins of his neck and the veins under his tail between his hind legs. Most of what you are doing is splashing lukewarm water all over his body, especially his neck and between his legs and on his forehead, and then scraping it off, to drop his temperature. You can see more about this in the ten-minute break segment of the eventing section.

## WINTER PRECAUTIONS

If you are in a cold situation, use the same common sense of keeping your horse's temperature even. If he needs blanketing in the winter, then put blankets on him as soon as you get done with your test.

Frequently, for winter schooling shows, people will use what is known as a "quarter sheet" that is designed to go under the saddle during their warm-up exercise so the horse's back muscles get a chance to be warmed up before the test. Then, just before the test, the quarter sheet is removed, just as a runner would switch from warm-up sweats to lighter running gear.

## SHIPPING

You will notice also that most of the horses are bandaged for shipping, usually in some form of a standing wrap that goes up to the knees and down over the hooves. They also have their tails wrapped as well. Dressage horses frequently are high-strung and they are not terribly good shippers. They must go very long distances, and the longer the distance, the greater the chance of a trailer injury.

If you have a horse that does not ship well in a single stall, cut out the bottom section of the barrier between the stalls so there is basically just the bar that runs parallel to the horse's body and goes back to the tail chains. The horse will be able to spread his legs out farther and will ship better. Another alternative if you are shipping only one horse is to push the barrier all they way over to the right and give the horse the left-hand stall. That way, he can spread his legs out and balance himself a little better.

## RESTING BETWEEN CLASSES

Frequently, dressage horses will have hay nets to keep them occupied when they are between classes. However, they cannot have great quantities of it at all times since they are going to be competing at various times during the day. You will find that many of the trailers have a sun roof that, when opened, will dissipate the heat within the trailer.

Quite a few dressage horses are more comfortable in the temporary stabling. However, some horses get very insecure in the temporary stabling and will demolish it. So you need to get to know your horse a bit better to decide which way to go with him.

## ENTERING A SHOW

When you enter a dressage competition, start at the lowest level and give yourself an opportunity to become comfortable in a new environment. You will be able to ride three or four tests at the novice level and get a feeling for whether or not you enjoy dressage.

## LEARNING THE TEST

When you are learning the tests, you will find that frequently it will help if you make a spot in which you can walk that is in the same shape as your dressage arena. Imagine, if you will, that you are the horse and rider and then pretend to ride your whole test in this imaginary arena. For instance, you could do this in your living room and put up little cards around where the different letters are on the dressage arena. This way you could trot from A to X, halt and salute, and then work your way through the whole test, section by section, with your test in your hand to make sure that you are memorizing it properly.

Now, the benefit of this particular method of learning the dressage test is that if you memorize it right to begin with, the motion is going to feel correct when you are doing it on horseback. You want the test so clear in your own mind that when the horse does something that is not perfection, your subconscious will still keep directing you on the correct test. By walking the exact steps that you are going to be doing, it will be easier for you to maintain that subconscious flow.

Try to work with one test at a time. Have it memorized and then go ahead and ride the test with your horse after you have got it memorized at home with all of the letters up in a dressage arena. You will find that the things that seemed terribly easy when you were reading them, suddenly become much more difficult when you have to do them on horseback, and require a lot more preparation and timing.

It helps if you keep a copy of your test in your pocket so that you can refer to it as you need to when you get distracted. You will frequently find that when you start working on a test, developing the precision the test calls for will require doing a particular movement many times to get it correct and requires lots of preparation ahead of time to have the exactness that you want.

For example, to make a perfectly straight entrance in at A, you need to read your test to discover whether, at the far end of the arena, you are going to the left or to the right. This is because you want the horse to maintain a bend in that direction, so, for instance, if you are going to the right, you will be making a right-handed circle outside the dressage arena for your entry and that will be on the right side of the arena. As you straighten out, you will be coming down the midline of A but with just a hair more bend to the right. This way, when you do your halt and continue on, you do not have to flex your horse in the opposite direction. This becomes particularly important when you have to enter at a canter and have the lead correct.

When you are schooling the figures that are called for in your test, work on each one for a while rather than just one for a very long time. Your horse will get sour and so will you in that particular movement. He will then remember being miserable when you make it in the actual test.

If you can, try not to ride the test in the exact sequence the test is to be ridden in during the competition. Your horse will memorize your test very quickly. When you get to the actual test in the dressage show, he is likely to anticipate and rush his movements, occasionally leaving out sections to get to the next one.

When you are first learning and you are riding a horse that may not be the most wonderful mover in the world, an important part of your score is going to be on suppleness and obedience as well as going forward. To get the obedience and to raise your score, go for the accuracy in the movement. With a lot of work, you can pick up a 9, 10 being the ultimate in praise, for a halt, and that will compensate for a less than wonderful passage later on where a showier mover might be able to be more dramatic than your horse.

When you are doing your halt, it has to be perfectly square with your body exactly in the cross hairs of that point. A lot of work goes into having that kind of precision. When you are doing your trotting across the diagonal, use your corner before and your corner after to get the horse lined up and straight before going across the diagonal so he has the maximum opportunity of showing his movement.

If you have a trot across the diagonal, make your change at the end of the diagonal unless your test calls for it in the middle. This way, the horse will be undisturbed during his long movement.

Practice your transitions up and down from gait to gait while you walk, trot, canter, to develop the precision that you are going to need. You can expect that you are going to need at least three half halts to be able to have a down transition, and at least two to be able to cue for an up transition.

The more information you give your horse ahead of time to anticipate that something new is coming up, the more time he has to get prepared. Always remember that your horse is a lot bigger than you are and it is going to take him time, like a large boat, to make his turns and to make the movements that you want. He cannot just whip around a corner like a bicycle and expect to do well on a test.

Your dressage instructor will help you with developing the balance and the forwardness within each gait. As your horse's balance improves and he carries himself better, you will find it easier for you to be able to sit his trot and to maintain your own quietness in your seat and in your hands.

## THE TEST

While performing the test, remember to breathe. Try to breathe in rhythm to the horse's movement. This will help you stay relaxed. If you can muster it, a smile does wonders. You might start enjoying what you are doing, relaxing your muscles further.

When doing your entering and finishing halts, make steady eye contact with the judge. Once you are organized at the halt, make a grand moment of the salute. Smile and you will look more in control. This is a moment of showmanship.

After finishing the final halt, you are still being judged until you leave the arena. Walk the horse forward straight to C and then be precise about turning and following the side of the arena to the exit. Do not rush to the exit. The walk counts as a movement.

Frequently, the judge will stop you at C and chat a moment. This gives you an offer of further discussion after the class. Remember after the chat to still have a proper exit.

Once you have cleared the arena, give your horse a big pat on the neck and tell him how marvelous he is. Even if you weren't pleased with the test, your big friend deserves some encouragement. Like a boy at ballroom dancing class, your horse needs all the praise he can get.

Extended trot: Olympic combination Hilda Gurney and "Keen" at the moment of suspension.

Collected canter.

# THE JUDGE

The dressage judge will score each movement on a scale from 0 to 10. The free walk counts double, as do the general overall impressions. The judge will comment on each movement. At the end of the test, usually the judge will make suggestions for improvement or comment on things done well. It is acceptable and appropriate to speak with the judge after the class about your test. You can ask questions and learn more. Try to be positive when you speak to the judge and you should get a positive response.

If you are judged by the same judge over the years, frequently the judge will remember you. Then she might especially comment on the areas you have improved.

If the show offers video cassettes of your rides, by all means order them. Your instructor can use them to help you understand any problem areas. They will help suggest new methods of tackling trouble spots.

Since dressage is the first test of eventing, in addition to being an Olympic sport in its own right, there is more information in the eventing section.

# 12

# Showing Hunters and Jumpers

---

MANY RIDERS enjoy taking their horses to horse shows, to compete in hunter or jumping classes. The American Horse Shows Association is the overseeing body for recognized showing in the United States. Showing hunters has evolved from having a nice field hunter that one wants to show in competition into a totally separate endeavor. The kind of horse most often used is a full Thoroughbred. Occasionally, a near-Thoroughbred will also do as well.

In cross-country riding, fox hunting, steeplechasing, and other sports out in the open, the rider must instinctively make the correct moves at the right time. He needs to develop enough skill to operate automatically as the element of surprise comes up.

For showing a hunter, the rider has a different set of problems. In the show ring, what the successful hunter rider is looking for is a consistently precise, elegant ride that gives the impression of smoothness, control, and grace, with a strong emphasis on consistency.

Everything in the ride should remain exactly the same in the onlooker's overall view. The jumping movements should all appear to be exactly the same over the fence. The horse should never appear to be the least bit ruffled or worried about a fence. All the strides between the fences should look identical. The moves of the rider are so subtle that it looks as if the horse is doing all of the movements on his own and the rider is just serenely going along to enjoy the ride. It is akin to watching a ballet dancer move with grace across the stage.

The viewer feels that the dancer just floats along. In a hunter round, that floating feeling is the achievement.

The hunter round is also different from dressage in that the horse is not going in the same frame. As you recall, in the dressage, the horse has a vertical face and much more of a compression and extension to his body. The changes of the movements are much more exaggerated than in the show hunter.

The show hunter moves long and low with his nose and neck slightly outstretched. There is light contact between the rider and the horse's mouth through the rein. The rein is not loose and floppy. But there isn't the tightness of control that one sees in the dressage.

Show hunters as a result do not develop their neck muscles in the same way that a dressage horse will. They are expected to balance themselves, but they do not need to cant their weight as much to their hindquarters as dressage horses will. The show hunter is usually shown with a standing martingale, which helps to stabilize it with its nose out.

To achieve the perfect hunter round, the rider has to be able to exactly analyze, similar to a computer program, his ride for the number of strides needed to have the ride appear to be the same all the way around. The size of the fences will change the bascule of the horse and how much ground he will cover from the time he leaves the fence to the time he lands.

In addition to the basic training and flat work that was mentioned in the dressage chapter, the showing hunter has to have flying changes and counter-canter in order to be able to complete a course in a recognized show division. The horse's form over fences is also judged and the show hunter is expected to keep both of his knees up, preferably tucked up high under his chin.

The reasoning for the flying changes is that the rider cannot cue his horse to change leads in the air over the fence as the subtle weight shift is sufficient to change the horse's form in the air. He is more likely to tip or drop one foot and not keep his knees up quite as tightly.

You want the bascule over the fence to be perfectly placed, so the center of the arc is directly over the center of the fence. Whether the fence will be a wall, which rides like a vertical or a gate, or a rolltop, which rides like a spread fence, will influence the shape of the bascule and where the horse will land. Then he will have a shorter or longer distance from the takeoff point to the next fence. This is where the rider's precise control comes in, influencing the size of the jump as well as the strides in between the fences. So while a line on a fence may be three strides, it may be ridden, depending on where the horse landed from the first fence, as a steady three strides, a holding three strides if the horse landed too far in the line, or a forward three strides if he landed close to the first fence and needs to cover a bit more ground to be at the correct spot to take off for the next fence. All of these rider cues are very subtle and should not be readily apparent to the eye unless the observer is a keen one.

The hack class in the hunter division requires three eyes, one on the judge, one on the horses around you, and one on your mount.

Schooling classes give the horse and rider a chance to practice before hitting the big time of the "A" circuit.

# SCHOOLING SHOWS

There are many different divisions for hunters depending on the skill level of the horse and rider and how many years they have been competing. At the bottom rung are the nonrecognized schooling shows that have classes such as "schooling hunter," "schooling jumper," "baby green hunter," or "chicken little hunter." These are designed as the lowest of the classes. The fences are quite small, starting as small as two feet to sometimes three feet. Generically, they are known as the three feet or less divisions.

There is a quantum leap from unrecognized showing to the recognized AHSA classes. Much of your ground work is done at the schooling shows where things are considerably more relaxed and you have more of an opportunity to get suggestions and help from other people.

# TYPE OF HORSE

Most of the horses that you see will be full Thoroughbreds, as these are the preferred style for show hunters. Occasionally, you will find near-Thoroughbred, around three-quarters or fifteen-sixteenths Thoroughbred. One does not find the quarter horse, field hunter type, or the Appaloosa type being shown in the hunter division. The horses that are selected to be show hunters look elegant and refined and carry with them a sense of quality. They are graceful to the eye but not particularly powerful. They may be more fine-boned than what you will find in the hunt field or as an event horse. Their conformation is more of the classic racing Thoroughbred than it is of the powerful field hunter or jumper.

They also tend to be fatter and less well muscled than the jumpers or other varieties of competitive horses. This layer of fat they carry hides structural imperfections and gives them a round shape. They also will normally have a very glossy coat with lots of highlights.

They are expected to be extremely quiet when they are showing and give the impression of being so cool, calm, and confident that they are a little bored by the whole proceeding. Since Thoroughbreds have a more enthusiastic attitude than that, it requires a lot of the rider's time to ride the horse to the point of being quiet, yet not allowing the horse to get too fit. Most show hunters will only be ridden for thirty to forty-five minutes a day. That can vary from two to three days a week for a made horse to four or five days a week for a green horse. Since the horses are shipped a great deal and spend a lot of time in stalls, it is important that they not get sufficiently fit to go stir crazy.

Ideally, the show hunter that you would prefer to have will be very kind, trusting, and willing to help you with the program. A well-made show hunter can watch other horses take the course before he has to go and analyze the course almost as well as you can.

# BUYING A SHOW HUNTER

Show horse prices tend to be much higher than those for the dressage or eventing or fox hunting animals.

The most expensive of the hunter division horses are the model conformation horses because they have to be physically perfect. This state of perfection requires tremendous amounts of careful nurturing to bring a show hunter to competition readiness. Horses that have successfully shown in recognized shows are more expensive than the horses that have just gone to schooling shows. If the horse has shown at a recognized show, the lowest level that he will have been in will be first-year green hunter. There is second-year green hunter, then the horse moves out of that division and the rider chooses another division to go into. The horses that go to the schooling shows with no prospect of going on to the recognized shows are not as tidy with their knees or may not have had their training sufficiently confirmed to be able to handle the recognized shows, or their rider is just learning the ropes.

You will need the services of a professional to help you locate the best horse for you within your budget constraints. The professional will usually charge a 10 percent commission as his finder's fee. He will also know which horses have a good track record for your style of riding and which horses are more sound than others, therefore his advice is usually worth the price. If you find a horse you like, have the professional try the horse before you to prescreen him. Frequently, the professional will decide that a particular horse won't be appropriate for you because the horse's style and yours are not complementary to each other; or your learning curve doesn't match that particular horse's ease of handling. Ideally, you want the most made horse you can get your hands on. So if the horse is older—ten to twelve years— and is still sound, he will be a better investment for your dollar than an exquisite four-year-old or five-year-old, who really needs the help of an extremely experienced rider, perhaps to realize the potential that your twelve-year-old has. An older horse can compensate for your mistakes and frequently will make the ride infinitely easier for you. These older horses often can be leased for the competitive season as well and your professional will know where to look to find one that is still sound enough to do what you require of him.

If you go to enough horse shows before you buy a horse and check who the trainers are of the horses that do well, you will find that you'll be able to discern who does the best job with his horses and then ask that particular professional for help. If he is too busy to help you, he still may have a suggestion as to who would be competent to act as your agent.

You will still need to have a very thorough vetting of the horse to make sure he is sufficiently sound. Also, with a show horse, it is a wise idea to pay the extra money to have drug tests run on him as well. Since the horse is such a major investment, later on, when you decide to sell, it will make it easier for you since the horse doesn't need to go on drugs to be able to perform. The drugging of horses is prohibited by the AHSA, but since you are in a noncompetitive situation when you're buying, you need to keep your guard up.

Ideally, you want to ride the horse as many times as possible before purchasing. Occasionally, you will find a seller willing to let you ride the horse for up to a week. If it is at all possible to have a trial period with the horse, by all means ask. Very few sellers will allow their horses to go on trial to someone whom they don't know because of the danger of the horse being injured. The seller has no way of knowing whether or not you are a competent horse person or not. The horse will be going as well as possible when you try him, so if you have any problems at all at this stage of the game, you can be sure that it isn't going to get any better. For example, if a horse refuses a fence for you in the trial period, you can bet he will be refusing fences for you after the trial period.

## HUNTER DIVISIONS

Since showing hunters is not an Olympic sport, nor a world championship sport, there are many professional riders. There is no requirement to stay an amateur. As a result, many of the classes have large stakes, such as $100, $300, $1,000, stakes class, so the professional rider has a chance to earn some money for the owners of the horse. As a result, the riding is much more competitive. Also, the horses are judged rather than scored, and it is totally at the discretion of the judge what he likes about a horse. He doesn't have to produce a scorecard for the riders to look at, similar to either the show jumper or any of the Olympic sports.

The hunter courses are very quiet, very conservative and have no color. Instead, there are many flowerboxes that add the color to the fences. Hunter division jumps are frequently gates, walls, and rolltops, which are designed to be either a natural or white color.

### Novice Division

Some of the hunter classes that are available to adults are the novice and the green hunter divisions for riders and horses that are just starting out. The novice divisions exist mostly in unrecognized schooling shows. Normally, riders do not want to take their horses to the recognized shows until they are fairly certain that their training is sufficient for their horse to win a ribbon. Therefore, a lot of thought goes into the transition point of horse and rider from schooling to recognized shows. The novice classes frequently are two-foot divisions as far as the heights of jumps; they will not have in and outs. The lines from the fences will be fairly easy and the distances will ride true.

### Green Hunter Division

In the green hunter division, three-foot-high fences are the norm. The lines will still be easy lines, but in the recognized shows, in order to place, one will have to have one's flying changes, countercanters, and some lateral work in order to make the distances between the fences ride evenly and smoothly. At this level, the riders start do their influencing of the horse's stride when the horse is on the ground rather than in the air so that his position over the fence doesn't change.

## Amateur Owner and Working Division

In the recognized shows, the next divisions up feature four-foot fences; some of them are three feet, nine inches. These include amateur owner, for the amateur rider who wants to compete with other amateur riders instead of against the professionals, and the working hunter division. The amateur owner division is still very competitive and has many good horses in it. The horses are not conformation horses. They must be sound enough in the judges' opinions to be able to handle a day of fox hunting, but they are not judged on their beauty the way a conformation horse is judged. They can have blemishes, scratches, or scars, as long as it doesn't affect working soundness.

What does matter is performance. Horses are judged on how well they move and how well they jump the fence. They are expected to be well broke and mannerly so that if the judge were thinking of riding them for a day of hunting, he would think that that horse would be comfortable for the entire day. Therefore, the horse must not look as if he's pulling or executing any jerky movements. If a horse has high knee action and climbs the air, he will be less comfortable to ride for extended periods. Therefore, the judges would mark him down over a horse that moves long and low.

The working hunter division is highly competitive and is open to professionals. The distances are frequently somewhat difficult to make and may require greater finesse of horse and rider to give the appearance of smoothness and elegance. Since this is a performance class, the conformation of the horse does not count other than suitability to be a hunter.

## The Handy Hunter Division

The handy hunter classes are designed to show the handiness and tractability of the hunter. Frequently, tests in this particular class include opening and closing gates without getting off the horse, having to take a very wide jump, and having to come to a halt afterward or taking two fences that require sharp angles or jumping the fence at an angle. The courses are usually very tight and very cluttered. The horse needs to be especially well trained on the flat.

## Model Conformation Division

Conformation horses compete in two separate divisions. One is judged in hand, which are called the model classes and are really breeding classes. They show stallions with their offspring or mares and young horses that are

Sometimes the hunter divisions serve also as practice before moving up to show jumper divisions or across to stadium jumping. This hunt team rider shows elements of all the different specialties.

Watching Grand Prix show jumping can be breathtaking. This USET team rider is not interfering and has to keep soft contact with the mouth even though his form is unorthodox.

suitable to become hunters. They are the beauty pageant of the horse world. These classes are usually judged by professionals with many years of experience in showing the horses in hand, because it is so difficult to do it well.

After the horses have graduated from the in-hand breeding classes, they move to the division known as conformation hunter. At this point in their training, they have learned to be ridden on the flat and to jump. They are judged 60 percent on their conformation, and any flaw is marked down, so the horses are kept very carefully from getting abrasions on their bodies. These horses are also kept much fatter than horses competing in any other working division because the fat will hide minor imperfections of structure.

### Hunt Teams Division

Large shows frequently offer special classes that do not count toward a championship, but are fun to enter. These include hunt teams, comprising three or four horses from the same hunt, family classes in which the entire family from smallest child up to grandparent may enter as a group, or hunter pairs, which is two riders over a course. Most of these classes require that all the riders in a numerical group, such as all the members of a family who are riding together, jump a fence together. This leads to some very interesting moments as contestants try to line up three or four horses to jump one fence at the same time. These horses are jumping abreast and they are judged on whether the riders are able to have the horses jump exactly at the same time so all the horses' knees are lined up over the fence.

In addition to these classes, there are a large number of junior divisions for riders who have not yet reached their twenty-first birthday, and pony divisions for riders who are still small enough to ride ponies and have not reached their twenty-first birthday.

## SHOW JUMPERS DIVISION

The other major division in horse shows is the jumper classes. Show jumping is an Olympic sport, and as a result does involve a large number of amateurs. The distinctions between amateur and professional are much more blurred in show ring than they are in dressage or eventing.

A jumper can be any horse that can comfortably jump a five-foot fence or larger course within the time constraints allowed. Very tall or very powerful horses, brave enough to face a seven-foot-high wall, but careful enough to keep their feet up so not to rub fences, make successful show jumpers.

These horses are quite rare and therefore they are also extremely valuable. The Natural, a horse that has done extremely well at the Grand Prix, the highest level of show jumping, was sold several years ago for a million dollars. When horses become this expensive, very few people can buy them individually. As a result, syndications are much more common for show jumpers than they are in other areas.

A syndicate will offer shares. At the end of the competitive time period, which will have been stipulated by contract, the horse is sold unless he has earned sufficient income and the syndicate decides to keep him. The jumper classes have very large cash awards, which makes it possible for the professional rider to make quite a bit of money for the owners of the horses he rides. There is a lot of excitement and prestige in the jumper division because of the grace under pressure shown despite the height of the fences and the time constraints.

Most of the horses of this division are Hanoverians, Selle Français, Trakehner, and warm blood crosses. There are a few Thoroughbreds, but, generally speaking, the horses are crossed with something heavier and more powerful than the typical American Thoroughbred. These horses are specialists.

Show jumping courses tend to have very tight distances between fences—fences that have odd distances to each other or require pirouettes or half pirouettes to be able to make the distances. The fences are very fanciful, brightly colored, and tend to appear somewhat spooky to the horses. Once one reaches Grand Prix, there will frequently be some changes in terrain, such as bank fences with a fence on top or a water fence. These, however, are the exceptions rather than the rule.

## Speed Classes

There are two basic types of jumper classes. In the speed classes, time is the most important element. The fences are around five feet tall, and they are placed in odd spots. The horses have to have a very high level of dressage training to be able to rock back on their hocks, turn 180 degrees, and jump another large fence.

The riding style changes somewhat. The rider has to decide on the smoothest possible way of getting from fence to fence so the momentum of the horse isn't totally broken and the horse still has enough propulsion to lift off. Starting and stopping take valuable time, so the art of the horsemanship is to do as much as possible without it and without unbalancing the horse. Since jumpers are scored rather than judged, the results of the round are available from the time monitors immediately during the round as well as after the round.

## Puissance Classes

Another type of jumper is the puissance expert. "Puissance" means "strength," and these horses can jump very high vertical fences. Occasionally, they can also jump high and wide oxers as well. Usually, there is a complete course and a jump-off of the top horses that successfully complete the course and then the last run-off will be over a large oxer and a large wall. If more testing is needed, only the large wall will be used. These walls are made from

Speed classes require the rider make use of time in the air. Here the rider is asking for a turn in the air and a lead change to the right. The horse has responded to the weight change by unfolding the right leg sooner in preparation for landing. The risky part of asking in the air for a lead change is that the horse may drop his hind legs too soon and drop rails.

large hollow blocks, so they fall down quite easily. It takes tremendous courage of both horse and rider to be willing to try to jump something that neither horse nor rider can see over. A puissance wall can be over seven feet high and some have measured as high as seven feet, six inches.

The riding style of the jumper rider is closely aligned to that of the balance-seat rider. The jumper rider needs to use a strong driving seat and greater collection of his horse. The precision and technical expertise needed to develop the impulsion and then handle the thrust of takeoff require that the rider be able to maintain his balance as the horse rockets out from under him. As a result, jumper riders frequently have their form drastically changed throughout the arc of the jump and, in their particular case, the changes usually pivot around their knees, even though their weight is in the stirrup. Because of the technical expertise that is needed and developed by the time the rider reaches the Grand Prix level, his control is superb. As a result, for an observer, it is much less nerve-racking to watch a Grand Prix course being ridden than it is to watch a preliminary jumper course. However, the rider will learn as much from the mistakes of the preliminary jumper class as he will from the observation of doing it well in the Grand Prix.

Occasionally, one will find superb riders who are able to maintain the position all the way through a course of fences. Riding show jumpers is extremely difficult and should not be attempted until the other levels of riding have been assimilated and confirmed.

Jumper classes are stair-stepped so that the horse and rider do not get overfaced. Some of the divisions are the junior jumpers for juniors under the age of twenty-one, amateur owner division, the preliminary division, the intermediate, and the Grand Prix. The Grand Prix is the same level that is used for the World Cup and for Olympic competition. Each of the levels is stair-stepped to make the course a little more difficult, the turns and pirouettes more frequent or harder. The distance between the fences becomes more and more off-stride, so the riders have to decide how much compression they need from their horses in order to make distances. They spend a lot of time watching the riders before them to decide whether the distance will ride best as the tight three-stride, for instance, or a longer three-stride. The training that one gets as a hunter division rider holds one in good stead for continuing on to the jumper division. The smoothness and precision of this division also give the basics for the higher levels of the jumper division.

## GOING TO A HORSE SHOW

Once the rider has made the decision that he is interested in participating in a horse show, he should take some time and go to a show without his horse. There he can see how the riders organize themselves in their preparation for the class as well as what they do in the class. Ideally, one would pick an A-rated show for this observation so one can watch the best of the riders. Most

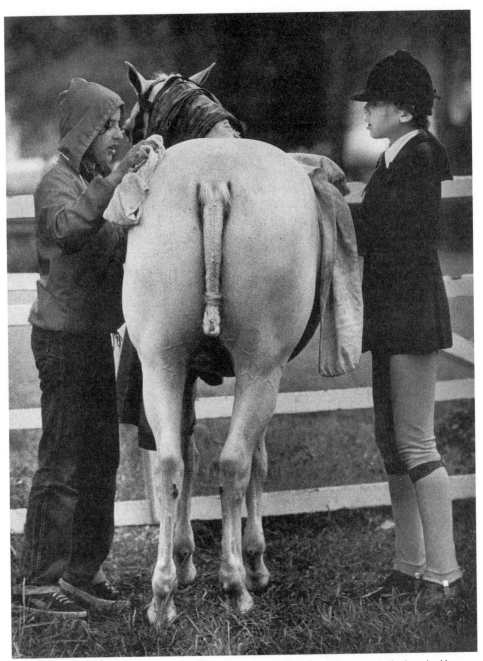

Participating in a horse show means staying perfectly groomed at all times—even in the rain. Here a young rider and her groom pull off the rain covers and dry the tack and horse. Note the meticulous mud-knot, practical when showing on a muddy day.

of the time, coaches are interested in new riders as students. Unless a coach is actively working with someone at the moment, he or she may be very approachable, especially if you are interested in having a longer-term relationship as a student. Be careful not to monopolize their time, however, since coaches are responsible for a large number of people.

## Riding Attire for Hunter Classes

Riding attire for hunter classes tends to be extremely conservative. It is form-fitting, and ideally it is custom-tailored to the rider, although a ready-made coat can be adjusted by a good tailor.

Custom boots look like custom boots and are much more comfortable than stock boots. They are worth the investment as your first specially made item. Properly cared for, they will last years. Ideally, they should be made from fine french calf, cuff-lined so they are very soft and flexible and easy to break in. The boots are plain black. They do not have a patent leather top for the ladies or a tan top for the gentlemen. Usually, they are the dress boot style, although some men will use a black field boot style instead.

One's hunt colors are not worn for horse showing except in formal attire classes, which are quite rare. Instead, the rider will wear a pinstripe or solid navy blue or gray coat with a plain collar. For men, a button-down shirt and a conservative tie are appropriate.

The ladies will wear the choker instead of the stock tie. The choker may be ornamented with their initials or a very conservative pin, such as a plain gold safety pin.

Breeches are usually buff, or light gray-beige—never white. Most breeches these days are of the stretch sort, although if one locates well-fitting breeches of the old school that are made out of natural fabrics such as wool or cotton, they are appropriate.

A safety helmet is preferred because of the possibility of head injury. Most of the riders wear a hunt cap type with a chin harness rather than a cross-country helmet with jockey cover. The hunt cap has its velvet cover permanently attached and has a smoother shape to it.

Riders may use dark leather gloves. The gloves can hide a multitude of sins with one's hands. Some riders prefer to ride without gloves, but their hands are much more visible. If your hands become sweaty, it is considerably more difficult to pull the reins.

Since a tidy, workmanlike appearance is what is strived for, ladies need to wear hairnets unless their hair is extremely short. Men also need to have their hair cut short enough to look tidy under a hunt cap.

For the ladies, there are English-style hairnets, which are a little more obvious than American hairnets. The good point of these English nets is that they can take tremendous abuse without tearing. They are also stronger, so if you have a lot of hair, they will hold it better. Even if a lady puts her hair up in some sort of braid or knot or bun, she will still need a hairnet to keep the little ends from popping out. If the lady decides to use an American hairnet instead, she needs to plan on one for each class because they literally self-destruct!

One of the dilemmas for riders who need help with their eyesight is whether to wear contact lenses or glasses. Many riders prefer contact lenses, although if the dirt gets in your eyes, you may have serious problems and not be able to continue your round. As a result, many other riders prefer to wear glasses instead. Although one may not be marked down specifically for wearing sunglasses in the show ring, it does not give as good a first impression as either plain glasses or contact lenses.

Many riders will carry a stick with them. It is usually one of the shorter jumping bats—about eighteen inches in length. It is usually a dark-colored leather so that it will blend into the horse's color and not be obvious. Most of these bats are clean-shafted, with just the leather tip at the end. The feathered bats that are required for racing are not as preferred, even though the theory behind them is that the feathers create more noise at the same time they slow the whip down in the air and cause less pain.

## Attire for the Horse

The horse's attire is very simple and conservative. Usually, the rider is using a close-contact saddle, although if he has only a cross-country saddle available to him, he'll be using that. The saddle should be a leather saddle of conservative style. The synthetic saddles are not appropriate.

The saddle will be resting on a white saddle-shaped pad. Ideally, this will be of sheepskin, although almost any plain pad is permissible. There should be no colors or trim on it. If one needs a foam pad to balance the saddle, that is placed on top of the sheepskin and should be covered in white so it is neutral to the eye. Many saddle pads have pockets designed already in them for this purpose.

The bridle that the horse wears is a quiet, conservative leather-only bridle. It will have only a regular cavesson, not a drop cavesson, not a flash, not a figure eight. The regular cavesson can be adjusted quite snugly and be almost as effective as any of the other nosebands.

The reins on the bridle can be any sort of leather—braided, laced, or smooth—depending on the rider's preference. However, reins that are webbed with leather are inappropriate. Rubber reins are inappropriate even if they are in brown or black.

The rider can use either a snaffle or a Pelham, although preference is given to the snaffle. If the snaffle is used, it should be adjusted properly in the horse's mouth so that there are two or three wrinkles at the edge of his mouth where the bit comes up to join the cheekpiece. If a Pelham is used or other straight bar bit, there will be only one wrinkle at the corner of the mouth.

A standing martingale or no martingale at all is correct. No other form of martingale is appropriate, including running martingale, Irish martingale, bib martingale, or German martingale. The standing martingale is normally adjusted so that when the horse's head is relaxed as he is standing still, the martingale can be lifted up to two inches away from the horse's throat latch. The standing martingale is attached to the girth, run through the breastplate, and attached to the noseband of the bridle. Some standing martingales attach directly to a hunting breastplate on a ring attachment.

A hunting-type breastplate is allowed, without brass fittings. Again, the fittings on it should be quiet, small, and conservative as possible with little flash. Like every other part of the horse accoutrements, it needs to be well fitted to the shape of the horse's body without excess.

Any sort of leather girth is appropriate, although most riders prefer to use an elastic-end girth because it holds its position better when the horse jumps. Ideally, the girth is a dark leather and will blend into the color of the horse.

### Grooming the Horse

The turn-out for the horse actually starts many months before in a good feeding, vetting, and grooming program. Ideally, the horse has developed muscling and topline through his exercise program as he has been trained. He also will have been fed well to put enough fat on him to give him a roundish appearance and hide some of his smaller blemishes. With proper nutrition, his coat will have a natural gleam all of its own. The rubbing and grooming will bring the glow up. Ideally, the horse will even be dappled. So the final grooming is just the final touches as opposed to the making of a horse from scratch.

Most horses are shown in the spring through the fall, when their coats are short. If the rider elects to ride in the winter, frequently the horse is given a total body clip. However, if the rider does clip his horse, he needs to be extremely careful to keep him well covered with blankets through the winter. The clipping job should be done by a professional or experienced groom. Never attempt to clip your own horse the first time before a horse show. The results are mortifying if you do it yourself and an insult to the judge.

Show horses have their manes braided for recognized shows. For unrecognized schooling shows, especially those held middle-of-the-week, as long as the horse's mane lies over, it is unnecessary to braid. Many riders will keep their horse's mane in rubber band braids to train it to lie flat on the correct side of the horse's neck. In order to braid a horse's mane, the mane has to be correctly pulled from underneath so that the top hairs all look even, but the mane itself is much thinner. Either the *Event Groom's Handbook* or the *Grooming to Win* book or video has excellent instructions on how to braid and pull a mane.

The braiding style for the Thoroughbred in a show ring uses more and smaller braids than event style. If a horse has a long swan neck, you can use fewer braids to emphasize the neck. If a horse has a short, fat neck, then you use many braids. An average Thoroughbred mane will normally take about thirty braids.

The mane will be four to six inches in length. If you pull it too short, there is nothing to hold on to, and if it is too long, you may have to put in too many braids.

For showing, the mane is braided in yarn, although old-school riders will occasionally sew with thread, which is much more difficult to take out later. The yarn matches the horse's mane or the rider's coat if the rider's coat is sufficiently dark. Never use rubber bands for braiding manes in horse show competition.

The horse's tail is only braided for important classes, because every time you braid the tail, the hairs tend to break off. If you do the tail too often, you will end up with a fuzzy mess at the top of the horse's tail instead of something you can work with. As a guideline, four times in one week is too much. The pulled tail that's banged at the bottom, which is a style that is used for event horses, dressage horses and show jumpers, is not often used for hunters in the United States, although it is appropriate in England. Occasionally, riders will have their horses' tails put up in a mud knot, which emphasizes hindquarters.

The horse's ears, mouth, fetlocks, and spare facial whiskers are trimmed as often as needed to give a smooth appearance. In conformation classes, one will occasionally see horses that have had a thin coat of petroleum jelly, which has been rubbed on a towel, used for highlights on their heads. Petroleum jelly is also used in the ears to keep gnats from biting. With petroleum jelly, use a very thin coat, as it will melt, run, and attract dust.

Ideally, the horse has had a bath—usually a day or so prior to the show. If the rider uses some Show Sheen, then all the rider needs to do is be up early the morning of the show to get out the extra manure spots and have the mane and tail braided. The Show Sheen will prevent most stains, tangles, and give highlights. It is also very slippery.

Just before entering the show ring, the rider's groom will paint the horse's feet and put a final polish on the rider's boots and clean off any smudges of foam or debris on the horse's coat and mouth.

## WHAT TO LOOK FOR IN A GROOM

When you first start competing with your horse, you can go to the competition by yourself and manage him yourself. However, you will find that it will be a lot easier and more fun if you take along another person who is knowledgeable and helpful at the lower levels. You can make do with anyone who is concerned with your best interest, has spent a little time with you and your horse, and knows the ropes about what you want.

At the novice level, the time spans between different tests are long enough for you to relax along with your horse in between events. There is often enough time for you to have a picnic and enjoy meeting some new friends. It is also wonderful to have someone hold your horse when you are called away for whatever reason.

As you progress in eventing, or if you are riding many classes in a dressage show or a hunter show, you will find that it helps a great deal to have a groom for the occasion. Ideally, if money were no object, you would have a groom full time so that you could ride more horses. For many people, this is a lovely pipe dream and not a reality, but it is possible to persuade somebody to groom for you in competition. What you are looking for is someone who is competent and either has ridden at the same level you want to compete at or has groomed for someone on a regular basis. The groom has been trained to know what you are going to need and when you are going to need it.

Frequently, Pony Club members make ideal grooms because they have had a lot of training and stable management and they have competed as well. They are usually very cheerful and willing to work for a very small sum.

Perhaps even a very small sum is out of your budget, as well. But once you have gone to a couple of competitions and talked with people, you will start making friends on the circuit. You can work out a buddy relationship with another rider. He or she will help you at one competition if you will do the same at the next. Both of you will benefit from the arrangement and may end up with a close friendship as well.

The higher the level in which you want to compete, the more professional the groom needs to be. That is to say, the groom needs to have had some previous experience at the same level. They may not need to have actually ridden it before as long as they have had experience grooming for someone who was competent at that level.

Since grooms are a notoriously fickle bunch, almost as difficult to entice as farriers, they also have to be treated with great courtesy. In the United States, the groom in one competition may be the rider in the next competition, so there is equality between grooms and riders that is not often seen in other parts of the world.

As a competitor, you will need to educate yourself on all aspects of grooming. This way, you will know what you want done and when. You also will know if the tasks are done properly before the critical moment in competition. Remember that the groom needs to know what your peculiarities, needs, and requests are. Each rider is different.

## HORSE SHOW SCHEDULE

The show schedule of a horse that is just starting out will depend to a certain extent on his soundness. One is doing schooling shows if the horse is eligible—for example, baby green or schooling hunters and jumpers.

The horse can handle two divisions, which would give the rider four jumping classes plus two hacks. If the hacks are going very well, the rider can opt out of the hack classes and just concentrate on the jumping.

Since there is a quantum leap from a schooling show to the recognized show, one will try hard to soften the transition by looking for a B-rated show. These B-rated shows are extremely hard to find. A horse can go horse showing every weekend. Where the stamina comes in is if you are going to an A-rated show where you have to show four or five times a week; in which case, you will go to a schedule of fewer shows depending on the soundness of the horse.

The caveat of never taking one more jump than necessary with your horse is one to notice. There is a strongly held theory that a horse only has so many jumps in his entire lifetime, and if you use them up too quickly on inappropriate fences, then the horse will become unsound and you will lose a large part of his competitive life. There are many horses that are still competing in their teens because their riders were careful with their jumping.

## TRAINING PREPARATION FOR A SHOW

In preparation for the typical hunter division classes, the rider will be emphasizing the basic training of the horse, although in a slightly different form from the classical dressage. The horse will have its nose forward of the vertical position and will be encouraged to go in a long and low frame. He will still need to be straight on his straight lines and not bulge out on his turns or cut in. So the rider will still be continuing to use his aids to keep the horse in a frame, although the frame is a long one.

Since the judge is looking for long and low in the strides and the ease of the horse's handling, the rider will use the basic warm-up schooling exercises, serpentine, voltes, and circling on a twenty-meter circle to establish pace and transition. Instead of reversing direction by cutting across the ring, the rider will do a turn on the haunches or a turn on the forehand to show the higher level of training of the horse. This also serves to balance the horse again before he sets out a new pace in the opposite direction.

In the over-fences classes inside an enclosed area, the judge is looking for the uniformity of pace from the starting circle throughout the ride, including the lines and the turns. He expects smoothness in the jumping bascule. Each fence is to be consistently taken the same as the one before. You are looking for a perfection ride where everything is elegant and understated and looks effortless. The course will be defined to have questions on the lines of fences, the smoothness of the turns, and the rider's capabilities at organizing the horse without it being obvious. Since in the indoor arenas the horses do not move forward, the stride used tends to be about twelve feet, especially on smaller courses. For the larger four-foot or three-foot, nine-inch courses, the striding opens up to a thirteen-foot stride, which means that the horse has to be going more forward and you are moving at a faster clip. This translates into a normal hand gallop for the fences for a horse standing sixteen hands, one inch. In order to have the jumping form be correct, the horse has to reach the right takeoff point in order to maintain a perfect arc.

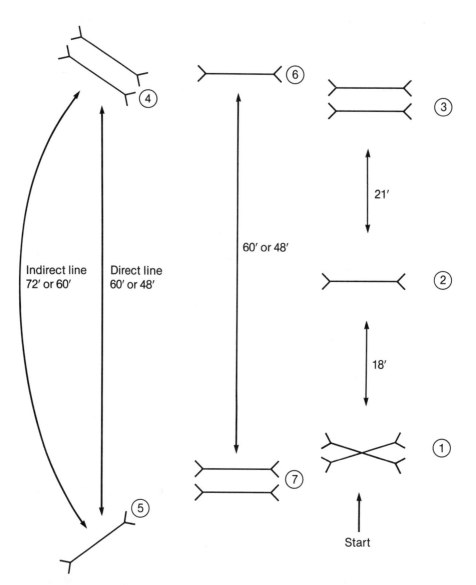

A schooling course with a variety of options. You can practice shortening and lengthening strides, curving indirect or angled direct lines. Fences should be set so that they can be ridden in either direction, so the horse does not overdevelop one side.

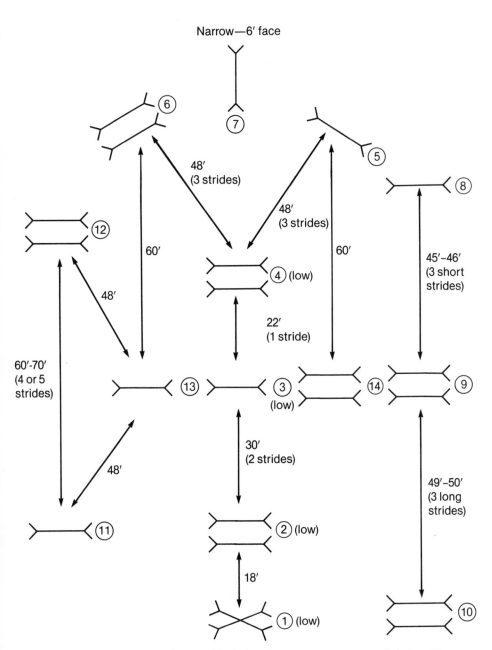

Narrow—6' face

⑥

⑦

⑤

⑧

48'
(3 strides)

48'
(3 strides)

⑫

60'

④ (low)

60'

45'–46'
(3 short
strides)

48'

22'
(1 stride)

60'-70'
(4 or 5
strides)

⑬

③
(low)

⑭

⑨

48'

30'
(2 strides)

49'–50'
(3 long
strides)

⑪

② (low)

18'

① (low)

⑩

If you are lucky to have lots of jumps, this design gives an enormous array of choices. You can change the order of jumps around without moving any of the equipment.

## OUTSIDE COURSES

For courses on the outside, which are held in a fairly large open field, the distances are greater between the fences. These classes are few and far between now, as it becomes more difficult for organizers to locate sufficient land to place the fences. The horse is expected to move on between fences, but still maintain the same pace all the way around.

The outside course requires being able to jump from a gallop, maintaining the pace without having your horse flatten over his fences. It requires as much practice as working on the regular hand gallop inside the show ring fences. Frequently, riders become undone on an outside course because of the variations in terrain, which will lengthen and shorten strides. Also, these courses tend to be too long to memorize all the striding between the fences. The rider has to be able to maintain the pace until he gets within a range to judge his distance. He needs to know what he is doing five to six strides out from a fence and confirm it three strides out from the fence. The rider has a different horse's mental attitude to contend with as well. Horses tend to be somewhat surprised at being outside the show ring environment and tend to be a bit more assertive even to the point of aggressively taking fences.

## FENCE DISTANCES

Overall, in the recognized hunter divisions, riders can expect to have related distances in combination fences such as in-and-outs that are one-stride or a one-stride to a two-stride. Frequently, the distances between the fences can ride very short, which requires the horse to handle a trappy situation with ease. The horse is able to do this because of the previous training and collection allowing him to shorten his frame. Most recognized shows do not have changes in terrain and the classes are on almost exactly level ground.

## HUNTER SEAT RIDER POSITION

In the hunter seat riding style, as opposed to the balance seat riding style, the judge expects the rider over fences to have his back parallel to the horse's back, with his arm and hand extended farther up on the horse's crest than that of the balance seat. Since the hunter seat rider is working on level ground, he can tip his body to that parallel position without worrying about a change in terrain that would cause him to fall. The line from the bit in the horse's mouth to the elbow of the rider is maintained straight, but the rider's upper body is very close to the horse's neck, allowing the rider's seat to come out of the saddle and be parallel to the horse's back. The rider still looks up and in the direction he is planning to go. This helps to maintain his balance and keep his weight in his heels. One of the problems with this style of riding is maintaining enough weight in your lower leg and heel so that you don't tip over the front of the horse or get left behind.

It is because of this particular riding style that most riders prefer a close-contact saddle that allows them to make adjustments more subtly and return more quickly than they would in a cross-country saddle. Also, they don't need to have the knee roll support, since they don't have the concussion of drop fences or of banks.

Their hands continue to be soft and yielding to the horse's mouth, with light contact allowing the horse's nose to be ahead of the verticals well.

The hunter seat over fences does not work well for cross-country riding or any terrain change. The riding style of the balance seat is much safer; however, the balance seat is not as beautiful to watch since the movements for cross-country are more extreme in their nature to compensate for the changes of terrain and speed. Many wonderful show ring hunter riders have discovered that their horses will run away with them in the hunt field unless they modify their riding style to suit the new demands. Likewise, balance seat riders have to modify their riding style in order to go into the show ring and have a prayer of doing well and perhaps pinning. Both methods over fences work well, each for its own specific requirements.

## FLYING CHANGES

In addition to the basic suppling exercises that are mentioned in the dressage chapter, the horse needs to be confirmed in his flying changes and able to do some lateral work. Ideally, the rider will have bought a horse who already has his flying changes. These take a long time to teach. Most horses will take an entire summer to get the hang of doing a flying change.

The flying change requires that the rider switch his aids from the one lead of canter to the aids of the other lead. To review, the aids for a canter depart are:

- The outside leg behind the girth,
- The inside leg on the girth,
- The inside rein bending the horse's head slightly to the inside so the rider can see the eyeball of the horse.

The rider can then deepen his seat and cue with the outside leg, allowing the horse to rise up underneath him in the canter depart.

Before asking for the canter depart, the rider has to have a slow, collected trot so the horse has impulsion for the rise into the canter. It is quite difficult to do a proper canter depart from a posting trot or a trot with any speed.

At higher levels of training, the horse is cued for the canter depart from the pressure of the inside leg, which gives a straighter depart. The inside leg aid canter depart is used just a hair behind the edge of the girth. At this higher level of canter depart, the horse does not need to have as much bend in his head and neck and his haunches do not move outward.

The goal of the dressage canter depart is straightness and the maintenance of pace. Most horses will try to speed up on a canter depart and the rider has to be careful to settle the horse in the first stride for the exact pace he has in mind.

### Teaching the Flying Change

The flying change of the canter is ideally a reversal of the rein and leg aids in the shift of the rider's weight to the new outside hipbone. In teaching the flying change, the rider will work frequently on a figure eight pattern, the center point of which will have a rail on the ground perpendicular to the horse's crossing point. The rider will first canter a circle of the figure eight, down-transition to a trot for the two strides over the rail, and then pick up the canter again on the other side of the rail to go in the new circle direction. After the horse has gotten the concept of trotting over the rail and changing leads, the rider can then shorten the trot strides down to one stride and then pick up the canter. When the horse has absorbed that piece of information, the rider can then ask for the canter depart just before the rail, so that the stride over the rail acts as the canter depart stride. The horse, in effect, has a small jump over the rail to help him with the canter depart.

Another method of teaching the flying change is to canter the horse toward a wall and use the wall to force the change. Again, the rider switches his aids to cue the horse a stride or two before the wall. It is important before giving the canter depart signals that the horse is properly set up with a number of half halts and has enough collection to be able to make the transition.

Some riders will use the canter on a diagonal across the arena, and then, as they reach the turn of the arena for the short side, they will ask for the canter depart and the corner of the arena will reinforce the lead change. Most horses will try to evade a canter depart signal, especially for a flying change, if they are not properly prepared or don't understand the signals, by running out, so the rider needs to use a lot of half halts to keep the horse in proper frame.

## COUNTERCANTER

The countercanter is occasionally used. This figure requires that you start on the correct and true canter with the inside leg to the inside of the circle, then will gradually start a serpentine the length of the arena, allowing the horse to move toward the center point of the arena and then come back to the wall. The bend of the horse's head and the position of the rider stay the same for the canter aids all through the exercise. By using very gradual curves in the serpentine, the horse will learn to move away from your leg drifting to the center of the arena and then back again. Once he is comfortable with that

230

movement, you can then make the curves a little more pronounced. Eventually, you will be able to touch the far side of the arena at the center point and then come back to the true circle again.

If a horse is not given sufficient support from the rider to maintain the countercanter aids, he will either switch leads or fall down. The falling down is most likely to happen if you make your corners too sharp for him to be able to handle. With the countercanter, *never make a sharp corner when the horse is on the false lead or the horse will fall down.*

## LATERAL WORK

In lateral work, with the horse on the bit, the rider should be able to move the horse with the rider's outside leg so that the horse will move sideways to the centerline of the arena. The horse's head and neck are bent in the direction that the rider wants to move toward, although this is slight and it is usually a matter of the rider seeing the horse's inside eyeball. Ideally, the horse's body is straight except for the curve of the head, which is just enough to show the eyeball. Many riders have trouble with their lateral work, in that the haunches will lead or trail instead of maintaining a straight line. The horse needs to maintain forward motion as well.

When he is able to move forward and sideways at the same time with his legs crossing in front of each other, he has developed a half pass. This requires a degree of collection. Usually the half pass is started at a walk for a few strides, and then the horse is praised and allowed to go straight for a while and then asked again. Eventually, the horse will be able to do the half pass at a trot and also at a canter. The half pass becomes useful if the rider decides he needs to buy a little extra space to add an extra stride between fences. This way, he can drift a little to the outside or a little to the inside and purchase six inches per stride, without appearing to shorten stride. The formal dressage half pass is much more collected than the informal longer and lower version used in the hunter ring.

## GETTING INVOLVED

### Entering the Show

When entering the show for the first time, plan to call ahead to the organizer and inquire if you can bring your horse over a day or so before to acclimate him to the show grounds. Frequently, if the organizers know you have a green horse that hasn't been to a show ground before, they will allow you to come and school a course. They actually set up a specific time for all the green horses to come and school.

When you enter your divisions, you will want to choose the beginning ones with the most flat classes. Then, if you feel comfortable over fences, choose the classes that have the lowest fences you're eligible for.

### The Warm-up

On the morning of the show, you will want to go early to school in the show ring, in the schooling classes. These give the horses an opportunity to become familiar with the show grounds, with all of the commotion, and for the rider to check his lines and distances. At the "in" gate will be posted all of the courses for the day, and the rider can pay special attention in his warm-up rounds to any particular lines or turns or transitions he will be needing later in the day.

The horse going into a flat class is expected to very, very quiet. The rider will need to ride the horse down to subdue him enough for this particular class. In doing so, the rider concentrates on his work on the flat without fences, saving the horse's legs by not jumping him. The flat work exercises will pay off later on in the jumping classes as well. If the horse is very fresh, the rider may need to lunge the horse before he gets on to ensure that the horse doesn't start the day by bucking or other disobedience.

There is a lot of hurly-burly in the warm-up arena when the show is on and the rider needs a second person to raise and lower the fences and help him with this schooling. One needs to be aggressive in the warm-up arena in order just to get the job done; however, don't monopolize the fences so much no one else can work. If you are going to be showing indoors, try to get permission to ride in an indoor arena beforehand. Horses will not like an indoor arena; nor will they like mirrors, which are frequently at the corners of the indoor arena and they will shy from those particular areas. The rider needs to drive the horses into the corners during his warm-up time so that the horse becomes acclimated and knows that he can still work. Later on, the horse will be much more willing during his classes to make the turns that the rider needs. Horses will also spook at pigeons that roost in the eaves. They are much less willing to go forward generally than they are at an outdoor show and the rider needs to be quite aggressive.

### The Flat Class

When warming up for a flat class, ideally the rider will have his horse moving forward before he comes into the arena. He can do this by some posting trot work outside the arena in the warm-up area just before going in, if he has a horse that tends to be laid back. If he has a horse that is too much on the muscle, then he will have to do some walking to calm him down. From the time the horse enters the arena, consider yourself as being judged. If your horse has a particularly good extended trot, show it off. If he does a nice turn on the haunches or on the forehand, show that off.

Ideally, you will place yourself in the holes between the groups of riders as they space around the arena. It takes three eyes to be able to ride a flat class: one on your horse, to have him performing at his best; one on the judge, to be in the right spot at the right time; and one on the other riders, to make sure you won't get cut off. Place your horse to the inside of the pack whenever possible. While it is permissible to cut across the arena to find a better hole for your horse to be shown in, if you do it too often, you will annoy the judge.

Showing on the flat requires a certain theatricality. The presentation of the horse and rider has to be immaculate. The tidiness and conservative elegance give the horse an extra bit of polish, which makes the difference between being out of the ribbons and being in the ribbons if everything else is equal. The rider has to know what his horse does not do as well and hide in the pack for a problem until he gets the problem solved. When asked to do a reverse of direction, the rider can use a turn on the forehand or on the haunches to show the horse's education and mannerliness.

Occasionally, the horses are asked individually to go from a hand gallop to a halt and then return to the lineup. Ideally, the horse is sufficiently trained that when the rider gives the signal to halt, the horse will halt almost instantly. It is the icing on the cake if the horse will walk quietly on a loose rein back to the lineup. Some riders will exaggerate this to the point of having the reins on the buckle for their return to the lineup. In a flat class, remember the judge is looking for a horse that is going to be comfortable to hunt all day, so the mannerliness and the precision of the transitions will be important as well as the ground-covering quality of the strides.

## Warm-up for Over-Fences Classes

In the warm-up for the over the fences classes, the rider will want to get the horse going forward tidily. He will probably start out by some limbering-up exercises on the flat, like the walk, trot, and canter emphasizing his transitions. A touch of lateral work to make sure the horse is moving through the gears sideways as well as forward, then the rider probably will start with the small crossrail fence and he will work up to a vertical and then an oxer. As soon as the horse is moving quietly over his fences with both knees up, the rider should stop the jumping. If there is an angle fence in the class, the rider can practice that to remind the horse that there is an angle coming. Ideally, the rider will not take any more warm-up fences than absolutely necessary to get his horse prepped for the class. After the warm-up over-fences work is complete, the rider will then walk his horse just before entering the arena so the horse gets a chance to mentally relax, but is still on his toes.

Since the rider will watch a few horses go prior to getting on his horse, the rider should have a feel for how many strides it will take between fences to produce the kind of ride that he wants. He will watch to see whether the striding is a "tight three strides," for instance, or a "nice three strides," or a "steady three strides." Horse shows are required to post their courses at least an hour ahead of the class. The order of go will be rotated throughout the day, so you will need to check this before each class so that you are in proper sequence, therefore giving you plenty of time to memorize the course.

Usually, you will want to get on your mount as the order reaches ten horses before you're due to get in the arena. This will give you plenty of time to be prepared and catch your breath just before you go in. If you have to ride before the ten-horse mark, get on early and sit on your horse and watch a couple of horses go. Many horses will do better if they sit awhile waiting to go into the arena. Remember, it is better to be ready a little too soon and wait a bit than it is not to be ready on time.

If your horse is an old campaigner and gets restless after you get him ready, you can have someone walk him while you stand and watch the horses go. Then you pop on and give him a walk or a touch of a trot just before he goes in and he will be ready to do his showmanship. A horse who is a little on the lethargic side may need a tap with the crop just before entering the arena to get him awake and going forward. A horse who is sharp and strong and tends to be aggressive will need to be soothed, stroked on the neck, and then allowed to go in.

## Classes over Fences

When you enter the arena, from the moment the gate opens, you are being judged and you will be making a circle approximately one-third the size of the arena to develop your pace. Most horses will be trotted in at a posting trot, slowed down to a slower, more collected trot, and picked up the canter lead. Once the canter is achieved, the rider will smoothly and quickly bring the horse up to the pace necessary for the line of fences. Once that pace is achieved, the rider does not vary it throughout the rest of the ride. Waiting until after your second fence to do a stride adjustment is too late. If you have to adjust your stride to have the fences come out well, you probably have already lost the class and should consider the rest of the ride a schooling exercise to improve your overall riding.

When showing a horse, you want to hide your mistakes and faults, and emphasize the horse's good points. When you are in the ring, it is not a good idea to pick a fight. You try to finesse whatever is possible if you run into a problem. When riding your course, you want to remember to keep your eyes up, looking where you are going, and getting a feel for maintaining your pace. If you keep those two things in mind, the course will probably ride well for you.

Remember that your turns and angles are just as important as your straight lines. You can use your turns and angles to set the horse up again and balance him for the next straight line, just as you would do if you were riding a dressage class. The balancing, however, is a little more subtle, in that your weight and shoulders will shift back to a slightly more upward position, bringing your weight deeper into your heels. You also are using your half halts with your hand very gently before your turn to help with the balancing of the

Water jumps require speed and impulsion.

The preliminary jumper classes give stair-step practice for jumping bigger fences.

235

turn. Most horses like two or three half halts as a warning that something is coming up and to balance themselves before you ask them to do whatever the new problem is.

If you are going to need to shorten your strides after the horse lands after a fence, give him a half halt to collect himself. If each of the strides needs to be shorter, you will still be keeping your leg strong to keep the momentum up so that he doesn't tip on his forehand and stall out on you. If your horse has a very long stride and it is difficult for you to shorten him, instead of using a direct line from one fence to another, you may opt to use an indirect line, drifting slightly out to put a bow in your line, thus creating a little more distance. This should be practiced at home many times before you do it in a horse show, because you can drift yourself right out of the optimum line—it would look as if your horse is refusing by running out. If your horse has a tendency to dwell in the air or to feel as if he is stalling, you will need more momentum to get over your fences and you will need to encourage the horse as he lands to pick up the distance that was lost in his jumping. Since the stall will have caused him to land close to the fence, his strides will have to make up for the difference. This is why watching a couple of horses go before you is important. If you see a horse whose stride matches your horse's stride, or whose style over fences is similar, you can then pick out the information you need to have your round go better.

It is very helpful to have someone on the ground watching you ride. It is even better to have someone videotape the ride for you so that later on you can look at it, and figure out what needs correcting. It is also helpful to your instructor if you have a videotape because he can then more precisely target for you the program to improve your riding skills. There are many subtle things that the rider will not see as he is making the trip, that the videotape or the ground person might pick up—if the horse opened his mouth a bit and looked in resistance, or if both legs didn't come up equally over the fences, or if the bascule was not of the proper shape or was too early or too late.

Some horses like to rub fences. This will count as a fault unless the horse is absolutely perfect in every way and the rub was a very light one. Generally speaking, if you have a horse that rubs fences, it is a wiser course of action to only run him in classes with lower fences than the ones that he rubs. For example, if he rubs a three-foot, nine-inch fence, don't show him at that level, but instead at three feet, six inches. If he habitually rubs, but still keeps his knees up and you're frustrated, you may want to change him to event riding instead, where if he rubs a solid obstacle, it is going to sting sufficiently for him to give up the idea. A horse rubbing a fence does not necessarily mean he's a coward. Frequently, the problem is just the opposite—he is more bold than he is careful. It can be corrected to a certain extent by lots of gymnastic exercises.

USET rider shows his hunter background in his style.

## After the Course of Fence

After you have ridden the course, and if you are fortunate enough to be called back, most classes will require that the horse be hunting sound and jogged out for soundness. If you are called back, you will want to have your saddle off your horse. Your groom will wipe the horse off and tidy him up. Meanwhile, you will tidy yourself up enough to run on foot back into the ring. The horse will be stood up for the judge to look at, and the judge will then ask you to trot the horse out for him. As long as the horse trots sound at that moment, you are still in the running. If, at that moment, the horse does not trot out, then you are eliminated. Sometimes the judge will rearrange the order of the line before he announces the pinning.

Since there is a lot of free time at horse shows, especially if you are riding only one horse, use the time productively by watching other riders and other classes. You can learn a lot about the conformation of the horses by watching the model classes. There is much to be learned on technique from both the professional hunter riders and the jumper riders. Frequently, it is helpful to pick a particularly good rider and follow him throughout the show to learn his techniques of preparation warm-up and then actual performance. Watching other riders' grooms prepare the horses before and after the classes may also be helpful.

## After the Show

After the show is over, collect your photographs, videotapes, and other information that is available to you to peruse later in the week. Give this information to your instructor if the instructor was not at the show. The instructor will more effective in helping you with your training.

One needs to keep in mind the concept of sportsmanship. Winning, although wonderful, is not everything and merely improving accounts for a lot. If you can improve just one area each time you go, eventually you will have the whole package put together. Horse showing, being a perfectionist sport, takes years to be able to perfect. While you can improve the odds by having your horse trained to the best possible level, or having bought the top horse in the area, it is still going to be up to you, as the rider, to improve yourself sufficiently to ride him.

# 13

# Combined Training and the Novice Event

COMBINED TRAINING is an Olympic sport that is derived from the exams given to cavalry officers. Also known as "the military," and "three-day eventing," the tests were given on three successive days. These were to establish the degree of horsemanship the officer had attained.

When the cavalries of the world were disbanded after World War II, the national teams were taken over by civilians. The tests were then adjusted to civilian needs.

The first test, dressage, simulates the parade ground movements of the officers' charges. It requires suppleness, obedience, and balance. The horses move more forward than they would if trained for pure dressage. Similar to compulsory figures in figure skating, the fluidity of strides is matched by precision. If the horse doesn't do well in the first test, he is likely to have trouble completing the other tests.

The second test is the cross-country or speed and endurance test. This test simulates the cavalry horse and his officer taking an important message cross-country from one battle station to another. The test itself includes a steeplechase phase, usually about two miles long, and has hurdle fences that are about five feet high. The horse has to brush through these fences at speed.

It also has two sections of what is known as roads and tracks, walking and trotting for several miles at a time. These sections are metered and timed so it is a bit like a car rally. You have to be at the right place at the right time.

Torrance Watkins and "Poltroon." This combined-training Olympic medalist combination broke many myths. "Poltroon" is quite small, just above fifteen hands, and a pinto with asymmetrical markings. Her brilliance and charisma combined with incredible jumping form won the hearts of all who saw her. Their impeccable turn-out is finished to the fine details, down to Torrance's earrings (permissible in dressage). "Poltroon"'s mane was braided in the same two colors of thread as her mane, so the braiding would not distract the eye.

These phases served as connecting, warming-up, and cooling-out phases to the steeplechase.

The final phase of the cross-country is held after a compulsory rest break and veterinarian exam to ensure that the horses are fit enough to continue. This last and most difficult phase is known as cross-country. Horses and riders gallop at a preselected speed over natural terrain, jumping any obstacles that are flagged. These can include six-foot drops into water, water fences, large open ditches, jumps up and down revetted banks, and maze fences. The fences would have height, width, and depth and frequently are in combination.

On the final day, the horse will be checked by a veterinarian to ensure that he is sound. Stadium jumping simulates that the officer's mount is still able to function after having performed the rigorous tests of the two previous days. The stadium phase has a short but difficult course utilizing brilliantly colored show jumper–type fences. Stadium jumping courses are usually held on open fields. The ground undulates, changing the distances and lines between the fences. It requires constant balancing of the horse.

Not officially part of the testing, yet critical to successful completion of it, is the rider's knowledge of keeping a horse sound.

One of the interesting aspects of three-day event riding is that the teams can be composed of women as well as men. There is no segregation of sexes for the competition. All that is necessary is that the riders meet a certain weight requirement, which is usually 165 pounds. This can be met by the lady riders by using lead-weight pads over their saddle pads.

## ORGANIZATION

In 1950, with the disbanding of the U.S. Cavalry, the U.S. Cavalry riders became the coaches and advisers to the new civilian organization called the U.S. Equestrian Team (USET).

In 1959, the USET decided to concentrate only on fielding the international teams for all three Olympic disciplines—dressage, show jumping, and combined training. The U.S. Combined Training Association (USCTA) was formed to take over the grass-roots training and support to bring the riders and horses up to international competition. The mandate of the USCTA provided for a stair-step methodology so that the horse and riders would not be overfaced at any one location along the stair. This method of nurturing the training of horse and rider has been most effective. The United States has placed many gold medal teams in international competition as a result of the breadth of this program.

In addition to the USCTA's program, there is the United States Pony Club Program, which is basically from the British system. Both the Pony Club and the USCTA use similar divisions. As an adult rider, if you can find a Pony Club near you, you can observe and learn many of the practical aspects.

# THE NOVICE EVENT

The novice one-day event is the lowest rung of the U.S. Combined Training Association's stepladder of divisions. In the author's opinion, it is easier than fox hunting. The basic requirements of the level are: in dressage— that the horse and rider are able to walk, trot, and canter in both directions in the ring, and be able to stay in the ring. The rider needs to be able to halt, salute the judge, and work the horse in a low-training-level frame.

In the jumping tests, the jumps are very inviting and quite tiny—most are smaller than two feet, six inches. The water jump has no steep sides on it, and is really more of a stream crossing. There will be distance between the fences to allow for corrections. The stadium jumping will have approximately twelve jumping efforts and no combinations.

One is ready to ride in a novice competition when one can successfully remember and complete: the dressage test; a course of twelve fences; a walk, trot, and canter in the open in addition to having schooled water fences, little ditches, and banks. (These are very tiny—about the size of small verges off driveways or dirt roads.)

Novice is divided into novice horse and novice rider, so that the novice rider does not have an anxiety attack from discovering that the person in front of him is the world champion on his newest acquisition. The USCTA has been very considerate and gives the novice rider every opportunity to be quietly nervous all on his own and in like company. All his peers are going to be feeling equally jelly-legged. He will quickly discover a certain amount of camaraderie similar to the experience of final exams in college. The other reason is an equally beneficial one to the novice rider. The USCTA recognizes that the most wonderful horse in the world, who is exquisitely trained, still will not go as well for a novice rider as a less well-trained horse will for an expert rider. Every effort is made by the organizers to make the novice rider feel comfortable, at home, and very much wanted as part of the U.S. Combined Training Association.

The USCTA *Omnibus,* issued several times a year, lists novice events and combined tests that do not include the cross-country. The combined tests are just the dressage and the stadium jumping. These are usually held at the beginning of the event season for your area and during the hot weather. Eventing is usually done when the weather is cool so the horses have an easier time with their breathing and recovery and are not stressed so much by the hot weather. It is also timed so that the ground is not frozen, to minimize damage to horses' joints and reduce injury possibilities.

It is great practice for getting yourself organized for doing a three-phase. These are usually very low-keyed and a lot of fun with ample opportunities to have a picnic with new friends and ask questions and learn. Event riders are a friendly bunch and are very willing to help each other. Camaraderie is one of the attractions of the sport.

If you have been to a few low-level tests at a dressage show, you will have

Novice helsinki: this little cross-country fence is built on the gentle slope of a hill. It looks odd, but rides easily. Most helsinkis are verticals instead of spreads.

gotten over the nerves of a first competition. If you haven't, you will find that getting ready for the dressage test is very similar to what you would do if you were just going to a dressage show. Your dressage will also be improved by the lack of need to do galloping or conditioning with your horse.

The cross-country is both designed for speed and type of fence to be ridden at a trot at 350 meters per minute. You will be alternating between trotting, cantering, and walking, depending on how your horse reacts to his new fences and how much you need to keep him going forward. The speed is specifically designed so the horse does not need to be rushed around the course and the novice rider does not need to deal with the meters-per-minute requirements of learning his various speeds of gallop. At the novice event, he doesn't have to gallop at all. A canter is more than sufficient for a horse. The ponies don't even need to be pushed very hard.

At this level, you do not need to worry about overwhelming fences. Fences are very small and very inviting to the horses and you will be fighting more your own nerves than your horse's nerves. By being well prepared and having done each of the segments before, so that you can repeat until you are comfortable, you will make yourself feel better about coming to a competition where each part depends on the next part.

If you can find a cross-country course near you for schooling, arrange to go out with a friend or instructor to practice a school over the course before you actually have to compete over it. Your nerves will be a whole lot better and your horse will be more likely to have a successful go his first time out. If you haven't had an opportunity to find a cross-country course to work over, at least concoct the types of fences you will be needing to ride over at home.

You can dig a ditch that is approximately twenty feet wide, two feet deep, and eighteen feet long, and line it with plastic. Put in about a foot of gravel-sand mixture and fill it with a little water, about six inches worth, and you will have your water fence to practice in if you cannot find a stream.

Another alternative is to construct a little box that is painted blue on the inside, which is quite low, about four inches in height, and you pop that underneath one of your verticals. It will give some of the effect of having a stadium water fence. You can put it just before the fence or just after the fence to give different practice. The little blue box will not work for practicing a water jump, however, where the horse does have to get his feet wet, so you still have to at least find a substantial stream or mud puddle to work in.

The bank jumps you can probably practice off the small side of a hill or the sides of a driveway. The driveway will also give you a minor ditch to work with as well if you can find a safe spot. Most of the stone walls and oxers can be simulated through your stadium jumping courses as far as the type of fence is concerned.

### Accustoming the Horse to Competition

In preparation for a novice event, it is helpful if you have had previous experience with your horse by going to a little dressage or hunter show. There,

244

you can enter in many classes and your slate is wiped clean from each class so each is a new effort. In eventing, if whatever you do at the beginning is tallied up against the other two phases, you are much more locked into your performance than you would be to start fresh each time in a regular show. In addition to which, eventing is scored on negative points, rather than positive points, so the lower the number, the better you did; as opposed to a dressage show in which the higher percentile, the better you did.

Ideally, by taking your horse out to fox hunt or to a show, you are, in addition to working on that particular element, teaching him company manners. He becomes accustomed to being in a large group of horses, doing something different from what everyone else is doing, and paying attention to you. The dressage work that you have done at home will have helped him with understanding that he has to pay attention to you rather than look at the crowd. These first times out, you need to be patient with your horse if he hasn't been out in company. It will be a very heady experience for him and he won't settle down for quite a while. You may spend several hours getting him calmed down enough to actually ride him. Frequently, riders will take unentered horses to shows just for the experience of being on the show grounds.

One method used when taking a nervous horse off the trailer is attaching a lunge line to the halter to take the horse off rather than a lead shank. If the horse flies back out of the trailer, from surprise at all the commotion around him, the person unloading him still has control of him. Frequently, the horse is brought to the show grounds with his saddle and bridle already on him. A second or third person is enlisted to adjust the tack so that he isn't all over your feet and all over you.

Frequently, the rider will use the lunge line hooked onto the bridle the same way he would lunging at home and lead the horse around the show grounds, being careful not to get in anyone's way, so that he gets a chance to be accustomed to the area. Then the rider will start lunging in a quieter area, to develop control over him. As he settles and gets back into a working mode, the rider can move him from one lunging spot to another so that he gradually gets used to working in a strange environment. After he is quiet on the lunge, you mount and walk him around, expecting him to shy and spook at every new thing he sees.

After the horse has walked about, you can school him in dressage at one of the warm-up areas and get him used to working. Then, just let him watch a few classes and call it a day and take him home. He will benefit immensely from the exposure and so will you.

A horse who has miles and miles of campaign experience will probably be keen, but not difficult to handle. A younger horse or a horse who has had less social experience or has not been out in a long time can be expected to have more distraction problems.

The more times you get your horse out in public before competition, the easier you will find the whole endeavor. For one thing, you learn to pack your car and trailer and get yourself on the road at the appointed time. You also learn what the checklists are that you need for your own particular kinds of equipment before you get to a competition. It is very frustrating to pay to be entered and suddenly discover you forgot your bridle or horse. For the novice rider, just organizing those first trailer trips is a major accomplishment and the rider should give himself a pat on the back for mastering this skill.

### Preparations

When you are ready to enter a novice-level event, you need to start several weeks in advance getting your horse's mane and tail pulled, since a horse does not like this done all at one time. You also need to invest in some camphorated body wash so that your horse dries off quickly. This way, between different parts of the competition, you can give him a quick sponge bath and make him feel better and get the sweat marks off so that at each test, he is fresh and comfortable.

At the novice level, the equipment that you will be needing will be your regular saddle and bridle. At this level, you do not need to go out and buy a specialized dressage or jumping saddle. An all-purpose one will be more than adequate. Any saddle needs to be level and comfortable. Frequently, riders will first buy their jumping saddle because they can do their dressage in it. They may not score as well because their legs will be too far forward, but they will be safe on the cross-country. Whereas, if you buy your dressage saddle first, it is extremely difficult to be safe jumping cross-country because there is no place for your knee to go when you have shortened your stirrups.

You will want to check all of your tack to make sure the stitches are holding and there are no stray parts, that it is all in good repair and is placed properly on the saddle or bridle. Eventing is stressful on a horse and rider, and you are more likely to have breakage than you would on a quiet little hack. It is important that your leather goods have been well oiled several weeks prior to the competition so that they are at their maximum strength and flexibility and the oil has had a chance to penetrate. Also, the oil is less likely to stain your breeches if it has had a couple of weeks to soak into the leather.

You will want to bring along a hay net for your horse to occupy him between the phases. You will probably want to have a fishnet sheet, otherwise known as an Airtex, and a regular sheet or a cooler for him so that after he has been washed, you can keep him covered so he doesn't chill as he's drying.

In addition to the usual hoof picks and brushes in your grooming box, you will probably want to have two clean rags—one for your boots and another for wiping off the horse's mouth and any last-minute mud removal. You will want to put hoof dressing on the horse's feet just before he enters the ring to make them look shiny, unless you are using an epoxy finish, which you can apply before you get to the show. The idea is to have that last little bit of slick and shine before you enter the ring.

Do not use a silicone hair polish product on a horse that you are planning on eventing other than for those parts of the body that you might not need to grab on cross-country.

Novice bank: the horse has not done one of these before and is not certain when to put his legs down. The rider has come in fast and is in a strong driving position. The horse is as enthusiastic as the rider.

In addition to the usual grooming box, you will need to bring water from home for your horse and hot water for washing him. If you fill up a five-gallon jug with just hot water, you can mix it with cold water when you need it and it will keep the horse from being uncomfortable when you wash him. Cold water on a horse's muscles will cause them to cramp up and he may tie up from the sudden chilling.

You also need to think of your personal needs as the rider. It is very important that you get enough sleep the night before so that you are mentally quick as well as remembering to eat. If your blood sugar drops, you will become weak and foggy-headed at a time when you really want to be at your very best. Many riders pack snacks that are rich in either proteins or carbohydrates. These include cheese or some other easily digested protein and honey for a quick fix about fifteen minutes before a ride. If you overdo the sugar, you will get a quick flush of energy followed by an equal drop, which you don't want to happen on your cross-country. So you have to be careful not to abuse your amount of sugar intake. While some events will have food on the grounds, never assume that that will be the case, and always pack your own lunch. If you put in enough food to share, you may be able to have a picnic with some new friends. You will also probably want to have something to drink for yourself. Some people like the electrolyte drinks such as Gatorade. Other people find them difficult to drink and prefer either soft drinks or mineral water. Occasionally, you will find riders who are thrilled with orange juice. In your preparation, you can experiment as to what beverage you like best.

Since keeping your riding clothes clean up until the moment of competition can be difficult, most riders have an alternate set of clothes that they wear in between rides. These can be either blue jeans or overalls that protect the white breeches. Changing clothes in a horse trailer has its surprising moments. Your horse may deposit a trickle of hay in your breeches when you are otherwise occupied. This leads to a most memorable ride.

Lady riders need to remember to wear a hairnet unless they have extremely short hair. Even short hair will present better under a hunt cap or other headgear if it is confined by a hairnet. There is one minor, but very noticeable, finishing point; women should not wear ornate or dangling earrings—it is very distracting. Likewise, if a lady needs a bra, she should wear one that will support her. Few things look worse than watching someone bounce about the ring in syncopated time.

### The Dressage Test

Always consult the USCTA rulebook before attending a dressage event. There is a lot of material that needs to be memorized to keep the sport safe. There are illustrations of all the different kinds of saddlery that are allowed. In addition to the simple snaffle bridle and saddle, you are allowed a breastplate to keep the saddle from slipping back. Carrying a whip into the ring is not permitted. Some riders will practice with their dressage whip and drop the whip just before they enter the arena. If you are worried about remembering to drop your whip, ask a friend or a groom to take it away from you when they take the tail wrap off, before you do your final circuits outside the ring.

For planning your timing for the event, the event secretary will have sent you a card that will give you exact times or you will have called in to get your times. These times are precise to the minute: instead of going at 3:30 P.M., you may be going at 3:32 P.M.—and they really mean 3:32 P.M. There is no fudge factor for being a little late. If you miss your time, you are eliminated. The good point of such exact timing is that you can warm up your horse exactly the way you want to, and have him peaked for his performance and not have to sit around waiting once you have reached that peak. You have much greater control. In addition, by knowing exactly when you go, you can also organize the rest of the day and have a good idea of when you are going to be leaving to go home.

When setting up your time schedule, add to it blocks of fifteen to thirty minutes for each segment, so that you have built-in buffer time for yourself. Inevitably, it takes you longer to get organized and out in the morning than you have planned. The traffic is worse; you have to go slower with the trailer than you would in the car; you might follow the wrong trailer and get lost, even though you went to the course the day before to walk it. You can make mistakes in the morning because you are rattled. If you build the extra time in, it will help to keep your brain unscrambled and relax you.

### The Warm-up

When planning the amount of time you need to warm up at novice level, remember that most riders will be riding their horses anywhere from fifteen to thirty minutes. If you plan on the thirty minutes, you can use part of your time to stretch your horse leisurely out and walk from the trailer over to the warm-up area, without having to worry. That will help him get used to the situation. Take in all the new information about being in a competition, and start the two of you stretching out. Ideally, you will do stretching-out exercises and a considerable amount of walking and shoulder-in, working in a circle, running through your gears, checking your transitions, and then walking again to stretch the two of you out and keep your relaxation going.

The relaxation is emphasized because it is a critical part of competition life. If you get tense, your muscles are going to tighten up and send the horse forward more than you had intended. When you try to hold him back, he gets worried. He doesn't understand what is wrong and, in trying to please you, may end by blowing up, instead, out of frustration. He is also going to be much keener because of being in a new environment with lots of other horses around.

You have to work him back into those skills that you have been using at home for dressage, so he understands he has a job to do and what the job is. To keep him from shying, you can send him more forward into a trot, do a couple of transitions, some lateral work, or work on a figure eight. Anything to keep his mind distracted from the outside stimulation and concentrating on you is fair game. You intersperse with this long walks on a loose rein because you will have a free walk on a loose rein on your test. This is the hardest thing to get in a competition environment because the horse and you are so stimulated. Frequently, after you have done your faster work, he will have used up a little bit of energy and be more willing to settle for you.

Just before you go into the holding area for the ring, your groom will remove the tail bandage on your horse, do a final check on polish on his hooves, brush off your boots, wipe off any sweat marks, and generally give a last discerning eye to make sure you are turned out as well as you can possibly muster. The ring steward will call you about three minutes before your test and check your bit and, if you are using spurs, will check to make sure the spurs are not sharp enough to injure the horse.

If you are used to using spurs, you need to check them before you go to your competition, because spurs will corrode. This creates rough spots on the inside of the spur where it goes against the horse, and these rough spots can wound the horse's side. In addition to being terribly embarrassing for you, because you had not intended to hurt your horse, it will also eliminate you. Being eliminated for cruelty is one of the most embarrassing and potentially difficult things to live down. Probably in a novice event, if you have a kindly ring steward, they may take your spurs away from you and allow you to ride the test anyway after explaining what has happened to your spurs. But it is up to the ring steward's sole discretion whether or not to allow you to continue or whether you are eliminated before you even start.

Once you are allowed to be near the ring with your horse, you want to give him every opportunity to get used to the new surroundings. If your horse is a little sluggish, you can use the trot to move him forward, get him up into the bridle, and move him more enthusiastically. If you need to be more precise on your halts, you can do a trot to a halt to a trot again. Use your time between the time they allow you near the arena and the time you actually enter the arena to acclimate the horse. You usually circle the arena, sometimes several times, being sure to show your horse the judges' stand. He needs to survey the scene before he gets into the arena and suddenly decides that the judges' stand is a dragon about to eat him. Some horses are very upset by seeing an open trailer with a judge sitting in it. They will spook for the entire test every time they get to that end of the arena. If you have a horse that is really petrified, be determined, keep on going and keep a very steady encouraging leg on the horse. You will have to push him more forward than you would normally in order to keep him under control. You will especially have to support him with your inside leg on the turns at that end of the arena.

Novice competitions are usually held on grass and the terrain is not perfectly flat, which means your horse is going to naturally speed up and slow down, depending on the ground changes, and lose his balance. If you watch the horses before you—and when you walk the course the day before, go over and walk the inside of the dressage arena—you can tell where your dips are going to be. Wherever there is a dip, you will have to support your horse even more than you would on the flat, because he will tend to drop on his forehand and perhaps stumble.

### Riding the Dressage Test

Your purpose is to stay within the arena when you do your test and to try to make all of the movements. If you have managed those two things on your first novice event, you have really accomplished a great deal and you should be proud of yourself. Ideally, you will have picked up your pattern requirements close to the letter where they were asked. There is a lot of latitude in novice eventing, and not as much is expected of you as it will be later when you and the horse are more fully trained. There is a lot of forgiveness at this level. This is nice to remember when you feel you have just blown it by three strides on your transition up or your transition down, or you can not maintain an absolutely perfect square halt because your horse is still spooking at the judges' stand. Every time you go into the arena, it will get better and you have to believe that you will continue to improve. The judges frequently are very encouraging, too.

Judges will usually try to ring their bell to tell you to enter the arena when you are down at the end close to them so that you will be sure to hear the bell. Frequently, riders become very anxious about hearing the bell and will ask the person minding the entrance to the ring also to tell them the bell has rung so they have a safety net in case they can't hear. You have over thirty seconds to get from one end of the arena to the other, which is more than enough time to do it comfortably. You can trot your way around the arena getting yourself organized. Go out a distance from the arena and make a segment of a twenty-meter circle to make your turn to give you a straight entry. You want to be perfectly straight, with your horse aimed exactly to the center of the arena, before you cross the line into it. You need at least three strides outside the arena to accomplish that. If you are straight when you aim for the judges' faces or for the red marker behind the C, you will stay straight on.

Remember that the point of departure of each of the transitions is when your shoulders are even with the point, not the head of the horse or the tail of the horse. If you use your peripheral vision, you can pick up the side points that you need to be accurate. Remember to use extra half halts because your nerves will probably be up a bit for the entry. Try to keep your head up and maintain eye contact if you can with the judge. If you get a proper halt, make a lot of your salute, use your time to drag the gesture out a bit to make it more impressive. You need to have eye contact with the judge so that when he nods his head for you to continue on, you are ready to go.

Taking your hand off the reins is frequently one of the more traumatic experiences for a novice rider because your horse is most likely to wiggle from the weight change of your hand. Just try to stay very erect and at the same time think something relaxing in a mental image so that your horse doesn't feel a surge of adrenaline through your body. If, when making your halt, your weight is the least bit off, your horse will not halt square. You can ask him to move forward to correct the halt, but be careful not to ask him to square up his halt by backing up. Backing up will lose points, in addition to which he will end unbalanced and you still won't have a square halt.

When riding your test, remember to ride forward but don't rush. Keep the same rhythm and cadence that you have been working on all along and try to remember to breathe. Most novice riders are so petrified that they hold their breath for the entire test and end up looking quite blue by the end of it. In addition, that makes them even more tense and the test doesn't go as well. Many judges will try to smile to relax you because they are not allowed to help you any more than that during your test. If you smile back, you might start breathing again.

If you forget your test, it isn't the end of the world. You will lose two points and the bell will sound signalling you to stop. If you look totally blank and perplexed, you will be told where to start your test again, so you know what movement you forgot and get back on track again. You can forget up to two times. Should you forget a third time, you are eliminated, but will probably be allowed to continue your test anyway for the experience.

If your horse jumps out of the arena, just keep riding forward, jump back into the arena, and complete your test. Even though you are eliminated, you can finish your test and gain the experience from it. At some schooling dressage horse shows, you will see horses that are very big and very green end up on the wrong side of the dressage fence and the riders just keep maintaining the same arc and ride them back in again. You don't even need to change your gait to go over the fence since it is so low.

Frequently, novice competitions use a large numbered vest, or "penny" for identifying each competing rider. The penny is made in only one size and is frequently too big for lady riders and tends to slide down one sleeve during a ride. You can hold it in place by pinning each shoulder to your riding jacket before you start the test. It is also a good idea to do the same for any other use of the penny. The bandage pins that you use for your wraps and bandages on your horse will quite adequately handle a penny.

If you are given the cardboard small bridle numbers for dressage, you can put these in a number of places other than in the browband loop of your bridle. Some people put them on their boot, others put them in the center of their breastplate. Occasionally, people will put them on the side of their breastplate.

At the end of your dressage ride, the judge will frequently speak to you after you have done your salute. You are still being judged in your free walk as you leave the arena, so try to remember that you are still performing, even though the judge has scored all but one movement of your test. When you finish your test, you will walk forward toward C and the dressage judge. Use the whole turn and corner of the arena to turn and walk out on loose rein. Since this is part of your dressage test, remember not to speak until you have left the arena. Unless your horse is totally bombproof, don't pat him until you have cleared the arena.

You should now have a block of time between the dressage test and the cross-country, in which you can get your horse washed off or rubbed down, depending on the temperature, and go over to the cross-country course.

## Walking the Cross-Country

When you arrived at the competition the day before for the course walk, you would have walked it the first time with an official, learning all the changes that would be made to the course for your level. Frequently, the same fences will serve for many different levels and the fence judge will be responsible for lowering the fence for your level or changing the options so it is easier for your horse. So you need to pay particular attention to any little notes that might have been left by the organizer for you and it is important to have that first walk with the official if at all possible. The first time you walk a cross-country course, you will just be locating where the course goes and whatever special instructions the organizer has left for you. You need to walk the course at least twice more to memorize it.

When you are walking a cross-country course, you have to look at the course from the point of view of your horse when he sees it for the first time as he is jumping it. Consider all of the different options that your horse might possibly need. For each fence, you have to think, "What would happen if my horse refused or fell at this fence? How would I pick a route that is easier for him to go over?" Then, once you have picked what your options are, you need to figure out the lines that you want to use through the fences. When you are galloping along, you will know exactly where you want to go and where you want to leave the takeoff point. You need to analyze the course to decide where you are going to trot, and where you think you might need to canter. If at all possible, walk the course with another knowledgeable rider or instructor so you have the benefit of their experience when you go as well.

It is especially important when confronted with a water jump on the course that prior to taking your horse through it, you personally have walked through the water jump. When you are walking the course, plan on bringing along an extra pair of tennis shoes and socks or some hightop boots so you can wade. You would be surprised at how uneven the footing is in the water jump. There are spots that are good footing all the way through and then there are spots you can drop off and never be seen again.

Frequently, if the water jump passes through a pond, the organizers will have streamers on either side of the pathway to keep you on the straight and narrow. If the organizers do not do this, it is particularly important that you go out there and get your feet wet. Remember: the deeper the water, the better the chance of your horse flipping with you.

Try to memorize the fences in order, with their numbers, in case you have a bit of amnesia along the way. It will help you remember the number of the next fence and put it into order. Event riders occasionally forget. Usually, when their horse is giving them a hard time, they suddenly discover they haven't a clue where they are. This is not confined just to novice riders.

Even the Olympians, such as Mike Plumb, have made errors on major courses. At Middletown event one year, Mike was in first place on one horse and had several horses in competition. He forgot what course he was riding and jumped the wrong last fence, thereby eliminating himself. This has also happened at the Olympics with riders riding for their national teams. Virtually every rider who events for any length of time has had it happen.

Once you have decided on the lines that you want to use throughout the course, then you need to walk the course again by yourself, not talking to anyone and not stopping. Pretend that you are on the horse and on course. This is a very important course walk for you because it is almost going to feel as if you are out there really riding the course.

If there are fences that are particularly worrisome for you, you may want to visit those fences again. If there is enough time before your division, you can watch some other horses over those fences. If at all possible, check with riders who have ridden the course and see how it went for them. A rider just coming off the course will be happy to tell you what parts were muddy, what side of the fence is better than the other side of the fence, if they had a refusal and where. Your helper or groom will be able to gather this information as well, and that will be of use to you when you are planning your run. Pay particular attention to your water fence.

Walking courses can be physically very tiring if you are not used to walking. If you have been chasing your horse around a hilly pasture for the past couple of months, you will probably be fine. If you have your horse in a boarding situation and you don't normally walk as part of your daily routine, you may want to consider adding walking to your physical fitness program. If your leg muscles start to cramp up from the walking and then you have to compete, it can make it very difficult and painful for you as your legs are seizing up with cramps. Some of the cramping can be avoided, if this is a recurrent problem for you, by taking potassium. Some people eat lots of bananas and this seems to help. If you are still having trouble, you can get over-the-counter potassium tablets, which are potassium chloride. This is a variety of salt and it is important for keeping your lactic acid build-up at a minimum. You will be able to really feel the difference because when you get to the point where your legs would normally start cramping up, they will be able to go farther. Regular salt tablets are not as effective and are harder on your heart.

If you are a very nervous individual, you might consider using panto-thenic acid and the B vitamins to counteract the effects of competition-induced stress. They coat the nerve synapses and will literally aid the electrical impulse in making its jumps so that you remain calm. Sometimes avoiding all caffeine products helps, too. If you're feeling tired when you stop the caffeine, another vitamin, niacinamide, a variety of niacin, frequently will get your metabolism going and help with the tired feeling in the morning. It does not give you the rush of caffeine, but it also does not make your hands shake.

## Weather Conditions

Riding events tend to follow the football attitude of the event is on no matter what the weather. You, the rider, have to decide for yourself if the weather conditions are too miserable for you to go. If you have very muddy ground and you are a novice rider, you really should consider not taking your horse that day, even though you paid all that money to come to the competition and you spent so much effort to get to that stage. If you are eventing every three weeks or so, which is a normal novice schedule, losing one competition is not the end of the world.

If you go when the footing is very bad, it is hard for you to stand up, or it is raining so hard that the judges have the lights on in their car, your chances of being hurt are much greater and the chances of your having an absolutely miserable experience and not wanting to event again are excellent. In addition, your saddle turns to soup. You are riding a grease pit, and you cannot help your horse.

You need to consider that if it is below 32°F, ground conditions are going to change radically. You may have a greasy footing on top of frozen ground, which makes it difficult for the horse to get his hooves into it. If you do have a fall, you are more likely to get injured.

Likewise, if it is absolutely beastly hot, around 100°F, you and the horse are going to be highly stressed. If you had been practicing at 100°F, you and the horse were doing well with heat and you were wearing your safety helmet at the time, you can consider continuing on if you have built up your level of fitness. You need to be particularly aware of heat exhaustion for you and your horse.

## Cross-Country Warm-up

For the cross-country, you will want to warm up about fifteen minutes before you do the run. This will give you enough time to walk your horse from the trailer over to your starting area. Do some trotting, run the horse through the transitions, walk, trot, canter, and back down again. Make sure the brakes work and then go over a crossrail and a vertical to get him going forward and thinking in terms of jumping.

The jumps will be flagged and you will have to take them in the correct order or you will be eliminated. There is usually an official appointed to stand in the warm-up area to make sure everyone complies with the rules. The helpers may raise the fences to help their riders, but they cannot raise them beyond the height the horse is going to jump in competition. You won't be faced with any five-foot monsters as you are cantering down the line thinking you are going to be jumping something that is two and a half feet. If someone raises a fence higher than you can handle, you can ask them to lower it back down to something more appropriate. Frequently, you will end up with a person beside each fence raising or lowering the fence for each horse that is going over.

The warm-up area can be a real zoo, and that's why the rules of the road are so important to keep from getting hurt. When you are in the warm-up area, pay attention to what the people are doing around you, so you don't end up getting a horse astride your saddle that you hadn't planned on meeting.

### Riding the Cross-Country

When you have the horse up in the bridle, go over to the cross-country starting box and let them know you're ready to go. At your appointed time, they will give you a ten-second warning to get into the box, turn your horse around, start your stopwatch, and then go. You want the horse to be ready to move out of the box, but you don't want him to lunge out of control, and then have to fight for control down to your first fence. It is better to take a little extra time, since at this level you do have time, and start him gently at a trot down to his fence. You don't need to do any of the course at breakneck speed. You also have time to say thank you to the starter who started you. It will not eliminate you to be polite. Many people start their stopwatch at ten seconds before they begin so that they know whether the stopwatch is working before they actually go. This also makes it possible to have both hands on the reins for your start. You just need to remember when you are looking at your stopwatch that you have added on an extra ten seconds.

Many times at novice, people practice with their stopwatch, but they don't really need one to make it around the course because the course is so short and the time allowed is so great. Ideally, the organizer has placed a halfway point marker so that you can practice checking your watch at that time and see how you're doing and if you need to press on harder. This is a courtesy by the organizer and is not necessary at this level. It is seen usually at higher levels.

When calculating your strides as you are going cross-country, you need to remember that horses shorten their stride going uphill and lengthen their stride going downhill, so your fences will be organized to have two short strides if you're going up something rather than one long stride. And you as the rider need to plan on having your horse ride it with two short strides rather than one long stride for it to work out successfully. Also, if you are coming out of water to a fence, you can expect the horse to have very little impulsion to take the fence. All of his momentum will have been broken by the force of the water.

As you are riding the course, the three or four times you have spent in walking the course will hold you in good stead because subconsciously you will keep yourself on track while you're doing the actual adjustments your horse requires. It is very similar to dressage in that you are mentally working at two different levels at the same time: to keep the minor adjustments of your horse

Training level drop: this rider is having so much fun that he is going too fast for the obstacle. The speed and form is appropriate for a much bigger oxer on level ground. He will be fine on landing because the drop is small. His lower leg has dropped back, giving him a less secure position.

going at all times, and the subconscious requirements of making sure that you get to the right fence at the right time. Ideally, when you have walked the course, you have plotted exactly where you want the horse to go and you are looking up for that point so you can steer the horse to the fence without wobbling. All the training that you did on your gymnastic lines, looking ahead and over the fence at a point beyond the fence at eye height, will prove useful.

One of the important rules in cross-country is to keep your weight back. Do not try to be forward over your fences in a hunter ring style. If you are forward, you will look pretty all the way to the ground.

Riders have discovered, to their surprise, that if they become unseated on a small cross-country course, but still come down more or less on the horse, if they cling to the mane, they might be able to get themselves back in the saddle. This is much harder to do if you have applied Show Sheen to your horse's mane and neck. You can't keep contact because the hair becomes so slick. A fall on cross-country that is within the penalty zone of the jump will cost you sixty penalty points and thereby throw you out of competition. A rider will do anything to stay on for the required number of feet to get out of the penalty zone. It is when you are clinging to the side of your horse, trying not to touch the ground, that you really appreciate the time that you spent teaching him to lunge and his learning his voice commands, because a horse who is on voice command will slow down to a walk if you ask him and halt when you ask him. When you have cleared the penalty zone, you can then fall off, hop back on and continue. If he is on voice commands, you don't even have to wait to put your feet in the stirrups before you're under way again.

If you have been doing your work without stirrups in preparation, your leg muscles will be strong enough so that you will find you can actually jump without stirrups and not disturb your seat. Just plan on grabbing a large piece of mane halfway up the neck and holding on. This even works for bank fences where you jump up and jump off. As long as you are clear of the penalty zone, the only fault you will have will be for time rather than jump penalties. So you can have a fall and still place in the whole competition.

Try not to be distracted by the crowd or photographers. It is very tempting to wave and enjoy your friend's admiration. Usually, just after you've waved to your friend, grinned, and said "Hi," you discover you are on the wrong lead, make a turn, and your horse falls down. It is very embarrassing to have your horse fall when there isn't any jump in sight anywhere.

If you have a refusal at a fence, immediately circle your horse and take the fence again. Remember that you will need more impulsion, more bat, more leg, and your voice to encourage the horse forward. He is going to be in "stall" if left to his own desires. You have to make the jump more desirable than the consequences if he doesn't take it. Ideally, present him at a slightly different point than where he refused. It will make it much easier to get over the fence. If there is an easier option through the fence, take it. You have already lost all hope of having a place in the final pinnings. You might as well have a good learning experience out of it for you and the horse.

258

If the next horse on course is coming through, the fence judge will wave you aside and let the next horse go through. So don't be surprised if the fence judge speaks to you and asks you to move aside. You are allowed three tries at a fence. On failing the third one, you are eliminated.

You can frequently go back after they have gone through the cross-country phase of the competition and school your horse on course again to get him over that particular fence. If you do intend to school your horse, do not plan on doing it by yourself. Make sure you have at least two other friends along with you to provide encouragement and ideally someone you respect as an instructor to help you. Your horse is going to be recalcitrant about going over a fence he has already decided he doesn't need.

Make sure as you are coming up to the face of the fence that you are planning to jump that the segment is designated for you. Frequently, the little notes that are on the face of a wide fence will say that the flags are going to be moved and the face you are supposed to take is much narrower and a different place altogether than you had planned. So, look before you leap. You do not get bonus points for taking a harder face than the one that was designated for you.

If there are people in your path that are spectators, it is all right to yell at them rather than just running over them. Frequently, spectators at novice events don't know that they are in the pathway of the horse. If they are crossing in a spot where the fence judge has little control, you may find that you need to yell "Horse on course" to get their attention. This will not eliminate you.

When you are riding for the finish after your last fence, you do not need to speed up your horse. You will not be gaining enough time to make it worthwhile. It ruins the whole training exercise for your horse without gaining anything for you. Make sure that you do go through the finish flags. Frequently, novice riders are so relieved at having survived the course that they forget that they have to go through the flags.

## Cooling Out

After you have gone through the flags, bring your horse to a walk, slowly going through the gaits. Do not pull him up abruptly because he is more likely to injure himself. After he has pulled up, hop off and loosen the girth and start walking him. He will need the walking to help get his heart rate back to normal.

Your groom can take over at this point and put a halter over the bridle. As the horse is walking, you can run the stirrups up on both sides of the saddle and loosen the girth further if necessary. You also need to loosen his noseband, so he can breathe better. If the weather is cool, throw a cooler over him.

As he cools out, you can start offering him a sip of water every once in a while. You don't want him to drink a half bucket of water all at one time because he may develop colic. If you drag the sips out a bit, he will be fine.

As he cools out and his breathing becomes more normal, you can take the saddle and extra tack off and start washing him down with a camphorated body wash such as Vitrolin. This will dry his coat quite quickly and help with the cooling-out process. If the weather is at all cool, you can put an Airtex sheet, or a cooler, or a combination thereof, over him to help him cool out evenly so his muscles don't tie up.

Frequently, at the higher levels, you will find horses who run on cross-country with large quantities of grease down the fronts of their legs, both hind legs as well as front legs. This traditionally has been petroleum jelly, which is extremely difficult to get off. The theory behind the grease is that if your horse hits a fence, he will slide rather than cut himself. While it does make a difference, it is overkill for the small novice-level fences, so you probably don't need to bother with it. Some of the high-level event riders have experimented with water-soluble ointments. Your veterinarian can make a recommendation of some of the varieties of cow udder balm that are available. You can buy these in large-enough quantity that the expense is not so great.

To remove the grease is a long and painful process for horse and rider unless you use a water-soluble product. If at all possible, do not clean the petroleum jelly off with your own personal Turkish towels as they will do a real job on your washing machine. It takes many washing cycles to get the petroleum jelly out. So for days afterward, you are going to have petroleum jelly in all your clothes. A commercial laundry may be the answer here.

If you use galloping boots and bell boots on cross-country, you will want to take them off and rinse them clean and rinse the horse's legs off to get all the dirt and grit out of his hair to keep it from rubbing when he gets ready to do stadium. All of his tack is going to need a quick once-over-lightly to get it tidy enough to go into stadium. Riders will frequently use Horseman's One-Step Cleaner and Dressing for this particular purpose. The Tanner saddle soap will also do a quick job. If you can come up with two pairs of riding boots for yourself, it will also cut down on some of your time spent getting ready for stadium as well. If you have used a silicone base with your mink oil or shoe polish, it will be easier to get the boots back up to competition shine in short order with a buffing cloth.

Have someone keep an eye on your scoring for cross-country. If you should disagree with the way you were scored, you can file a protest, if need be. There is a charge for filing protests and filing a protest is a serious matter.

### Walking Stadium

While your groom is cooling your horse off and tidying up your tack, you need to go over and walk the stadium course. This will probably need walking at least three or four times, too. Ideally, you would like to watch other horses go before you ride it to make sure the lines that you have decided upon will work. Again, since you have time, give yourself as much space as you need to make nice curves into your fences. Use your twenty-meter circle arc or large segments to make your turns, so that your horse arrives balanced and with at least three straight strides before each of the fences he needs to take. You should find out where the judges are going to be for the salute, and you also need to know where your start and finish flags are.

Be sure to notice where the perimeters of your stadium jumping area are. Occasionally, some good-hearted soul will take the tapes down, and if you go through the area where the tape was, you are still eliminated for leaving the arena, even though you didn't see the tape. Occasionally, judges will take pity on you and will explain what went wrong and perhaps not eliminate you. Anywhere above novice level, you will be eliminated as knowing the rules better.

## Order of Start

Since you usually know what time you're going to go dressage and cross-country, you have your day fairly well mapped out. With stadium at the lower levels, the horses can either go in numerical order as they do in dressage or they can go in reverse order of standing. For each event, you need to ask the organizers which way they are going to run the stadium order so that you can allow the right amount of time to warm up. Occasionally, if it is a very busy event and the riders are riding at many different levels, you will have horses that will go out of order. This is because they are needed somewhere else at the time they are supposed to do stadium or a person has two horses in the same division.

One of the nightmares of event riders is that they will be so tightly scheduled that while they are riding one division, they will be called to ride in another. This particular nightmare actually does happen on occasion. The way to solve the problem is to talk to the official in charge of stadium and tell him that you suspect that you will have a conflict. They will reschedule your stadium run so that you are not eliminated for not showing up at the right time because you are on cross-country. The officials are not going to be upset with you for asking for a change in order of go, so don't feel shy about asking if you think you need it.

## Food and Energy

Also remember to factor in time for eating. Lunch or snacks help immensely in keeping your blood sugar level up, which you need to turn in your maximum competitive performance. Most riders have an electrolyte-base drink or some suitable calorie-laden drink. They also will have protein-carbohydrate food to eat. Never assume that food will be available at a competition through the auspices of the auxiliary. Frequently, the organizers have trouble getting someone to come in and cook for the occasion. Also, you might have such constraints on your time that you won't have time to go over and wait in line. Generally speaking, it is much easier for you to have your own picnic basket with the things that you like that give you energy.

You also need to remember that after the competition is over and the adrenaline level finally drops, you are going to be more tired than usual because you have used up so much energy. Adrenaline is wonderful, when it is working. When you come off an adrenaline high, you really feel the drop. It is a good idea to have a cup of coffee or tea to keep you from falling asleep on the way home. You will find that you will be very tired that night and will be anxious to sleep as much as possible.

### Stadium Jumping Warm-up

Plan on getting on your horse about ten horses ahead of you in the order of start.

For your warm-up for stadium jumping, you will want to be stretching your horse back out again at a walk. You will use a warm-up ritual similar to the one that you use for dressage. You will want to do shoulder-in, serpentines, and some lateral work to have the horse limbered side to side. Work through your transitions so that he is in tune with your shifting his gears.

Once you have all the muscles stretched out, you can take him over a few small fences so that he knows that he is going to be jumping. You would use a crossrail, and then a vertical, and then an oxer. As soon as he does it right, you don't need to jump him anymore. Do not wear your horse out before the testing stadium course. He is going to be more tired than usual because he has done so much in one day. So you will need to conserve your horse to a certain extent. As soon as you have what you want, up in the bridle, paying attention, has jumped correctly over the little fences, you can pull him up and go back to walking again to keep his muscles stretched. Ideally, you will be keeping an eye on the order of go in the ring and how the horses are jumping the fences. Particularly observe if a large or small circle segment to a fence works better, if two short strides ride better than one long stride. When riding, remember that if there is a bounce, come in slowly enough so that the horse lands in the correct place. If there are any particularly difficult turns that you need to think about, turn your head while you are in the air over the jump to make sure the horse lands on the correct lead. If the arena seems very cramped, you will need to have the horse more on your hand and leg, using as much impulsion and collection as you can muster, so that he has lots of rpms coming into the jumps but doesn't have much in the way of speed. He is much less likely to quit in front of a fence if you have kept him rocked on his hindquarters and moving forward than he is if allowed to go on his forehand. Also, notice how fast the riders who seem to have smooth rounds are going. The stadium can be ridden so that it looks terribly easy, smooth and flowing, a little like a ballet, or it can look very choppy. Try to emulate the smoothness. See what the riders are doing and try to copy them.

### The Stadium Test

When you first come into the arena, you will have to pull up and salute the judge. Since you will be wearing a safety helmet, you won't have remove

Do not forget to have a snug throat latch on your bridle. This rider had a fall and took the bridle with him. His horse promptly left, preferring the middle on the in-use dressage arena. After a quick pas-de-deux, he then headed for the trailers, eliminating the rider's hopes of completing the test.

your hat; you just tip your head and drop your hand. Your horse will probably be bouncing a bit because you have him up in the bridle. You do not need a perfectly still dressage halt to make your salute. Then plan your circle to start your canter well back from the starting flags. Ideally, you want to give your horse a chance to look at all of the fences before he has to jump any of them, so he has a chance to look at the lay of the land. He will understand what is being asked of him after your first time on a course and will be keen to move on. After you have completed the course, you will need to bring him down to a walk before leaving the arena. While you can go galloping out of the arena, this is very dangerous. It is much better form to have your horse under control before you leave. Don't forget to go through the finish flags at the end of the course.

Frequently, it takes awhile for the scores to be posted. If you think you have a chance of placing in the top ten, then keep your horse saddled unless the stadium officials have told you they do not expect to have you riding back into the arena to receive your ribbons. This is a matter of preference by the organizers as to whether they make a presentation ceremony where you are on your horse or if they just pass the ribbons out to you at some other location.

Remember that you need to turn in your competition penny and bridle number at the end of the competition. When you do this, you will receive a copy of your dressage scores. Most dressage judges are very helpful in their comments and will make suggestions at the bottom of the sheet about things you can work on to improve your ride. If you have any questions, it is permissible to go up to the dressage judge and ask specifically about your ride. You will find that dressage judges can frequently be a big help to you in understanding whatever your particular problems are. They may suggest some alternatives on how to correct those sections of your ride.

Occasionally, you will develop very strong friendships with the judges and some of them do teach as well. If you are a student of a dressage judge, you cannot ride underneath that judge for points. You would have to go *hors concours,* which means you are not in the competition to place. You are just there for the experience. For this reason, in the *Omnibus Schedule,* the organizers will name all of the judges, so you know ahead of time what you need to do. The eventing community works very hard to keep things as honest as possible. This is one of the ways to keep from having an unfair situation.

It is not at all unusual at your first competition or so to make sufficient mistakes to have been eliminated four or five times by the end of the competition. You will find all of the technical staff, the judges and the fence judges and the warm-up judge, will explain whatever the mistake was and how to correct it and encourage you to come back and try again. The whole purpose of the novice level is to encourage you.

One of the purposes of the novice-level event, other than to encourage, is to give you positive feedback about the areas you can improve in. You are riding against yourself at your own level of education in horsemanship rather than riding against other competitors. It is a subtle difference and means there

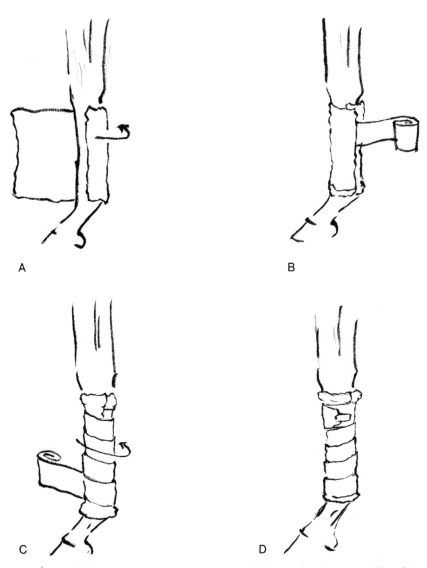

A

B

C

D

Wrapping an exercise or standing bandage: A) use a thick layer of cotton wrapped from front to back, inside to outside. The cotton should go from knee to fetlock; B) previously, roll the bandage inside out, end to beginning with slight equal tension. Start the wrap near the top of the cotton and wrap front to back, inside the leg to outside the leg. Take the bandage first up to the top of the cotton leaving a one-inch border, then wrap down the leg. You want a 50 percent overlap; C) once you reach the bottom of the leg, start back up; D) you should finish with the wrap midway to the top of the leg. If the bandage comes out in the wrong place and you are using pins to secure it, you can fold the excess bandage under itself. This creates the ideal length so that the bandage can be pinned on the outside of the leg behind the bone. Place masking tape over the pins to keep the horse from removing the bandage. Bandages will slip if they are put on too loose or get wet. If they do slip, they need to be adjusted immediately or they injure the horse.

is tremendous camaraderie among the riders. Everyone is facing the course rather than each other. Frequently, riders will develop very strong friendships. They will help each other out at competitions and pass on the tips that they have learned worked for them. If they are very good friends and you discover you have forgotten your tack somewhere along the line, they will frequently bail you out. If you borrow someone's equipment, be sure to return it immediately—they will be needing it again in the near future.

## Preparations for Shipping

After stadium, you can cool your horse out and wrap his legs. Many riders will use either an alcohol-base rub on their horse's legs or a liniment to ease the tendons. Horses frequently have their legs wrapped for the trip home, even if you normally do not wrap your horse's legs for shipping, because of the strain he's had. It is more of a preventive medicine. If it is a long way home, frequently the riders will use a poultice rather than an alcohol-base rub.

There are many rubs on the market. A few of the brand names are Bigeloil and Absorbine. If they seem too strong for your horse, you can cut them in half with alcohol to make them milder on the horse's skin. Again, this is something you can experiment with before you get to the competition.

Your vet can show you how to wrap a horse's leg properly. It is very similar to wrapping an elastic bandage on a person, except that you use a thick layer of cotton between the bandage and the horse's leg to minimize the chances of pulling the tendons and the blood vessels out of position and actually making the whole situation a great deal worse. Wrapping a horse's legs requires a great deal of practice with an expert eye watching you. Most veterinarians are very happy to help you learn how to do this.

Also, there are several schools of thought on how to keep the bandage in place. The new bandages use Velcro, which works out beautifully, as long as you organize the bandage to end where the Velcro pieces can touch. Before the advent of Velcro, you had to use two large bandage pins per leg with the points going away from the front of the horse, toward his rear, on the outside of the leg. These were then covered with pieces of tape, usually masking tape, but almost any strong adhering tape will do. Scotch tape does not have sufficient adhesion to work. Some riders don't like using even the pins and instead will use the masking tape around the leg. Since masking tape breaks easily, it requires closer supervision than using the pin method.

A poultice is more drawing for the legs and is the next step up in care from an alcohol rub. This is applied by an upward motion of the hand, putting the poultice against the grain of the hairs of the leg. Poultice resembles clay and reminds you of your first-grade modeling class. If you treat it the same as you did in first grade, by adding water to make it more slippery, it is easier to work with, and you will find that you are less frustrated. It is very messy to work with. You cannot use a poultice on any cuts, unless you have gotten a special kind from the veterinarian, which is designed to go over cuts. The

Poultice: the thick claylike mixture draws the swelling and helps to keep the legs tight after a stressful day.

Wrapping legs: while the groom on the right is using a standard-length cotton, the one on the left is improvising with a longer, thicker shipping cotton. She has pulled it up around the knee to match the other wrap. Normally, the shipping cotton would cover the whole pastern and the top of the hoof to the cornet band.

clay base will more likely infect a cut than help a situation. Solidly cover the tendon area, most of the way around the leg between the knee and the fetlock.

You then take a little piece of Saran Wrap just large enough to close over itself to cover the poultice. You don't want a piece so long that it actually acts as a wrap that would go all the way around the tendon with the excess. The reason for this is that the Saran Wrap can twist and you don't want to hurt the tendon inadvertently by having uneven pressure. After the Saran Wrap is in place, it will protect your cottons from the poultice, as well as keep the drawing powers of the poultice working longer because the poultice won't dry out as quickly. After the Saran Wrap, you then wrap with your cottons and with your regular bandage. You will find other riders at the competition working with this and you can observe them and learn how to do it.

Poultice is very hard to take off as well. Generally speaking, a high-pressure water hose does wonders for removing it. Unfortunately, at many competitions where you are in temporary stabling, you have no water pressure. You need to allow forty-five minutes to get the stuff off the legs. It is almost as difficult to remove as petroleum jelly.

### Looking Forward

Most horses are comfortable competing every three weeks. That gives you a week to regroup and two weeks to grow between competitions. It gives you a chance to assimilate the lessons you learned from the previous event.

When you feel that you have learned as much as you can from the novice level, you can move up to the training level. Each of the stair-steps of eventing is carefully planned to give horse and rider the best possible chance to learn new skills in a safe fashion. You will find certain riders you admire for their organizational skills, the way that they can turn a horse out to perfection and ride it well. They consistently will be winning or placing. If you ask them, they usually will teach and pass on their knowledge.

As you get to the higher levels, having a competent instructor gets more and more important. Virtually no one makes it to the middle levels of eventing without having outside instruction from a very knowledgeable person in this field. Frequently, older riders have more experience to draw on to help you. One does not need to be an Olympic-level rider in order to teach well. Someone who has ridden to high levels previously and is now bringing along younger horses or younger riders will frequently have more observations to make that may be of use to you.

Choosing an instructor is like any other partnership. The personalities of student and instructor have to meld together to get the maximum out of the relationship. If you are uncomfortable with the style that your instructor is using, find another instructor. You do not have to do something that makes you feel uncomfortable. Frequently, having a number of instruction opportunities with different people, such as clinics, will help. It gives you many different viewpoints on how to correct the problems that you are working on.

# Radnor Preliminary and Young Rider
## Cross-Country Obstacles

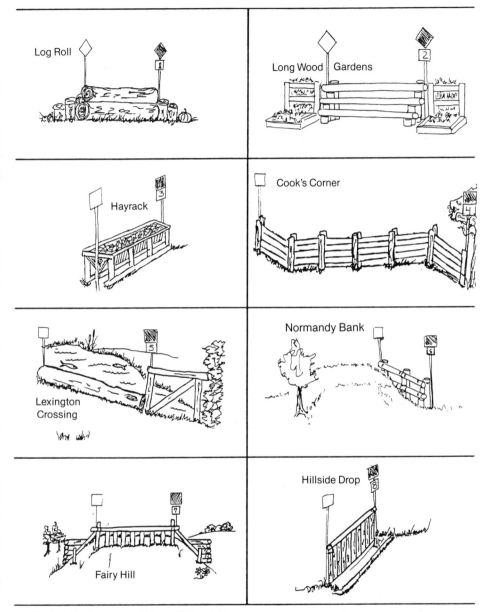

Log Roll

Long Wood Gardens

Hayrack

Cook's Corner

Lexington Crossing

Normandy Bank

Fairy Hill

Hillside Drop

Radnor Preliminary and Young Riders 3-Day cross country course. As you move up levels, the course becomes more complex. The course is designed to put the easiest obstacles at the beginning and the end, with the most difficult in the middle. Still inviting to the horse, there are more options.

# Radnor Preliminary and Young Rider
## Cross-Country Obstacles

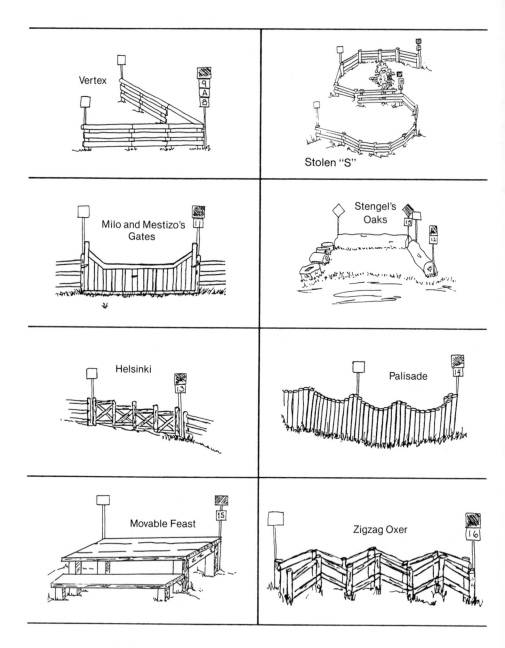

Vertex

Stolen "S"

Milo and Mestizo's Gates

Stengel's Oaks

Helsinki

Palisade

Movable Feast

Zigzag Oxer

# Radnor Preliminary and Young Rider
## Cross-Country Obstacles

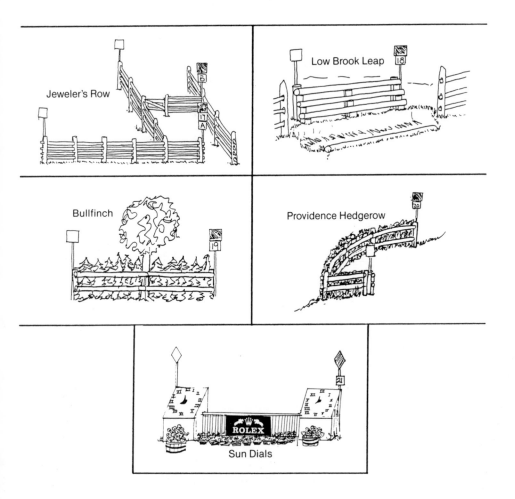

Jeweler's Row

Low Brook Leap

Bullfinch

Providence Hedgerow

Sun Dials

If you decide that you like eventing enough that you want to run several horses at the same competition, you need to be careful not to confuse your courses and tests, thereby eliminating yourself for riding the wrong one. This is frequently the nemesis of the high-level riders who are teaching students. When you first start riding several horses, try to keep them all at the same level until you adjust to the added pressures. Training-level cross-country courses are similar in height and degree of difficulty to fox hunting. It is a very easy schedule to fox hunt all winter, pick up eventing in the spring and fall, and then do some dressage and horse showing in the summer. Your horse can go all year round and be getting fitter, as will you.

# 14

# Upper-Level Eventing, International Competition, and the Olympics

---

$\mathbf{F}$REQUENTLY, lower-level riders are interested in what lies ahead if they decide to go up the skill ladder levels in eventing. When one reaches the preliminary level, a whole new order of magnitude of riding experience comes into play in that you now have a choice between riding in a one-day horse trial and riding in a three-day. A one-day horse trial does not require as versatile and clever a horse, nor the same degree of endurance and fitness work that a three-day will. Many horses can handle preliminary one-day horse trials. The one-day format does not severely stress them and it can be very enjoyable without having to go out and purchase a new horse.

## THE THREE-DAY EVENT

A three-day requires that the horse and rider make a much greater commitment to the amount of time spent on horseback and getting the horse fit.

The advanced level oxer massif. This fence requires galloping on speed and half halts to free the forehand for lift-off. This rider has a powerful position. Her leg is right where it should be and supports the horse. Her hand position maintains contact. She is using a bridge, since there is a substantial dip on the landing side. With her parallel back, she could be riding show jumpers. Bea Perkins, USCTA team rider at the Blue Ridge Selection Trials.

## Event Scheduling

Also, the higher the level at which the horse is being competed, the fewer times per year he can go out because of the maintenance of that level of fitness. So if you are going intermediate, you may only go three or four times a season with a three-day at the end of the spring, and a three-day at the end of the fall season, so your horse will have very little total time off. Whereas a horse at the low levels can go many, many times per season for the experience because the fences are smaller and the level of fitness required is less. It is similar to the marathon runners who routinely will do five miles as their warm-up, but rarely will do twenty-four miles or more on a regular basis.

At this level, one starts using interval training seriously to be sure that the horse has been properly stressed and built up for the endurance phases. His gallop times change from just the four-minute, 450-meters-per-minute gallop into working up into higher speeds, and the rider needs to be able to do more intricate dressage work, including extension and some collection. The steeplechase phase is new at this level; it will be the first time the rider and horse will go at a high speed over hurdle fences. It requires having a groom to help you in the vet box for the ten-minute break. There is too much to do for just the rider to be able to refresh the horse enough to go back out on course. The rider needs the ten minutes in the vet box to rest and regroup himself.

Three-day event riding is exhilarating; it is a whole new adrenaline high. It requires more commitment but gives more back, too. One of the fun things about eventing in a three-day is that people come in from other countries and other parts of the United States to ride in them. Several competitors' parties will give you a chance to get to know the other competitors. In addition, some of the events such as the Lexington Horse Trials, which have been sponsored by Rolex, are on television, and it is great fun that evening to watch yourself on TV if you have had a good go.

A three-day is the culmination of an entire year's worth of work. If you want your horse to do well in a three-day, it takes a managed program over the previous year to build the level of fitness and experience.

At preliminary, you start to get fences that are complicated, and that have multiple options. The amount of leeway for the different lines through the combination fences will be six inches or so, as opposed to the entire face of the fence being jumpable. For a particular line, you will have a much smaller safe passage for each of the options. Bounces will be used on cross-country and also in stadium. Frequently, in stadium, you will have a triple fence that will be a bounce to a one-stride. These may be set on uneven ground and you will have to be able to collect the horse or extend the horse's stride to compensate for the undulation in the ground.

Also, at this stage, you will get more difficult fences. There may be a vertical before a drop, a vertical before or after a water fence. Occasionally, you will have a big drop at the water, a couple of strides out and over a fence.

A preliminary one-day can be done without a groom, although it is exhausting for the rider. A preliminary three-day should not be attempted without extra ground support.

### Order of Start

Frequently, people have preferences as to where in the order of start that they would ideally like to go. Some riders prefer going very late in their divisions so they can watch other horses. Other riders feel that their chances of having better footing is best if they go first, and they pray that they have analyzed the course correctly.

One of the things that sometimes influences your order of start is the name of your horse, because frequently the organizers will go in alphabetical order. If you name your horse Arzab, you can almost be certain that you will always be the first horse on course. If you name your horse Zeus, more than likely you will be the last horse. Often, when one has a sponsor, the sponsor will ask to have the horse named for the sponsor or the sponsor's product. You will run across horses that are named Sony—whatever the horse's real name is, such as Sony Pegasus. If you have a sponsor whose name does not fall in the section of the alphabet you wish to ride, you can always reverse it and have it be Pegasus Sony. The USCTA publishes every year the list of horses and their grades. You can see what names are currently popular so that you don't end up being the fifteenth with the same name for your horse. This can lead to confusion if the other riders are in your area and are likely to be riding the same competitions that you are.

Going from the lower levels of novice and training to preliminary is a new order of magnitude. At preliminary, there is so much new information that one needs to absorb that it is difficult to do well without having instruction. But by the time you reach preliminary, you usually have zeroed in on who would make a good instructor for you.

### The Three-Day Horse

A preliminary three-day horse needs to be bold; he needs to want to attack his fences aggressively but wisely. At this point, you start to realize how much brain power your horse has in deciding how to work his way through a maze. It is also at preliminary you discover if he is athletic and has the discipline to be able to switch from each of the three disciplines.

Usually, it is at preliminary three-day that you discover that the horses placing are all or partially Thoroughbred. Many event horses are three-quarter breds and have tremendous jumping ability. They need to be clever in their jumping and able to bring their knees up and out of the way if they get in tight to a problem fence. You also need a horse who has a ground-covering, long, easy, fluid stride to make your gallop times. This is where the Thoroughbred cross comes in. He needs to be energy-efficient for maintaining a gallop without exhausting himself and be able to have sufficient energy level that he can draw from within himself for multiple fences and other exertions from the obstacles.

It is at preliminary three-day that you will be covering a great deal more ground at higher speeds than you normally do. With the addition of steeplechase and the two road and track phases, by the third day you will be riding a more tired horse than you are used to. You, yourself, need to have a fitness program during your year of preparation so that you have sufficient strength and energy on the last day to compensate for your horse's tiredness. It is much more difficult to ride a tired horse, because he is less willing to leave the ground. He tends to get in a little closer to his fences or to flatten in his jumping style. Sometimes he will try to throw himself over his fences rather than be careful. Your horse is more likely to make errors in judgment and rely upon you for more precise information than he normally does.

## The Training Schedule

When you start to go preliminary or higher-level, you will need to increase your training schedule. Most riders start as soon as the weather breaks in the winter. Frequently, the horses will have either December or January off, depending upon the weather conditions of the area. In late January and early February, they will start their walking out, stretching exercises, and gradually build up to working hills at a walk in the proper frame and at trotting. Your base for fitness is your walking and trotting work, not lots of galloping. The galloping tends to shorten a horse's tendons, and if they are not sufficiently stretched by the walking and trotting, you are more likely to have a bowed tendon early on and lose the whole season.

## Interval Training

One can get a horse advanced-level fit with a walk/trot program and only touching on the gallops the last week before you go to your competition. Most riders want to throw gallops in their schedule so that they themselves can tune in to their internal clocks to make sure that they are going the right speed for the different distances. There are several ways of developing fitness.

One of the methods that is used by the American teams is interval training, which starts with timed trots that are five minutes long, separated by three-minute walk intervals. Gradually, you increase the length of the trot time but keep the three-minute interval. You watch the horse's flank to see how many respirations per minute he has at the end of the stress period for the trot, and he should come back quickly to his regular breathing pattern for a walk within that three minutes.

The five-minute trots will help you stretch out your legs, if instead of posting at the trot, you use the half seat and practice stretching your legs down. The half seat is very similar to gallop position and can be interchangeable with gallop position. It is hard to maintain at the trot until your legs strengthen.

When doing your dressage work after the horse has been in work for a month, you can start sitting your trots without stirrups. This exercise you need to wait to start until the horse's back is flexible and swinging and he is in the proper frame. If you try to do it before he has stretched his back muscles and is going in the proper frame, both of you will be miserable and it will be an unsuccessful use of the time.

With the interval training in the trot work, you can increase the strenuousness of the exercise by using hills, trotting up and down in frame, rather than increasing speed. Some advanced riders have worked their way up to an hour and a half at a trot to build sufficient fitness for a three-day very successfully. They have added their gallop work only in the last two weeks before the competition. As a result, the horses have pulled with enthusiasm on roads and tracks and come into the vet box refreshed rather than tired.

When doing the interval training of the gallop work, you use the same methodology of doing your trot work first, after fifteen minutes of stretching out at a walk. When you start your gallop work, you will be going very slowly in gallop position, starting at 350 meters per minute, which is really a canter, working your way up to 400 meters per minute, which is a very slow hand gallop. Usually, you start with a four-minute gallop with a three-minute walk interval in between and you do three of these. Ideally, you want to do these on hills so that you get the maximum amount of breathing and fitness in with the minimum amount of speed.

The week before your competition, you can start with the 400 meters per minute on your first gallop, slide your way up to 450 meters per minute on your second gallop, and do your third sliding up and touching 520 meters per minute and sliding back down again. You want to have enough time working at gallop that you understand the pace you need to maintain.

When you stop the horse after each of the gallops, you want slowly to bring him down the gears, rather than stop him abruptly, because it is easier on his legs and his breathing. When he has come down to a walk, you can hop off, circle him around you at a walk, and then make him stand briefly while you take his respiration rate. You can do this by looking at his flank and keeping a stopwatch running for fifteen seconds. He should be no higher than twenty-two breaths in fifteen seconds. After you start walking him out, at five minutes, his breathing rate will be slightly more elevated than it was at the end of the gallop. Then, at ten minutes, his breathing should be back down into normal range again. You need to check the breathing every time you do a gallop to make sure that he is not being overstressed, and as the horse becomes fitter, his breathing rate will drop dramatically anywhere between five and ten breaths in the fifteen-second time frame.

### Computer Use in Training

Another way of checking on the fitness of your horse so that you don't overstress him is using the portable on-board computers that have been used by other sports. These are now becoming available through veterinarian supply houses. Frequently, endurance riding aficionados have used them. These have electrodes that go under the saddle in the hollow of the horse's withers and in the midline in the girth on his chest and give you a feedback on computer of how many heartbeats per minute the horse has. The computer can be set so that it has high and low parameters. If you stress your horse too much, an alarm will go off and if you haven't stressed him sufficiently, an alarm will go off. The computer itself is worn on your thigh or hip, hanging from a belt. Endurance riders use them a lot because of the accuracy. Ideally, you can learn pace and the amount of effort for your horse to do things, and then apply the knowledge that you gained in training actually to being out in competition. The computer will also give you a feedback. If, for instance, you are doing a combination fence, it will report the horse's heartbeat in the effort getting over the fence, and that of getting over the other elements of the fence. You will find that the stress level of jumping the obstacles makes very large peaks in the readout.

### Dressage

The dressage test requires extension and the beginnings of collection plus some lateral work. You will be using all of the new dressage movements either in your stadium jumping or in the cross-country in order to get around the course safely. At preliminary, the accuracy of the movement begins to become a dividing point on the placing of the riders. It becomes more important that the lines be very straight and that there is depth to the corners instead of a shallow curve. The horse's frame tightens with collection and greater flexion. The lateral work is usually shoulder-in.

It is difficult to ride a dressage test properly from this level on up without having a ground person help you to make sure that your geometric shapes are as accurate as possible. Since the figures become smaller and quicker with less transition time, the test requires greater memorization, and you don't have as much regroup time if you have an error. You learn to creep your hands down the reins to keep a constant contact, especially coming from the walk into a collected trot.

Because of the added difficulty of the dressage and jumping tests, most riders change their saddles from an all-purpose saddle to a pure dressage and jumping saddle. Because the positions are so much easier to maintain, other riders frequently find a large increase in their good marks in the dressage just from the change in saddle. Frequently, there is about a fifteen-point difference in overall scores.

At the low levels, whoever does well in dressage tends to hold the lead all the way through the competition. This becomes less and less true at the higher levels, where jumping tests become more important. By the time you reach preliminary three-day, cross-country and endurance phases usually change all of the placings from the dressage. If you have a very good cross-country horse, you can improve your overall placing through your jumping. As long as you are within the top ten in placing at the dressage, you will have

# Radnor CCA and Intermediate
## Cross-Country Obstacles

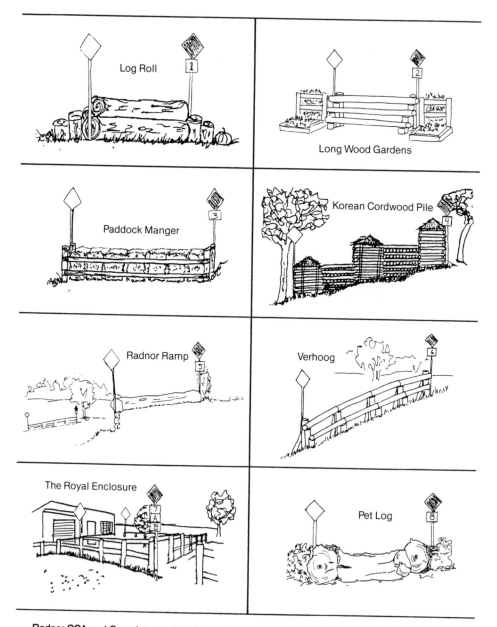

Log Roll 1

Long Wood Gardens 2

Paddock Manger 3

Korean Cordwood Pile 4

Radnor Ramp 5

Verhoog 6

The Royal Enclosure 7 A B

Pet Log 8

Radnor CCA and Open Intermediate Championship course: a CCA is an international FEI designation. Individual riders from other countries compete as well as Americans. The course is very big with many options. Many of the locations of obstacles are difficult.

# Radnor CCA and Intermediate
## Cross-Country Obstacles

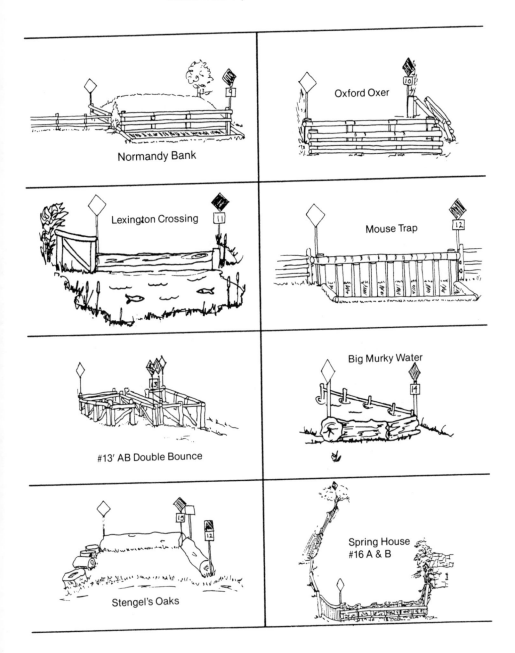

Normandy Bank

Oxford Oxer

Lexington Crossing

Mouse Trap

#13' AB Double Bounce

Big Murky Water

Stengel's Oaks

Spring House
#16 A & B

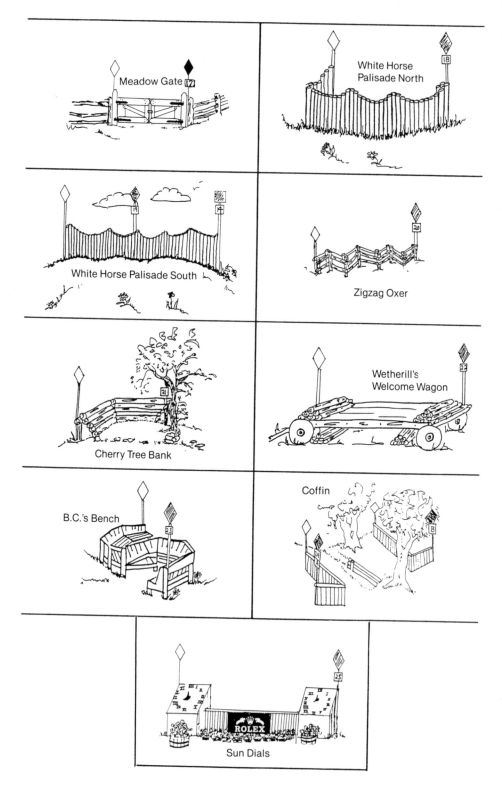

Meadow Gate

White Horse Palisade North

White Horse Palisade South

Zigzag Oxer

Cherry Tree Bank

Wetherill's Welcome Wagon

B.C.'s Bench

Coffin

Sun Dials

an excellent chance of placing much farther up by the end of the competition. As a result, event riders tend to first look at the horse's jumping ability rather than its dressage. They feel that they can perfect the dressage test, but they can't make the horse jump the fences if he is not inclined to do so on his own, and does not have the athletic aptitude and brains to be able to figure out the combinations that are presented to him.

## Analyzing the Cross-Country

The accuracy that you are striving for in dressage comes through for you in the jumping. It makes possible very precise lines through your fences and enhanced attentiveness from your horse.

Frequently, at the higher levels, the fences are set with odd ground lines and distances between fences, which makes it much more difficult to organize the horse between fences. From intermediate on, the distances between the fences are not true and frequently require tremendous finesse to have your horse in the right frame to safely get over the fence. You will find on the cross-country that there will be a variety of jumps that require that you come in on short strides or downshift to a trot to work your way through the maze. Then there will be other fences that require that you extend the stride and come in with a rolling gallop. Often the tightness of the turns that are used reflect the dressage training that you have done. If your horse is really awful at dressage, he will probably be really awful on the jumping because he is not paying attention to you in either place. The obedience becomes critical at the higher levels, yet you still need to maintain the willingness to go forward, on which you are also graded in the dressage.

As you go up in the levels, not only do you continue to walk all of your courses three or four times, but then you normally have to spend time with a fence to analyze all of the possible ways of taking that obstacle and compare which way you think that your horse will go through it best. Frequently, you will find riders who just sit beside a fence for a while and think through all of the different patterns. If a fence is really bothering you, then try to watch some horses over that particular fence or send out a delegate for you to watch it and then report back to you before your turn to ride. Often, your observer can tell you if the footing of one side of the fence is getting too chewed up to use, if holes have developed in a water fence, if the side is breaking away from a bank fence, or what the best option is. He can also let you know at what speed to come to the obstacle and whether the horses are taking it with short, choppy strides and how many, or whether they have gone for more speed and an extended stride.

## Relief from Heat

When competing in hot weather, one of the extra benefits that you can provide for your horse is some relief from the heat. If you are in a stable that has any electrical power at all, you can place a fan on his stall, gate, or wall to get some air flow. This gives him the choice of being in the breeze. If the barn itself is extremely hot, you may have problems with getting his temperature down before you will even start on cross-country. It is advisable to bring the horse out much earlier than you would normally before cross-country to cool him off, drop his heart rate, and adjust to the cooler temperature outside the barn before you expect him to run a cross-country course. Occasionally, you will find horses that are spun out of competition by the veterinarians before they even start cross-country, because the weather is too hot for them and they have already started having heat-related problems.

At this level, your horse also will be in need of electrolyte supplement in either his water or his feed. These dissolve easily in water but frequently horses do not like the flavor. It takes several days prior to a competition to have the horse adjusted to drinking the electrolyte-flavored water. If you have trouble getting the amount of water into him that you normally would, not to mention the greater amount that you need after cross-country, you may want to consider putting the electrolytes on top of his feed. It will be very salty and will help him develop an interest in drinking. If worse comes to worst, you can have a veterinarian help you with giving him a drench after cross-country. This is a last-resort suggestion. You can tell if your horse is dehydrated if you pinch the skin on the neck and it doesn't go back immediately, but instead stays in a little lump before it settles out.

Frequently, the horses need to have their grain levels raised and blood work done to make sure that they are not anemic from the extra work pressures. Their blood chemistry changes as they get fitter. Periodically, you need to have it checked by a vet to make sure you don't need to give a tonic with extra B vitamins and supplements. Many riders swear by $B_{12}$ and other B vitamins to put the pizzazz back in the attitude.

The morning of cross-country, often the horses are given a much lighter feed than usual and then are drawn without hay or grain before a competition so that they are not trying to digest a large quantity of feed while they are galloping around the course. Frequently, you will find horses who have muzzles on just before a cross-country to keep them from eating.

## Carrying Weights

At the three-day level, riders need sufficient weight to be 165 pounds for the jumping tests. For the lighter riders, this means using a weight pad. Ideally, your weight pad will be divided into three pockets per side. The pockets that are in front of the saddle place the weight over the horse's shoulders and can take two-thirds of the weight; the pocket behind the saddle can take one-third. Weight pads are tricky to use and they are very hard to put onto the horse if you are small and light. This is one situation where having some extra help makes a big difference. Read the rules and regulations to make sure you are not exempt from weight requirements. Juniors do not need to carry weight; and in some competitions, other riders do not need to carry weight.

If you are buying weights, frequently used are lead sheets that you can get from a plumber's supply house. The plumber will be happy to cut the sheets into the shapes that you need for your saddle pad if you bring your saddle pad to him. You also need to find a very good scale. Stand on it with all of your riding clothes and saddle and weight pads to make sure that you have the right amount of weights that you are taking with you to the competition.

Many is the rider who has taken all of his gear and his riding clothes over to his doctor's office to stand on his scales, since doctors' scales are probably more accurate than the scale you would find at home. The riders also make a point of checking on the scales on course before they tack their horses up the morning of the competition to make sure that the new scales do not have a different weight from the scales they have practiced with. Frequently, there will be a two- to three-pound adjustment from scale to scale.

In addition, you should bring extra weights with you in case you have lost more weight just before or during cross-country. The combined training rules reflect awareness of changes in weight on course. They have a compensation in that you are allowed to use your horse's bridle to make up a little bit more weight if you are desperate. A heavy cross-country bit helps a great deal to bring you into the correct weight.

You will have to drop your bat before being weighed in. No one is allowed to touch your horse until after you have completed the weighing-in. The course organizer will have a designated person to hold your horse, and to help you get your tack off for the weighing-in. Your groom is not allowed to touch your horse until the official person has released the horse to him or her.

Before you ride in a three-day, you will have ample opportunity to go to some three-days, either as pit crew for a friend who is riding, or as an observer. Take advantage of these opportunities to learn so that you can organize your own pit crew when the time comes. Most riders will try to have at least two to three people helping at the vet box.

One of those people might also be at the end of steeplechase to give a quick wash to the horse, a drink to the rider, and check all the shoes as the horse is walking away from the steeplechase. If a shoe is missing, an "Easy-boot" can be popped on so the horse doesn't stone bruise or tear his hoof wall further. The helper then races back to the vet box to arrange for a farrier to put a replacement shoe on during the ten-minute break. Some riders actually come to a complete halt for a short period of time to get all of this accomplished. Many horses like having a sponge full of water to rinse their mouths out after steeplechase.

If you have done a lot of trot work, especially on hills, you will find that your horse will pull on the second roads and tracks and will come in in good shape for your ten-minute break and veterinarian inspection.

## The Ten-Minute Break and the Vet Box

Plan to come early into the vet box. An extra minute makes a big difference. If you are very lucky, there will be a few hold-ups on course and

Analyzing fences is critical to success. Frequently, the riders will visit a fence four or five times and spend time with it if they are worried. The author contemplating an intermediate-level water-filled ditch and wall.

you can find out which fences are riding badly and what sections of fences ride better than others, in addition to having a little extra time. In the vet box, the rider's responsibilities ideally should be to refresh himself, drink an electrolyte or something similar, and to gather information from other riders, while keeping an eye on how his horse is progressing. Frequently, the horses will tie up in the vet box if they have been overstressed and the rider, by observing his horse, can see the minute changes that may signal a problem and get veterinarian help immediately if he needs it.

In the box, the veterinarians will be checking the horse's temperature, pulse, and respiration as soon as he comes from roads and tracks and then at periodic intervals throughout the ten minutes to see how he is progressing in his recovery. At the very end, the horse will be jogged out for the vet to make sure he is still sound and has not tied up.

If a veterinarian feels that your horse will experience difficulty on course, he can eliminate your horse. This is usually done in such a manner that you have the option of withdrawing rather than being eliminated. Alternatively, they will say, "Well, you can go, but much slower than you had planned." Heaven help you if you decide to ignore the veterinarian's advice. If you speed after an advisory of a slower speed, your horse will more than likely be spun at the veterinarian exam the next day. In addition, you will probably incur more injuries because your horse is not going out with a full tank of gas.

### Care of the Horse in the Vet Box

The care of the horse changes as well at the higher levels. He will probably be wearing shoes with screw-in heel caulks during the competitive season. When you get ready to do a three-day, you will have to have a second set of shoes made for emergency use in the vet box.

Frequently, horses with screw-in heel caulks will change from a road caulk, which they will use for steeplechase roads and tracks to a longer caulk for cross-country, if the weather conditions warrant. Many riders keep either spacers or cotton in the screw-in hole of the shoe when they do not have the caulks in place. They retap the screw threads before a three-day to make sure that the caulks can go in quickly and easily. Getting your caulks in place within the time allowed can be a difficult process and requires a certain amount of practice under pressure to fine-tune the skill.

### Vet Box Supplies

In addition, you will need a camphorated body brace such as Vitrolin mixed with warm water for rinsing the horse off and cooling him down; you will need another bucket with warmer water for doing the large muscle groups; and you will need a third for letting the horse have sips of water.

The veterinarian checks the temperature of the horse. The groom has placed a cool wet towel over the horse's neck to cool the blood in the veins as it circulates. One of the wash buckets and sweat scrapers is close at hand for cooling the horse down further.

Screw-in heel calks are changed to give maximum traction for weather conditions.

## Ice

When you go to observe three-day and it is very warm or hot, you will find riders frequently using ice on their horses. This is very judiciously applied to the areas with the most veins, avoiding large muscle groups and any of those that would be used for galloping and jumping. The ice is normally placed on a jugular vein on the neck and an ice pack on the horse's head and occasionally between the hind legs. Many horses resent having ice placed behind the hind legs, so one needs to be extremely careful when doing this. If it is an extremely hot and humid situation, the organizers and veterinarians have oxygen available for the horses. This is a rare situation that has mostly been remedied by the organizers moving competitions to cooler times of the year.

The grease that you are using is applied at the ten-minute break rather than earlier in the competition. In the riders' tack trunk in the vet box will also be an extra bridle, stirrup leathers and irons, girth, gloves, drinks, towels and rain sheet, coolers and sheets, a set of horse shoes, sweat scrapers and an extra halter and lead shank. When the trunk is lifted, it feels as if the kitchen sink was included, too.

## Cross-Country Timing

On the cross-country course, the way the riders make the time required on course is by galloping along at the higher speeds and then making their adjustments to be at the correct speed to jump the fence three or four strides out from the fence. This requires all of the dressage work that the horse has in order to make rapid transitions. The riders will also have chosen the most direct routes through the fences that they think their horses are capable of doing at that particular stage in the course. This also helps to keep them coming in at the correct time. There is no benefit in being too fast on cross-country in that you will have used up your horse's energy unnecessarily. In addition, if you are tied for placing, whoever is closer to ideal time will be determined as the higher place. On the high-level courses, there are markers around the course marking the quarter points and halfway points so that the riders can check their watches and see how they are doing in comparison to the ideal time. Usually, you want to be a little fast for the first half of the course to compensate for being a little slow in the second half.

Because the horses need to be at certain distance markers at exact times, during speed and endurance, riders wear a large note card taped to their arms. This has all the important times and locations on it. In addition, riders will use three watches, one with "real world" time, a digital chronometer for roads and tracks and cross-country, and a sweep-hand chronometer for steeplechase. The reason for the last watch is that at high speeds, one's arm moves too much to focus on a watch face. You can glance at the sweep hand as you reach the one-minute distance marker and tell if you are fast or need to speed up.

While riding the cross-country, the riders will also be listening to the

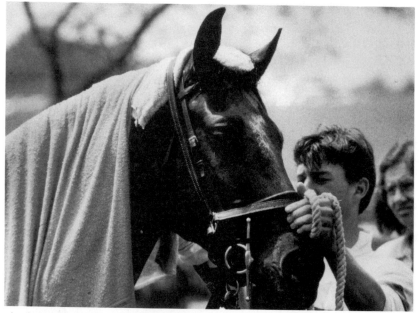

Ice is used to quickly cool the horse. An ice pack on the poll does help considerably in conjunction with cold-water-soaked towels.

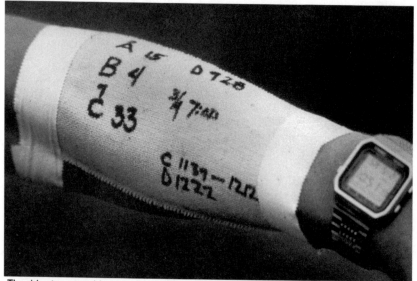

The rider tapes on his arm all the different times that he needs to be precise. "A" is the first section of roads and tracks, "B" is the steeplechase, "C" is the section of roads and tracks, and "D" is cross-country. The rider has also noted "real time" for "C" and "D" in case his stopwatch malfunctions.

290

motor to see how their horses' reaction times and exhaustion factors are. If their horses seem to be tiring, they will then switch from the most direct route to those with slower, easier options so that the horse safely gets around. In three-day, safely getting around is a major factor. The placings after cross-country are frequently quite different from the placings after dressage. A horse can come up from, for instance, fifteenth position to third place on a good cross-country run. Then he just needs to hold it together on stadium.

## Care after Cross-Country

After cross-country, the care of the horse is important to its being able to compete the next day in the stadium phase. After the horse has been walked cool and given a bath with Vitrolin or other camphorated body wash, the horse is cleared by the veterinarians for returning to the barn. There will be another veterinarian available at the barn in case you decide that you would like to give your horse the equine equivalent of an aspirin. There are a few legal drugs that you can use after cross-country to help the horse recover. This list changes from year to year, so you need to check with the veterinarian in charge to make sure that the drug you are planning to use is legal and you won't be eliminated.

In addition to the analgesic, you will also want to poultice the horse's legs. Many riders, in addition to poulticing the horse's legs, will also put clay or poultice on the bottom of their feet with a little piece of brown paper between the poultice or clay and the floor to help it stay in. If you have had some nicks and scratches on your horse from the cross-country, there are medicated poultices that are available that you can use for wound drawing that help to get the horse ready for the next day. At the very least, horses are wrapped with an alcohol wrap for overnight.

Most horses are happiest if they are given some time alone in their stalls to rest. Frequently, riders will give a warm bran mash after cross-country when a horse gets his regular feed on the theory that it makes his tummy feel just a little bit better and he is less likely to develop colic from it. The horse is also given free choice on hay. The hay may be dampened so that he doesn't inhale any dust particles that might possibly slow up his breathing for the next test.

Early the next morning, you or your groom should walk the horse to limber him because he will be very stiff. It also takes almost an hour to wash the poultice off and, ideally, you might have time to braid the mane before the vet check. Horses can be shown at vet check without the braids. The grooms can put the braids in before stadium jumping instead. At the vet check, the horses will be trotted on a hard surface. The veterinarians will decide if they think a horse is sound enough to continue or should be eliminated from the competition.

## Stadium Jumping Course Walk

There is normally a fairly long time between vet check and the running of stadium, which allows you time to go to the course walk for stadium. Walk

Wheeling the course: many riders measure the exact distance of the course to find the quarter, half, and three-quarter marks. The riders then can check against their stop-watches to see if they are too fast or too slow.

After the stress of cross-country, the horse's legs are poulticed and wrapped.

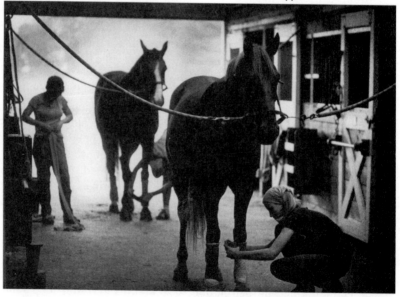

it four times to make sure that you have the exact distances and your battle plan in mind. One has to ride the stadium test very conservatively, because one's horse is tired and will not have the extra bit of zip to make the larger gesture over fences. This means that you choose small, controlled spots rather than long spots. It is also very hard to keep your horse from stalling from lack of impulsion. There is a lot of revving up, trying to keep the engine at optimum rpms without having a great deal of speed. Since your horse feels so radically different, three-day stadium jumping is a novel experience for many riders. The stadium test is set on uneven ground, with the fences designed for undulation. The distances are quite irregular and require much thought. If at all possible, walk it with an instructor or an extremely experienced friend. The more heads involved with analyzing the course, the better the chances that you will have the right program when you ride the course.

**Warm-up for Stadium**

At the upper levels, especially at three-day events for stadium, the horses go in reverse order of placing, which makes it a little more difficult to establish when you need to get your horse warmed up. Generally speaking, you will allow approximately five minutes for each horse in order to calculate when you need to start the warm-up. Alternatively, you can mount when the horse ten places ahead of you goes in the ring. Since your horse is going to be more tired if you have done a three-day, you will be using less speed work and less jumping to achieve your ends. You want to be careful that you don't use the last burst of energy that your horse has in the warm-up area instead of out on course.

**Vacation**

After the three-day is over, your horse is usually let down to relax for a month or so. Since he is going from a very fit stage to turnout, you do it somewhat gradually. Increase his turnout and take him for very short, quiet walks, out in the countryside if possible. If you stop work abruptly, your horse becomes very upset with you because he is so geared up. He is more likely to get into trouble. After a couple of days of the slow hacks, you will find that he is able to be turned out more without becoming stir crazy.

Some event horses do not like being off work. In their particular cases, the riders will arrange to have some semblance of exercise for them each day so that they still feel as if they are an important part of the rider's world. The actual work involved is very low-key. It is usually just hacking in the country-side at low speeds. Sometimes riders will decide to keep the horse up for an extra month in a slightly lower stage of fitness and fox hunt him, if it is in the fall, or pick up another three-day a little later. Occasionally, you can find three-day events that are a month apart. It is possible to keep the horse going that extra month, but then he is really in need of vacation after that.

Olympians Mike Plumb and "Better and Better" in harmony over a maze drop fence. Mike has his reins set for the bridge, but decides not to use it. He has a strong seat, carrying his weight close to the horse's back. His legs wrap around the horse supporting and ready to absorb the shock of landing. There is a straight line from the bit to his elbow giving support and suppleness. This is classic American drop fence style.

When your competitive season is finished, it is a good idea to have your veterinarian check the horse for any problems that are starting to show up from the wear and tear of competition life. That way, you know what you need to work on, to strengthen for the next competitive season, or what things are too difficult for him to do. Since the event horse has reached a high level in competition and has been on a rising work cycle for a number of years, his overall general fitness and stamina are those of an athlete. He is never really let down completely; he is only let down enough to regenerate and then worked back up to an even higher level of fitness.

**International Competition**

Many times, open intermediate acts as an introduction to advanced and the riders will move quickly from intermediate to advanced work. They will also frequently use the intermediate courses as a warm-up for a later advanced competition within the same season. At intermediate and beyond, one is riding with riders from other countries as well as the United States. The designations of the competitions change to the international as a result, and competitors from one national federation can be invited by another national federation to participate in its events.

When the horses travel internationally, they require passports and special veterinarian certificates. When one is competing abroad as an individual, one has to have a letter from the USCTA, stating that they have found that you and your horse are competent at the level at which you want to compete abroad. The USCTA will also make suggestions as to what competitions are appropriate for you from looking at your horse's competitive track record in the United States. Frequently, riders from other countries or high-level riders in this country can help you with targeting what competitions are worth your while to go over for the experience. These competitions include, at a highest level, Badminton and Burghley, England. These are the ultimate, other than World Championships for the three-day event competition. Unlike the World Championships, individual riders can enter as long as they are qualified.

One of the joys of riding high-level is the opportunity to meet riders from the other countries, visit them in their own countries when one is competing and learn more of their training techniques. One can literally go around the world visiting other three-day event riders who have come to competitions in the United States and Europe. Australia and New Zealand have very strong teams and breeding programs for their competition horses. Many of the horses at the highest levels come from England and Ireland. They are a cross between full Thoroughbreds and the Irish draft-type mares. They are mostly Thoroughbred, with just a touch of something else to give them substance, bone, and brains.

## The Olympics

Eventing, like dressage and Grand Prix show jumping, gives you the opportunity to look toward the Olympics, as these three disciplines are included in the summer Olympics. Therefore, one has the ultimate goals in mind when competing. The teams that represent the United States are picked just prior to each of the international competitions. There is no standing team year-round. After each competition, the team is disbanded and the new team is designated just before the next competition so the riders have to develop their horses totally on their own, without financial support from the United States Equestrian Team. There is very little in the way of financial support for any of the horse endeavors, especially for dressage and event riding. However, as you reach the higher levels, you may be asked to come for training sessions for either the jumping team, the dressage, or the three-day team, and these sessions will help you with developing your and your horse's potential.

Learning to ride at these higher levels takes many years of practice and experience. It is encouraging to remember that in horsemanship, one gets older and better simultaneously. There are dressage riders who have competed in the Olympics and World Championships during their seventies and eighties. Three-day event riders have ridden for their countries in their fifties and Grand Prix show jumpers have been in their sixties. There is a long time to keep improving. In riding, riders are like vintage wine—they get better with age.

# Glossary

**Bascule**   The shape of the arc that a horse makes while in the air over a jump. Looks like a rainbow.

**Bat**   A short whip used mounted to cue or discipline the horse. It does not have a thong.

**Borium**   A very hard metal soldered on to horseshoes. It will penetrate through frozen ground, ice, and asphalt, and will scratch steel and concrete.

**Bounce**   A very short-distance combination jump designed to have only enough space between elements to allow the horse to land and take off without taking a stride.

**Caliente**   Formerly, a brand name for jockey-type safety helmet, now used as a generic term.

**Cavalletti**   A series of jump rails laid on the ground to teach the horses cadence and balance in preparation for jumping.

**Cold blood**   Breed term for a horse of draft horse parentage.

**Collected**   The gathering together of the horse, compressing his body together through use of hand, leg, and seat of rider. These compress the horse's body like a spring, creating dynamic tension, elevation, and a shortened gait; shifts weight of horse to hindquarters with no change in rhythm or cadence.

**Colors**   Fox hunting term for insignia showing that a member of the hunt has hunted long enough with that hunt to be responsible for other members of the hunt and is familiar with the hunting territory. Denotes responsibility and is an honor.

**Conformation**   Breed term for the skeletal and muscular shape of a horse. The arrangement and congruity of parts.

**Diagonal**   A movement in the sequence of gait of the trot. The horse moves with a diagonal pair of front and back legs. The rider cues to influence the inside front diagonal pair of legs on a circle.

**Extend** Opposite of collect, stretching the horse's body and stride, covering more ground, releasing the spring of the horse's movement, with no change of rhythm, still using weight from hindquarters.

**Field** The followers of the hunt, usually mounted.

**Field master** Fox hunting term for person in charge of the followers of the hunt. Essentially the "second in command" after the master.

**Forehand** Front half of the horse's body.

**Fork** The front "V" shaped structure of the frame of the saddle tree. This part sits over the withers of the horse. The saddle tree acts as the structural support of the saddle.

**Frame** The shape of the horse's body in movement.

**Grand Prix** The highest level of competition in dressage. Includes pirouettes at the canter, change of lead every stride at the canter, passage and piaffe.

**Grand Prix** The highest level of competition in show jumping. Obstacles start at 5'5" with beginning spreads of 4' to 5'. Includes water jumps and multilevel obstacles within the arena.

**Ground line** A rail or other artificial indicator of the leading bottom edge of a jump.

**Gymnastic** A grid of small jumps with closely related distances between them used to teach a horse and rider appropriate takeoff spots and jumping techniques.

**Hand gallop** A slow gallop that is faster than a canter—around 520 meters per minute.

**Hindquarters** Rear half of the horse, haunches.

**Huntsman** Fox hunting term for person in charge of the foxhounds.

**Lead** The movement within the gait, especially for the canter and gallop of the front leg, which starts the gait sequence. This leg moves farther forward than the other front leg, hence the term "lead." The leading leg carries all of the horse's weight at one point in the sequence. The horse must have the inside leading leg on a circle in order to stay upright. Therefore, the "true" or "correct" lead would be the inside one. The rider's cues are timed to influence this moment in the horse's gait.

**Lunging** The on-the-ground training and exercising of the horse on a circle.

**Master of the hunt** Person—man or woman—in charge of the entire hunt and all of its relationships.

**Overface** Give too difficult a challenge to a horse's or person's level of expertise, thereby destroying self-confidence; the failure to achieve the goal.

**Penny** Numbered vest used in competition.

**Poultice** A clay compound used to reduce swelling and soothe legs.

**Pushing the horse into the rider's hand** Refers to the action of placing the horse on the bit. As the rider pushes the horse forward with his legs and seat, he vibrates gently the bit or asks for a shoulder-in to ask the horse to bring his head to the vertical face position. The feel of the reins is a soft contact with the mouth.

**School** To teach or train.

**Stocked up** Fluid filling in a horse's lower legs, usually from inflammation; can be caused by work too difficult for a horse's level of fitness, fever, illness, or allergy.

**Sweet feed**   Granola and molasses for horses; combination of grains usually oats and corn. Varies with manufacturer.

**To break down a horse**   Injuring a horse by pushing him beyond the fitness and capabilities of his body.

**To control a horse between the rider's leg and hand**   The leg generates the impulsion and energy to move, the seat increases the energy and cues forward or backward, while the hands provide cues for halt, collection, and direction. These natural aids give the corridors of power that cue the horse what is expected of him.

**Trailer**   Farrier term for a shoe adjusted so that the outside branch of the shoe extends a little beyond the outside of the heel. It turns the horse's foot to correct gait irregularities. It can put more stress on the joints of the legs, causing more problems.

**Warm blood**   Breed term for a horse of draft and Thoroughbred or Arab parentage.

**Whipper-in**   Fox hunting term for assistant to the huntsman. In charge of correcting the foxhounds and watching for foxes and other wildlife for the huntsman.

# Bibliography

HORSE ENTHUSIASTS are well served by an enormous selection of fine books by numerous authorities on a wide range of important subjects. The listing which follows is made up of outstanding books on general and specialized subjects of interest to those involved in the various aspects of equestrian sports. In addition, there are many more worth studying and every year brings new horse books to help you hone your riding and horse-keeping skills.

**General Interest**

British Horse Society and Pony Club. *The Manual of Horsemanship.* British Horse Society.
d'Eadrödy, Agoston L. *Give Your Horse a Chance.* Allen, U.K.
Foster, Carol. *The Athletic Horse.* Howell Book House.
Gianoli, Luigi. *Horses and Horsemanship Through the Ages.* Crown.
Giffin, James M., M.D., and Tom Gore, D.V.M. *Horse Owner's Veterinary Handbook.* Howell Book House.
Harris, Susan E. *Grooming to Win.* Charles Scribner's Sons.
Hawcroft, Tim, B.V.Sc., (Hons) M.A.C.V.Sc. *The Complete Book of Horse Care.* Howell Book House.
Hunt, Clifford. *The Keys to Good Horsemanship.* The Hunting Box.
Kane, Jeanne, and Lisa Waltman. *The Event Groom's Handbook.* Event Books International.
McBane, Susan. *The Horse and the Bit.* Howell Book House.
Pilliner, Sarah. *Performance Horse: Management, Care and Training.* Howell Book House.
Price, Steven D. *Get a Horse.* Viking.
Swift, Sally. *Cantered Riding.* David & Charles.
Thelwall, Jane. *The Less-Than-Perfect Horse.* Howell Book House.
Trippett, Frank. *The First Horsemen.* Time-Life Books.

**Horse Showing**

D'Ambrosio, Anthony. *Schooling to Show.* Viking.
Morris, George H. *Hunter Seat Equitation.* Doubleday & Co.

Richter, Judy. *Horse and Rider*. Arco.
Steinkraus, William, ed. *The U.S. Equestrian Team Book of Riding*. Simon & Schuster.
Wright, Gordon. *Learning to Ride, Hunt and Show*. Doubleday & Co.

## Hunting

Langley, Tim. *Good Morning . . . Good Night*. Blackthorn, U.K.
Mackay-Smith, Alexander. *Foxhunting in North America*. Good Printers.
McClung, Cookie. *Horses Are Different*. The Chronicle of the Horse.
Sinclair-Smith, Michael. *Don't Trample the Dogs*. Anvil Press, Canada.
————. *The Rider with the Little Bugle*. Anvil Press, Canada.
Young, James L. *A Field of Horses: The World of Marshall P. Hawkins*. Taylor.
Zelenak, Ernest, publisher. *Blue Ridge Hunt, The First Hundred Years*.

## Show Jumping

de Nemethy, Bertalan. *The de Nemethy Method*. Doubleday & Co.
Smart, John. *Showjumping*. Howell Book House.

## Dressage

de Kunffy, Charles. *Dressage Questions Answered*. Arco.
Froissard, Jean. *An Expert's Guide to Basic Dressage*. Wilshire.
Hamilton, Kate. *Dressage: An Approach to Competition*. Howell Book House.
Ljungquist, Bengt. *Practical Dressage*. Whittet & Shepperson.
Müseler, Wilhelm. *Riding Logic*. Arco.
Podhajsky, Alois. *The Art of Dressage*. Doubleday & Co.
————. *The Complete Training of Horse and Rider*. Wilshire.
Richards, Lockie. *Dressage*. David & Charles.

## Eventing

Bradwell, Judy. *Eventing: Preparation, Training and Competition*. Howell Book House.
Carruthers, Morris, Hogan, Thomson, Ed., John H. Fritz. *Designing Courses and Obstacles*. Houghton-Mifflin.
Kane, J. and L. Waltman. *The Event Groom's Handbook*. Event Books International.
O'Connor, Sally. *Practical Eventing*. Whittet & Shepperson.
————, editor. *The USCTA Book of Eventing*. United States Combined Training Association.
Phillips, Capt. Mark. *Captain Mark Phillips on Riding*. Arco.
Thomson, Bill. *Constructing Cross Country Obstacles*. Allen, U.K.
Wilcox, Sheila. *The Event Horse*. Lippincott.